ROMAN HOLIDAYS

AND OTHERS

W. D. HOWELLS

1st WORLD
LIBRARY
Literary Society

Roman Holidays and Others

W. D. Howells

© 1st World Library, 2007
PO Box 2211
Fairfield, IA 52556
www.1stworldlibrary.com
First Edition

LCCN: 2007927867

Softcover ISBN: 978-1-4218-4578-4
Hardcover ISBN: 978-1-4218-4494-7
eBook ISBN: 978-1-4218-4662-0

Purchase *"Roman Holidays and Others"*
as a traditional bound book at:
www.1stWorldLibrary.com/purchase.asp?ISBN=978-1-4218-4578-4

1ˢᵗ World Library Literary Society

Giving Back to the World

"If you want to work on the core problem, it's early school literacy."

- James Barksdale, former CEO of Netscape

"No skill is more crucial to the future of a child, or to a democratic and prosperous society, than literacy."

- Los Angeles Times

"Literacy... means far more than learning how to read and write... The aim is to transmit... knowledge and promote social participation."

- UNESCO

"Literacy is not a luxury, it is a right and a responsibility. If our world is to meet the challenges of the twenty-first century we must harness the energy and creativity of all our citizens."

- President Bill Clinton

"Parents should be encouraged to read to their children, and teachers should be equipped with all available techniques for teaching literacy, so the varying needs and capacities of individual kids can be taken into account."

- Hugh Mackay

CONTENTS

I

UP AND DOWN MADEIRA

No drop-curtain, at any theatre I have seen, was ever so richly imagined, with misty tops and shadowy clefts and frowning cliffs and gloomy valleys and long, plunging cataracts, as the actual landscape of Madeira, when we drew nearer and nearer to it, at the close of a tearful afternoon of mid-January. The scenery of drop-curtains is often very holdly beautiful, but here Nature, if she had taken a hint from art, had certainly bettered her instruction. During the waits between acts at the theatre, while studying the magnificent painting beyond the trouble of the orchestra, I have been most impressed by the splendid variety which the artist had got into his picture, where the spacious frame lent itself to his passion for saying everything; but I remembered his thronging fancies as meagre and scanty in the presence of the stupendous reality before me. I have, for instance, not even mentioned the sea, which swept smoother and smoother in toward the feet of those precipices and grew more and more trans-lucently purple and yellow and green, while half a score of cascades shot straight down their fronts in shafts of snowy foam, and over their pachydermatous shoulders streamed and hung long reaches of gray vines or mosses. To the view from the sea the island is all, with its changing capes and promontories and bays and inlets, one immeasurable mountain; and on the afternoon of our approach it was bestridden by a steadfast rainbow, of which we could only see one leg indeed, but that very stout and athletic.

There were breadths of dark woodland aloft on this mountain, and terraced vineyards lower down; and on the shelving plateaus yet farther from the heights that lost themselves in the clouds there were scattered white cottages; on little levels close to the sea there were set white villas. These, as the ship coquetted with the vagaries of the shore, thickened more and more, until after rounding a prodigious headland we found ourselves in face of the charming little city of Funchal: long horizontal lines of red roofs, ivory and pink and salmon walls, evenly fenestrated, with an ancient fortress giving the modern look of things a proper mediaeval touch. Large hotels, with the air of palaces, crowned the upland vantages; there were bell-towers of churches, and in one place there was a wide splotch of vivid color from the red of the densely flowering creeper on the side of some favored house. There was an acceptable expanse of warm brown near the quay from the withered but unfailing leaves of a sycamore-shaded promenade, and in the fine roadstead where we anchored there lay other steamers and a lead-colored Portuguese war-ship. I am not a painter, but I think that here are the materials of a water-color which almost any one else could paint. In the hands of a scene-painter they would yield a really unrivalled drop-curtain. I stick to the notion of this because when the beautiful goes too far, as it certainly does at Madeira, it leaves you not only sated but vindictive; you wish to mock it.

The afternoon saddened more and more, and one could not take an interest in the islanders who came out in little cockles and proposed to dive for shillings and sixpences, though quarters and dimes would do. The company's tender also

W. D. Howells

came out, and numbers of passengers went ashore in the mere wantonness of paying for their dinner and a night's lodging in the annexes of the hotels, which they were told beforehand were full. The lights began to twinkle from the windows of the town, and the dark fell upon the insupportable picturesqueness of the prospect, leaving one to a gayety of trooping and climbing lamps which defined the course of the streets.

The morning broke in sunshine, and after early breakfast the launches began to ply again between the ship and the shore and continued till nearly all the first and second cabin people had been carried off. The people of the steerage satisfied what longing they had for strange sights and scenes by thronging to the sides of the steamer until they gave her a strong list landward, as they easily might, for there were twenty-five hundred of them. At Madeira there is a local Thomas Cook & Son of quite another name, but we were not finally sure that the alert youth on the pier who sold us transportation and provision was really their agent. However, his tickets served perfectly well at all points, and he was of such an engaging civility and personal comeliness that I should not have much minded their failing us here and there. He gave the first charming-touch of the Latin south whose renewed contact is such a pleasure to any one knowing it from the past. All Portuguese as Funchal was, it looked so like a hundred little Italian towns that it seemed to me as if I must always have driven about them in calico-tented bullock-carts set on runners, as later I drove about Eunchal.

It was warm enough on the ship, but here in the town we found ourselves in weather that one could easily have taken for summer, if the inhabitants had not repeatedly assured us that it was the season of winter, and that there were no flowers and no fruits. They could not, if they had wished, have denied the flies; these, in a hotel interior to which we penetrated, simply swarmed. If it was winter in Funchal it was no wintrier than early autumn would have been in one of those Italian towns of other days; it had the same temperament, the same little tree-planted spaces, the same devious, cobble-paved streets, the same pleasant stucco houses; the churches had bells of like tone, and if their faqades confessed a Spanish touch they were not more Spanish than half the churches in Naples. The public ways were of a scrupulous cleanliness, as if, with so many English signs glaring down at them, they durst not untidy out-of-doors, though in-doors it was said to be different with them. There are three thousand English living at Funchal and everybody speaks English, however slightly. The fresh faces of English girls met us in the streets and no doubt English invalids abound.

We shipmates were all going to the station of the funicular railway, but our tickets did not call for bullock-sleds and so we took a clattering little horse-car, which climbed with us through up-hill streets and got us to the station too soon. Within the closed grille there the handsomest of swarthy, black-eyed, black-mustached station-masters (if such was his quality) told us that we could not have a train at once, though we had been advised that any ten of us could any time have a train, because the cars had all gone up the mountain and none would be down for twenty minutes. He spoke English and he mitigated by a most amiable personality sufferings which were perhaps not so great as we would have liked to think. Some of us wandered off down a pink-and-cream colored avenue near by and admired so much the curtains of red-and-yellow flowers—a cross between honeysuckles and trumpet blossoms—overhanging a garden-wall that two friendly boys began to share our interest in them. One of them mounted the other and tore down handfuls of the flowers, which they bestowed upon us with so little apparent expectation of reward that we promptly gave them of the

W. D. Howells

international copper coinage current in Madeira, and went back to the station doubtless feeling guiltier than they. Had we not been accessory after the fact to something like theft and, as it was Sunday, to Sabbath-breaking besides? Afterward flowers proved so abundant in Madeira in spite of its being winter, that we could not feel the larceny a serious one, and the Sunday was a Latin Sabbath well used to being broken. The pony engine which was to push our slanting car over the cogged track up the mountain arrived with due ceremony of bell and whistle, and we were let through the grille by the station-master as politely as if we had been each his considered guest. Then the climb began through the fields of sugar-cane, terraced vineyards, orchards of fruit trees, and gardens of vegetables planted under the arbors over which the grapes were trained. One of us told the others that the vegetables were sheltered to save them from being scorched by the summer sun, and that much of the work among them was done by moonlight to save the laborers from the same fate. I do not know how he had amassed this knowledge, and I am not sure that I have the right to impart it without his leave. I myself saw some melons lolling on one of the tiled roofs of the cottages where they had perhaps been pushed by the energetic forces of the earth and sky. The grape-vines were quiescent, partly because it was winter, as everybody said, and partly because the wine culture is no longer so profitable in the island. It has been found for the moment that Madeira is bad for the gout, and this discovery of the doctors is bad for the peasants (already cruelly overtaxed by Portugal), who are leaving their homes in great numbers and seeking their fortunes in both of the Americas, as well as the islands of all the seas. It must be a heartbreak for them to forsake such homes as we saw in the clean white cottages, with the balconies and terraces.

But there were no signs of depopulation either of old or young. Smiling mothers and fathers of all ages, in their

Sunday leisure and their Sunday best, watched our ascent as if they had never seen the like before, and our course was never so swift but we could be easily overtaken by the children; they embarrassed us with the riches of the camellias which they flung in upon us, and they were accompanied by small dogs which barked excitedly. Our train almost grazed the walls of the door-yards as we passed through the succession of the one-and two-story cottages, which dotted the mountain-side in every direction. When the eye could leave them it was lured from height to height, and at each rise of the track to some wider and lovelier expanse of the sea. We could see merely our own steamer in the roadstead, with the Portuguese war-ship, and the few other vessels at anchor, but we could never exhaust the variety of those varied mountain slopes and tops. Their picturesqueness of form and their delight of color would beggar any thesaurus of its descriptive reserves, and yet leave their beauty almost unhinted. A drop-curtain were here a vain simile; the chromatic glories of colored postal-cards might suggest the scene, but then again they might overdo it. Nature is modest in her most magnificent moods, and I do not see how she could have a more magnificent mood than Madeira. It can never be represented by my art, but it may be measurably stated: low lying sea; the town scattering and fraying everywhere into outlying hamlets, villas and cottages; steep rising upon steep, till they reach uninhabitable climaxes where the woods darken upward into the everlasting snows, in one whole of grandeur resuming in its unity every varying detail.

I dwell rather helplessly upon the scenery, because it was what we professedly went up or half up, or one-tenth or-hundredth up, the mountain for. Un-professedly we went up in order to come down by the toboggan of the country, though we vowed one another not to attempt anything so mad. In the meanwhile, before it should be time for lunch, we could walk up to a small church near the station and see the people at prayer in an interior which did not differ in bareness and tawdriness from most other country churches of the Latin south, though it had a facade so satisfy-ingly Spanish, because I suppose it was so perfectly Portuguese, that heart could ask no more. Not all the people were at prayer within; irregular files of them attended our progress to give us the opportunity of doing charity. The beggars were of every sort, sex, and age, and some, from the hands they held out, with fingers reduced to their last joints, looked as if they might be lepers, but I do not say they were. What I am sure of is that the faces of the worshippers—men, women, and children—when they came out of the church were of a gentleness which, if it was not innocence and goodness, might well have passed for those virtues. They had kind eyes, which seemed as often blue as black, and if they had no great beauty they were seldom quite ugly. I wish I could think we strangers, as they gazed curiously, timorously at us, struck them as favorably.

An involuntary ferocity from the famine which we began to feel may have glared from our visages, for we had eaten nothing for three hours, which was long for saloon passengers. At the first restaurant which we found, and in which we all but sat down at table, our coupons were not good, but this was not wholly loss, for we recouped ourselves in the beauties of the walk on which we wandered along the mountain-side to the right of the restaurant. At the point where we were no longer confident of our way an opportune native appeared and Jed us over paths paved with fine pebbles, sometimes wrought into geometric patterns, and always through pleasing sun and shade, till we reached a pretty hotel set, with its gardens before it, on a shelf of level land and commanding a view of our steamer and the surrounding sea. Tropic growths, which I will venture to call myrtle, oleander, laurel, and eucalyptus, environed the hotel, not too closely nor densely, and our increasing party was presently discovered from the head of its steps by a hospitable matron, who with a cry of comprehensive welcome ran within and was replaced by a head-waiter of as friendly aspect and much more English. He said our coupons were good there and that our luncheon would be ready in two minutes; for proof of the despatch with which we should be served he held up the first and second fingers of his right hand. Restored by his assurance, we did not really mind waiting twice the tale of all his ten fingers, and we spent our time variously in wandering about the plateau, among the wonted iron tables and chairs in front of the hotel, in being photographed in a fairy grotto behind it, and in examining the visitors' book in the parlor. The names of visitors from South Africa largely prevailed, for the Cape Town steamers, oftener than any others, touch at Madeira, but there was one traveller of Portuguese race who had written his name in bold characters above the cry, "Long live the Portuguese Republic." Soon after the Portuguese monarchy ceased to live for a time in the person of the murdered king and his heir, but it is doubtful if the health of the potential republic was as great as before.

That bright Sunday morning no shadow of the black event was forecast, and we gave our unstinted sympathy to our unknown co-republican. The luncheon, when we were called to it, had merits of novelty and quality which I will celebrate only as regards the delicate fish fresh from the sea, and the pease fresh from the garden, with poached eggs fresh from the coop dropped upon them. The conception of chops which followed was not so faultless, though the fruit with which we ended did much to repair any error of kid which may have mistaken itself for lamb. Perhaps our enthusiasm was heightened by the fine air which had sharpened our appetites. At any rate, it all ended in an habitual transaction in real estate by which I became the owner of the place, without expropriating the actual possessor, and established there those castles in Spain belonging to me in so many parts of the world.

There remained now nothing for us to do but to toboggan down the mountain, and we overcame our resolution not to do so far enough to go and look at the toboggans under the guidance of our head-waiter. When once we had looked we were lost. The toboggans were flat baskets set on iron-shod runners, and well cushioned and padded; they held one, two, or three passengers; the track on which they descended was paved, in gentle undulations, with thin pebbles set on edge and greased wherever the descent found a level. A smiling native, with a strong rope attached to the toboggan, stood on each side of it, and held it back or pulled it forward, according to the exigencies of the case. It is long since I slid down hill on a sled of my own, and I do not pretend to recall the sensation; but I can remember nothing so luxurious in transportation as the swift flight of the Madeira toboggan, which you temper at will through its guides and guards, but do not wish to temper at all when your first alarm, mainly theoretical, passes into the gayety ending in exultant rejoicing at the bottom of the course.

Our two toboggan men were possibly vigilant and reassuring beyond the common, but one was quite silently so; the other, who spoke a little English, encouraged us from time to time to believe that they were "strong mans," afterward correcting himself in conformity to the rules of Portuguese grammar, which make the adjective agree in number with the noun, and declaring that they were "strongs mans." We met many toboggan men who needed to be "strongs mans" in their ascent of our track, with their heavy toboggans on their heads; but some of them did not look strong, and our own arrived spent and panting at the bottom. Something like that is what always spoils pleasure in this world. Even when you have paid for it with your money, some one else has paid with his person twice as much, and you have not equalled his outlay when you have tipped him your handsomest.

A shilling apiece seemed handsome for those "strongs mans," but afterward there were watches of the nights when the spirit grieved that the shilling had not been made two apiece or even half a crown, and I wish now that the first reader of mine who toboggans down Madeira would make up the difference for me in his tip to those poor fellows. I do not mind if he adds a few pennies for the children who ran before our toboggan and tossed camellias into it, and then followed in the hopes of a reward, which we tried not to disappoint.

The future traveller need not add to the fee of the authorized and numbered guide who took possession of us as soon as we got out of our basket and led us unresisting to a waiting bullock sled. He invited himself into it, and gave himself the best of characters in the autobiography into which he wove his scanty instruction concerning the objects we passed. A bullock sled is not of such blithe progress as a toboggan, but it is very comfortable, and it is of an Oriental and litter-like dignity, with its calico cushions and curtains. One could not well use it in New York, but it serves every purpose of a cab in Funchal, where we noted a peculiar feature of local commerce which I hesitate to specify, since it cast apparent discredit upon woman. It was, as I have noted, Sunday; but every shop where things pleasing or even useful to women were sold was wide open, and somewhat flaringly invited the custom of our fellow-passengers of that sex; but there was not a shop where such things as men's collars were for sale, or anything pleasing or useful to man, but was closed and locked fast. I must except from this sweeping statement the cafes, but these should not count, for women as well as men frequented them, as we ascertained by going to a very

W. D. Howells

bowery one on the quay and ordering a bottle of the best and dryest Madeira. We wished perhaps to prove that it was really not bad for gout, or perhaps that it was no better than the Madeira you get in New York for the same price. Even with the help of friends, of the sex which could have been freely buying native laces, hats, fans, photographs, parasols, and tailor-made dresses, we could not finish that bottle. Glass after glass we bestowed on our smiling guide, with no final effect upon the bottle and none upon him, except to make him follow us to the tender and take an after-fee for showing us a way which we could not have missed blindfold. It was rather strange, but not stranger than the behavior of the captain of the tender, who, when he had collected our tickets, invited a free-will offering for collecting them, and mostly got it.

When we were safely and gladly on board our steamer again, we had nothing to do, until the deck-steward came round with tea, but watch the islanders swarming around us in their cockles and diving for sixpences and shillings, which they caught impartially with their fingers and toes. With so many all shouting and gesticulating, one could not venture one's silver indiscriminately; one must employ some particular diver, and I selected for my investments a poor young fellow who had lost an arm. With his one hand and his two feet he never failed of the coin I risked, and I wish they had been many enough to enable him to retire from the trade, which even in that mild air kept him visibly shivering when out of the water. I do not know his name, but I commend him to future travellers by the token of his pathetic mutilation.

By-and-by we felt the gentle stir of the steamer under us; the last tender went ashore, and the divers retired in their cockles from our side. Funchal began to rearrange the lines of her streets, while keeping those of her roofs and house-walls and terraced gardens. We passed out of the roadstead, we rounded the mighty headland by which we had entered, and were once more in face of that magnificent drop-curtain, which had now fallen upon one of the most vivid and novel passages of our lives.

W. D. Howells

II

TWO UP-TOWN BLOCKS INTO SPAIN

There is nothing strikes the traveller in his approach to the rock of Gibraltar so much as its resemblance to the trademark of the Prudential Insurance Company. He cannot help feeling that the famous stronghold is pictorially a plagiarism from the advertisements of that institution. As the lines change with the ship's course, the resemblance is less remarkable; but it is always remarkable, and I suppose it detracts somewhat from the majesty of the fortress, which we could wish to be more entirely original. This was my feeling when I first saw Gibraltar four years ago, and it remains my feeling after having last seen it four weeks ago. The eye seeks the bold, familiar legend, and one suffers a certain disappointment in its absence. Otherwise Gibraltar does not and cannot disappoint the most exacting tourist.

The morning which found us in face of it was in brisk contrast to the bland afternoon on which we had parted from Madeira. No flocking coracles surrounded our steamer, with crews eager to plunge into the hissing brine for shillings or equivalent quarters. The whitecaps looked snow cold as they tossed under the sharp north wind, and the tender which put us ashore had all it could do to embark and disembark us upright, or even aslant. But, once in the lee of the rocky

Africa breathed a genial warmth across the strait beyond which its summits faintly shimmered; or was it the welcome of Cook's carriages which warmed us so? We were promised separate vehicles for parties of three or four, with English-speaking drivers, and the promise was fairly well kept. The carriages bore a strong family likeness to the pictures of Spanish state coaches of the seventeenth century, and were curtained and cushioned in reddish calico. Rubber tires are yet unknown in southern Europe, and these mediaeval arks bounded over the stones with a violence which must once have been characteristic of those in the illustrations. But the English of our English-speaking driver was all that we could have asked for the shillings we paid Cook for him, or, if it was not, it was all we got. He was an energetic young fellow and satisfyingly Spanish in coloring, but in his eagerness to please he was less grave than I could now wish; I now wish everything in Spain to have been in keeping.

What was most perfectly, most fittingly in keeping was the sight of the Moors whom we began at once to see on the wharves and in the streets. They probably looked very much like the Moors who followed their caliph, if he was a caliph, into Spain when he drove Don Roderick out of his kingdom and established his own race and religion in the Peninsula. Moslem costumes can have changed very little in the last eleven or twelve hundred years, and these handsome fellows, who had come over with fresh eggs and vegetables and chickens and turkeys from Tangier, could not have been handsomer when they bore scimitars and javelins instead of coops and baskets. They had baggy drawers on, and brown cloaks, with bare, red legs and yellow slippers; one, when he took his fez off, had a head shaved perfectly bald, like the one-eyed Calender or the Barber's brother out of the *Arabian Nights;* the sparse mustache and short-forked beard heightened the verisimilitude. Whether they squatted on the wharf, or passed gravely through the street, or waited for custom in their little market among the hen-coops and the herds of rather lean, dispirited turkeys (which had not the satisfaction of their American kindred in being fattened for the sacrifice, for in Europe all turkeys are served lean), these Moors had an allure impossible to any Occidental race. It was greater even than that of their Semitic brethren, who had a market farther up in the town, and showed that a Jewish market could be much filthier than a' Moorish market without being more picturesque. Into the web of Oriental life were wrought the dapper figures of the red-coated, red-cheeked English soldiers, with blue, blue eyes and incredible red and yellow hair, lounging or hurrying orderlies with swagger-sticks, and apparently aimless privates no doubt bent 'upon quite definite business or pleasure. Now and then an English groom led an English horse through the long street from which the other streets in Gibraltar branch up and down hill, for there is no other level; and now and then an English man or woman rode trimly by.

The whole place is an incongruous mixture of Latin and Saxon. The strictly South-European effect of the houses and churches is a mute protest against the alien presence which keeps the streets so clean and maintains order by means of policemen showing under the helmets of the London bobby the faces of the native alguazil. In the shops the saleswomen speak English and look Spanish. Our driver, indeed, looked more Spanish than he spoke English.

His knowledge of our rude tongue extended hardly beyond the mention of certain conventional objects of interest, and did not suffice to explain why we could not see the old disused galleries of the fortifications. I do not know why we wished to see these; I doubt if we really did so, but we embittered life for that well-meaning boy by our insistence upon them, and we brought him under unjust suspicion of deceit by forcing him to a sort of time-limit in respect to them. We appealed from him to the blandest of black-mustached, olive-skinned bobby-alguazils, who directed us to a certain government office for a permit. There our application caused something like dismay, and we were directed to another office, but were saved from the shame of failure by incidentally learning that the galleries could not be seen till after three o'clock. As our ship sailed at that hour, we were probably saved a life-long disappointment.

Everywhere the rock of the Prudential beetles and towers over the town; but the fortifications are so far up in the sky that you can really distinguish nothing but the Marconi telegraphic apparatus at the top. Along the sea-level, which the town mostly keeps, the war-like harness of the stronghold shows through the civil dress of the town in barracks and specific forts and gray battle-ships lying at anchor in the docks. But all is simple and reserved, in the right English fashion. The strength of the place is not to be put forth till it is needed, which will be never, since it is hard to imagine how it can ever be even attempted by a hostile force. This is not saying, I hope, that an American fleet could not batter it down, nor leave one letter of the insurance advertisement after another on the face of the precipice.

There is a pretty public garden at Gibraltar in that part of the town which is farthest from the steamer's landing, and this proved the end of our excursion in our state coach. We found other state coaches there, and joined their passengers in strolling over the pleasant paths and trying to make out what bird it was singing somewhere in the trees. We made out an almond-tree in bloom, after some dispute; and, in fact, the climate there was much softer than at the landing, so insidiously soft that it required great force of character to keep from buying the flowers which some tasteful boys gathered from the public beds. There is a mild monument or two in this garden, to what memories I promptly failed to remember afterward; but as there are more military memories in the world than is good for it, and as these were undoubtedly military memories, I cannot much blame myself in the matter. After viewing them, there was nothing left to do but to get lunch, which we got extremely good at the hotel where a friend led us. There was at this hotel a head-waiter, in a silver-braided silk dress-coat of a mauve color, who imagined our wants so perfectly that I shall always regret not taking more of the omelette; the table-waiter urged it upon us twice with true friendliness. The eggs must have been laid for it in Africa that morning at daybreak, and brought over by a Moorish marketman, but we turned from the poetic experience of this omelette in the greedy hope of better things. Better things there could not be, but the fish was as good as the fish at Madeira, and the belief of the chops that they were lamb and not kid seemed better founded.

There had been an excellent bottle of Rioja Blanca, such as you may have as good at some Spanish restaurant in New York for as little money; and the lunch, when reckoned up in English shillings and Spanish undertones, was not cheap. Yet it was not dear, either, and there was no specific charge for that silver-braided dress-coat of a mauve color. An English dean in full clericals, and some English ladies talking in the waiting-room, added an agreeable confusion to our doubt of where and what we were, and we came away from the hotel as well content as if we had lunched in Plymouth or Bath. The table-waiter took an extra fee for confiding that he was a Milanese, and was almost the only Italian in Gibraltar; whether he was right or not I do not know, but it was certainly not his fault that we did not take twice of the omelette.

It is said that living is dear in Gibraltar, especially in the matter of house rent. The houses in the town are like all the houses of Latin Europe in their gray or yellowish walls of stone or stucco and their dark-green shutters. There is an English residential quarter at the east end of the town, where the houses may be different, for all I know; the English of our driver or the hire of our state coach did not enable us to visit that suburb, where the reader may imagine villas standing in grounds with lawns and gardens about them. The English have prevailed nothing against the local civilization in most things, while they have infected it with the costliness of the whole Anglo-Saxon life. We should not think seven hundred dollars in New York dear for even a quite small house, but it has come to that in Gibraltar, and there they think it dear, with other things proportionately so. Of course, it is an artificial place; the fortress makes the town, and the town in turn lives upon the fortress.

The English plant themselves nowhere without gathering English conveniences or conventions about them; Americans would not always think them comforts. There is at Gibraltar a club or clubs; there is a hunt, there is a lending library, there is tennis, there is golf, there is bridge, there is a cathedral, and I dare say there is gossip, but I do not know it. It was difficult to get land for the golf links, we heard, because of the Spanish jealousy of the English occupation, which they will not have extended any farther over Spanish soil, even in golf links. Gibraltar is fondly or whimsically known to the invaders as Gib, and I believe it is rather a favorite sojourn, though in summer it is frightfully hot, held out on the knees and insteps of the rock to the burning African sun, which comes up every morning over the sea after setting Sahara on fire.

All this foreign life must be exterior to the aboriginal Spanish life which has so long outlasted the Moorish, and is not without hope of outlasting the English. I do not know what the occupations and amusements of that life are, but I will suppose them unworthy enough. There must be a certain

W. D. Howells

space of neutral life uniting or dividing the two, which would form a curious inquiry, but Avould probably not lend itself to literary study. Besides this middle ground there is another neutral territory at Gibraltar which we traversed after luncheon, in order to say that we had been in Spain. That was the country of many more youthful dreamers in my time than, I fancy, it is in this. We used then, much more than now, to read Washington Irving, his *Tales of the Alhambra,* and his history of *The Conquest of Granada,* and we read Prescott's histories of Spanish kings and adventures in the old world and the new. We read *Don Quixote,* which very few read now, and we read *Gil Blas,* which fewer still now read; and all these constituted Spain a realm of faery, where every sort of delightful things did or could happen. I for my part had always expected to go to Spain and live among the people I had known in those charming books, yet I had been often in Europe, and had spent whole years there without ever going near Spain. But now, I saw, was my chance, and when the friend who had been lunching with us asked if we would not like to drive across that neutral territory and go into Spain a bit, it seemed as if the dream of my youth had suddenly renewed itself with the purpose of coming immediately true. It was a charmingly characteristic foretaste of Spanish travel that the driver of the state coach which we first engaged should, when we presently came back, have replaced himself by another for no other reason than, perhaps, that he could so provide us with a worse horse. I am not sure of this theory, and I do not insist upon it, but it seems plausible.

As soon as we rounded the rock of Gibraltar and struck across a flatter country than I supposed could be found within fifty miles of Gibraltar, we were swept by a blast which must have come from the Pyrenees, it was so savagely rough and cold. It may be always blowing there as a Spanish protest against the English treatment of the neutral territory;

in fact, it does not seem quite the thing to build over that space as the English have done, though the structures are entirely peaceable, and it is not strange that the Spaniards have refused to meet them half-way with a good road over it, or to let them make one the whole way. They stand gravely opposed to any further incursion. Officially in all the Spanish documents the place is styled "Gibraltar, temporarily occupied by Great Britain," and there is a little town which you see sparkling in the sun no great way off in Spain called San Roque, of which the mayor is also mayor of Gibraltar; he visits his province once a vear, and many people living for generations over the Spanish line keep the keys of the houses that they personally or ancestrally own in Gibraltar. The case has its pathos, but as a selfish witness I wish they had let the English make that road through the neutral territory. The present road is so bad that our state coach, in bounding over its inequalities, sometimes almost flung us into the arms of the Spanish beggars always extended toward us. They were probably most of them serious, but some of the younger ones recognized the *bouffe* qtiality of their calling. One pleasant starveling of ten or twelve entreated us for bread with a cigarette in his mouth, and, being rewarded for his impudence, entered into the spirit of the affair and asked for more, just as if we had given nothing.

A squalid little town grew up out of the flying gravel as we approached, and we left our state coach at the custom-house, which seemed the chief public edifice. There the inspectors did not go through the form of examining our hand-bags, as they would have done at an American frontier; and they did not pierce our carriage cushions with the long javelins with which they are armed for the detection of smuggling among the natives who have been shopping in Gibraltar. As the gates of that town are closed every day at nightfall by a patrol with drum and fife, and everybody is shut either in or out, it may easily happen with shoppers in haste to get through that they bring dutiable goods into Spain; but the official javelins rectify the error.

We left our belongings in our state coach and started for that stroll in Spain which I have measured as two up-town blocks, by what I think a pretty accurate guess; two cross-town blocks I am sure it was not. It was a mean-looking street, unswept and otherwise unkempt, with the usual yellowish or grayish buildings, rather low and rather new, as if prompted by a mistaken modern enterprise. They were both shops and dwellings; I am sure of a neat pharmacy and a fresh-looking cafe restaurant, and one dwelling all faced with bright-green tiles. An alguazil—I am certain he was an alguazil, though he looked like an Italian carabiniere and wore a cocked hat—loitered into a police station; but I remember no one else during our brief stay in that street except those *bouffe* boy beggars. Of course, they wished to sell us postal-cards, but they were willing to accept charity on any terms. Otherwise our Spanish tour was, so far as we then knew, absolutely without incident; but when we got too far away to return we found that we had been among brigands as well as beggars, and all the Spanish picaresque fiction seemed to come true in the theft of a black chudda shawl, which had indeed been so often lost in duplicate that it was time it was entirely lost. Whether it was secretly confiscated by the customs, or was accepted as a just tribute by the populace from a poetic admirer, I do not know, but I hope it is now in the keeping of some dark-eyed Spanish girl, who will wear it while murmuring through her lattice to her *novio* on the pavement outside. It was rather heavy to be worn as a veil, but I am sure she could manage it after dark, and *could* hold it under her chin, as she leaned forward to the grille, with one little olive hand, so that the *novio* would think it was a black silk mantilla. Or if it was a gift from him, it would be all right, anyway.

Our visit to Spain did not wholly realize my early dreams of that romantic land, and yet it had not been finally destitute of incident. Besides, *we* had not gone very far into the country; a third block might have teemed with adventure, but we had to be back on the steamer before three o'clock, and we dared not go beyond the second. Even within this limit a love of reality underlying all my love of romance was satisfied in the impression left by that dusty, empty, silent street. It seemed somehow like the street of a new, dreary, Western American town, so that I afterward could hardly believe that the shops and restaurants had not eked out their height with dashboard fronts. It was not a place that I would have chosen for a summer sojourn; the sense of a fly-blown past must have become a vivid part of future experience, and yet I could imagine that if one were born to it, and were young and hopeful, and had some one to share one's youth and hope, that Spanish street, which was all there was of that Spanish town, might have had its charm. I do not say that even for age there was not a railway station by which one might have got away, though there was no sign of any trains arriving or departing—perhaps because it was not one o'clock in the morning, which is the favorite hour of departure for Spanish trains.

When we turned to drive back over the neutral territory the rock of Gibraltar suddenly bulked up before us, in a sheer ascent that left the familiar Prudential view in utterly inconspicuous unimpressive-ness. Till one has seen it from this point one has not truly seen it. The vast stone shows like a half from which the other half has been sharply cleft and removed, that the sense of its precipitous magnitude may unrelievedly strike the eye; and it seems to have in that moment the whole world to tower up in from the level at its feet. No dictionary, however unabridged, has language adequate to convey the notion of it.

III

ASHORE AT GENOA

The pride of Americans in their native scenery is brought down almost to the level of the South Shore of Long Island in arriving home from the Mediterranean voyage to Europe. The last thing one sees in Europe is the rock of Gibraltar, but before that there have been the snow-topped Maritime Alps of Italy and the gray-brown, softly rounded, velvety heights of Spain; and one has to think very hard of the Palisades above the point where they have been blasted away for road-making material if one wishes to keep up one's spirits. The last time I came home the Mediterranean way I had a struggle with myself against excusing our sandy landscape, when we came in sight of it, with its summer cottages for the sole altitudes, to some Italian fellow-passengers who were not spellbound by its grandeur. I had to remember the Rocky Mountains, which I had never seen, and all the moral magnificence of our life before I could withhold the words of apology pressing to my lips. I was glad that I succeeded; but now, going back by the same route, I abandoned myself to transports in the beauty of the Mediterranean coast which I hope were not untrue to my country. Perhaps there is no country which can show anything like that beauty, and America is no worse off than the rest of the world; but I am not sure that I have a right to this consolation. Again there were those

"Silent pinnacles of aged snow,"

flushed with the Southern sun; in those sombre slopes of pine; again the olives climbing to their gloom; again the terraced vineyards and the white farmsteads, with villages nestling in the vast clefts of the hills, and all along the sea-level the blond towns and cities which broidei the hem of the land from Marseilles to Genoa. One is willing to brag; one must be a good American; but, honestly, have we anything like that to show the arriving foreigner? For some reason our ship was abating the speed with which she had crossed the Atlantic, and now she was swimming along the Mediterranean coasts so slowly and so closely that it seemed as if we could almost have cast an apple ashore, though probably we could not. We were at least far enough off to mistake Nice for Monte Carlo and then for San Remo, but that was partly because our course was so leisurely, and we thought we must have passed Nice long before we did. It did not matter; all those places were alike beautiful under the palms of their promenades, with their scattered villas and hotels stretching along their upper levels, and the ranks of shops and dwellings solidly forming the streets which left the shipping of their ports to climb to the gardens and farms beyond the villas. Cannes, Mentone, Ventimiglia, Ospedeletti, Bordighera, Taggia, Alassio: was that their fair succession, or did they follow in another order? Once more it did not matter; what is certain is that the golden sun of the soft January afternoon turned to crimson and left the last of them suffused in dim rose before we drifted into Genoa and came to anchor at dusk beside a steamer which had left New York on the same day as ours. By her vast size we could measure our own and have an objective perception of our grandeur. We had crossed in one of the largest ships afloat, but you cannot be both spectacle and spectator; and you must

W. D. Howells

match your magnificence with some rival magnificence before you can have a due sense of it. That was what we now got at Genoa, and we could not help pitying the people on that other ship, who must have suffered shame from our overwhelming magnitude; the fact that she was of nearly the same tonnage as our own ship had nothing to do with the case.

After the creamy and rosy tints of those daughters of climate along the Riviera, it was pleasant to find a many-centuried mother of commerce like Genoa of the dignified gray which she wears to the eye, whether it looks down on her from the heights above her port or up at her from the thickly masted and thickly funnelled waters of the harbor. Most European towns have red tiled roofs, which one gets rather tired of putting into one's word paintings, but the roofs of Genoa are gray tiled, and gray are her serried house walls, and gray her many churches and bell-towers. The sober tone gratifies your eye immensely, and the fact that your eye has noted it and not attributed the conventional coloring of southern Europe to the city is a flattery to your pride which you will not refuse. It is not a setting for opera like Naples; there is something businesslike in it which agrees with your American mood if you are true to America, and recalls you to duty if you are not.

I had not been in Genoa since 1864 except for a few days in 1905, and I saw changes which I will mostly not specify. Already at the earlier date the railway had cut through the beautiful and reverend Doria garden and left the old palace some scanty grounds on the sea-level, where commerce noisily encompassed it with trains and tracks and lines of freight-cars. But there had remained up to my last visit that grot on the gardened hill-slope whence a colossal marble Hercules helplessly overlooked the offence offered by the railroad; and now suddenly here was the lofty wall of some new edifice stretching across in front of the Hercules and wholly shutting him from view; for all I know it may have made him part of its structure.

Let this stand for a type of the change which had passed upon Genoa and has passed or is passing upon all Italy. The trouble is that Italy is full of very living Italians, the quickest-witted people in the world, who are alert to seize every chance for bettering themselves financially as they have bettered themselves politically. For my part, I always wonder they do not still rule the world when I see how intellectually fit they are to do it, how beyond any other race they seem still equipped for their ancient primacy. Possibly it is their ancient primacy which hangs about their necks and loads them down. It is better to have too little past, as we have, than too much, as they have. But if antiquity hampers them, they are tenderer of its vast mass than we are of our little fragments of it; tenderer than any other people, except perhaps the English, have shown themselves; but when the time comes that the past stands distinctly in the way of the future, down goes the past, even in Italy. I am not saying that I do not see why that railroad could not have tunnelled under the Doria garden rather than cut through it; and I am waiting for that new building to justify its behavior toward that poor old Hercules; but in the mean time I hold that Italy is for the Italians who now live in it, and have to get that better living out of it which we others all want our countries to yield us; and that it is not merely a playground for tourists who wish to sentimentalize it, or study it, or sketch it, or make copy of it, as I am doing now.

All the same I will not deny that I enjoyed more than any of the improvements which I noted in Genoa that bit of the old Doria palace-grounds which progress has left it. The gray edifice looks out on the neighboring traffic across the leanness of a lovely old garden, with statues and stone seats, and in the midst a softly soliloquizing fountain, painted green with moss and mould. When you enter the palace, as you do in response to a custodian who soon comes with a key and asks if you would like to see it, you find yourself, one flight up, in a long glazed gallery, fronting on the garden, which is so warm with the sun that you wish to spend the rest of your stay in Genoa there. It is frescoed round with classically imagined portraits of the different Dorias, and above all the portrait of that great hero of the republic. I do not know that this portrait particularly impresses you; if you have been here before you will be reserving yourself for the portrait which the custodian will lead you to see in the ultimate chamber of the rather rude old palace, where it is like a living presence.

It is the picture of a very old man in a flat cap, sitting sunken forward in his deep chair, with his thin, long hands folded one on the other, and looking wearily at you out of his faded eyes, in which dwell the memories of action in every sort and counsel in every kind. Victor in battles by land and sea, statesman and leader and sage, he looks it all in that wonderful effigy, which shuns no effect of his more than ninety years, but confesses his great age as a part of his greatness with a pathetic reality. The white beard, with "each particular hair" defined, falling almost to the pale, lean hands, is an essential part of the presentment, which is full of such scrupulous detail as the eye would unconsciously take note of in confronting the man himself and afterward supply in the remembrance of the whole. As if it were a part of his personality, on a table facing him, covered with maps and papers, sits the mighty admiral's cat, which, with true feline im-passiveness, ignores the spectator and gives its sole regard to the admiral. There are possibly better portraits in the world than this, which was once by Sebastiano del Piombo and is now by Titian; but I remember none which has moved me more.

We tried in vain for a photograph of it, and then after a brief glance at the riches of the Church of the Annunziata, where we were followed around the interior by a sacristan who desired us to note that the pillars were "All inlady, all inlady" with different marbles, and, after a chilly moment in San Lorenzo, which the worshippers and the masons were sharing between them in the prayers and repairs always going on in cathedrals, we drove for luncheon to the hotel where we had sojourned in great comfort three years before. Genoa has rather a bad name for its hotels, but we had found this one charming, perhaps because when we had objected to going five flights up the landlord had led us yet a floor higher, that we might walk into the garden. It is so in much of Genoa, where the precipitous nature of the site makes this vivid contrast between the levels of the front door and the back gate. Many of the streets have been widened since Heine saw the gossiping neighbors touching knees across them, but nothing less than an earthquake could change the temperamental topography of the place. It has its advantages; when there is a ring at the door the housemaid, instead of panting up from the kitchen to answer it, has merely to fall down five pairs of stairs. It cannot he denied, either, that the steep incline gives a charm to the streets which overcome it with sidewalks and driveways and trolley-tracks. Such a street as the Via Garibaldi (there is a Via Garibaldi in every Italian city, town, and village, and ought to be a dozen), compactly built, but giving here and there over the houses' shoulders glimpses of the gardens lurking behind them, is of a dignity full of the energy which a flat thoroughfare never displays or imparts. Without the inspiration lent us by the street, I am sure we should never have got to the top of it with our cab when we went to the Campo Santo; and, as it was, we had to help our horses upward by involuntarily straining forward from our places. But the Campo Santo was richly worth the effort, for to visit that famous cemetery is to enjoy an experience of which it is the unique opportunity.

W. D. Howells

I wish to celebrate it because it seems to me one of the frankest expressions of national taste and nature, and I do like simplicity—in others. The modern Italians are the most literal of the realists in all the arts, and, as I had striven for reality in my own poor way, I was perhaps the more curious to see its effects in sculpture which I had heard of so much. I will own that they went far beyond my expectation and possibly my wishes; but it is not to be supposed that it is only inferior artists who have abandoned themselves to the excesses of fidelity so abundant in the Campo Santo. There are, of course, enough poor falterings of allegory and tradition in the marble walls and floors of this vast residence of the dead (as it gives you the cheerful impression of being), but the characteristic note of the place is a realism braving it out in every extreme of actuality. Possibly the fact is most striking in that death-bed scene where the family, life-size and unsparingly portraitured, and, as it were, photographed in marble, are gathered in the room of the dying mother. She lies on a bedstead which bears every mark of being one of a standard chamber-set in the early eighteen-seventies, and about her stand her husband and her sons and daughters and their wives and husbands, in the fashions of that day. I recall a brother, in a cutaway coat, and a daughter, in a tie-back, embraced in their grief and turning their faces away from their mother toward the spectator; and doubtless there were others whom to describe in their dress would render as grotesque. It is enough to say that the artist, of a name well known in Italy and of uncommon gift, has been as true to the moment in their costume as to the eternal humanity in their faces. He has done what the sculptor or painter of the great periods of art used to do with their historical and scriptural people—he has put them in the dress of his own time and place; and it is impossible to deny him a convincing logic. No sophistry or convention of drapery in the scene could have conveyed its pathos half so well, or indeed at all. It does make you shudder, I allow; it sets your teeth on edge;

but then, if you are a real man or woman, it brings the lump into your throat; the smile fails from your lip; you pay the tribute of genuine pity and awe. I will not pretend that I was so much moved by the meeting in heaven of a son and father: the spirit of the son in a cutaway, with a derby hat in his hand, gazing with rapture into the face of the father's spirit in a long sack-coat holding his marble bowler elegantly away from his side, if I remember rightly. But here the fact wanted the basis of simplicity so strong in the other scene; in the mixture of the real and the ideal the group was romanticistic.

There are innumerable other portrait figures and busts in which the civic and social hour is expressed. The women's hair is dressed in this fashionable way or that; the men's beards are cut in conformity to the fashion or the personal preference in side whiskers or mustache or imperial or goatee; and their bronze or marble faces convey the contemporary character of aristocrat or bourgeois or politician or professional. I do not know just what the reader would expect me to say in defence of the full-length figure of a lady in *decollete* and trained evening dress, who enters from the tomb toward the spectator as if she were coming into a drawing-room after dinner. She is very beautiful, but she is no longer very young, and the bare arms, which hang gracefully at her side, respond to an intimation of *embonpoint* in the figure, with a slightly flabby over-largeness where they lose themselves in the ample shoulders. Whether this figure is the fancy of the sorrowing husband or the caprice of the defunct herself, who wished to be shown to after-time as she hoped she looked in the past, I do not know; but I had the same difficulty with it as I had with that father and son; it was romanticistic. Wholly realistic and rightly actual was that figure of an old woman who is said to have put by all her savings from the grocery business that she might appear properly in the Campo Santo, and who is shown there short and stout and common, in her ill-fitting best dress, but motherly and kind and of an undeniable and touching dignity.

If I am giving the reader the impression that I went to the Campo Santo in my last stop at Genoa, I am deceiving him; I record here the memories of four years ago. I did not revisit the place, but I should like to see it again, if only to revive my recollections of its unique interest. I did really revisit the Pal-lavicini-Durazzo palace, and there revived the pleasure I had known before in its wonderful Van Dycks. Most wonderful was and will always be the "Boy in White," the little serene princeling, whoever he was, in whom the painter has fixed forever a bewitching mood and moment of childhood. "The Mother with two Children" is very well and self-evidently true to personality and period and position; but, after all, she is nothing beside that "Boy in White," though she and her children are otherwise so wonderful. Now that I speak of her, however, she rather grows upon my recollection as a woman greater than her great world and proudly weary of it.

She was a lady of that very patrician house whose palace, in its cold grandeur and splendor, renews at once all one's faded or fading sense of the commercial past of Italy, when her greatest merchants were her greatest nobles and dwelt in magnificence unparalleled yet since Rome began to be old. Genoa, Venice, Pisa, Florence, what state their business men housed themselves in and environed themselves with! Their palaces by the hundreds were such as only the public edifices of our less simple State capitols could equal in size and not surpass in cost. Their *folie des grandeurs* realized illusions in architecture, in sculpture, and in painting which the assembled and concentrated feats of those arts all the way up and down Fifth Avenue, and in the millionaire blocks eastward could not produce the likeness of. We have the same madness in our brains; we have even a Roman megalomania, but the effect of it in Chicago or Pittsburg or Philadelphia or New York has not yet got beyond a ducal or a princely son-in-law. The splendors of such alliances have still to take substantial form in a single instance worthy to compare with a thousand instances in the commercial republics of Italy. This does not mean that our rich people have not so much money as the Italians of the Renaissance, but that perhaps in their *folie des grandeurs* they are a different kind of madmen; it means also that land and labor are dearer positively and comparatively with us, and that our pork-packing or stock-broking princes prefer to spend on comfort rather than size in their houses, and do not like the cold feet which the merchant princes of Italy must have had from generation to generation. I shall always be sorry I did not wear arctics when I went to the Pallavicini-Durazzo palace, and I strongly tirge the reader to do so when he goes.

He will not so much need them out-of-doors in a Genoese January, unless a *tramontana* is blowing, and there was none on our half-day. But in any case we did not walk. We selected the best-looking cab-horse we could find, and he turned out better than his driver, who asked a fabulous price by the hour. We obliged him to show his tariff, when his wickedness was apparent from the printed rates. He explained that the part we were looking at was obsolete, and he showed us another part, which was really for drives outside the city; but we agreed to pay it, and set out hoping for good behavior from him that would make up the difference. Again we were deceived; at the end he demanded a franc beyond even his unnatural fare. I urged that one should be reasonable; but he seemed to think not, and to avoid controversy I paid the extortionate franc. I remembered that just a month before, in New York, I had paid an extortionate dollar in like circumstances.

　　　　　　W. D. Howells

Nevertheless, that franc above and beyond the stipulated extortion impoverished me, and when we came to take a rowboat back to our steamer I beat the boatman down cruelly, mercilessly. He was a poor, lean little man, with rather a superannuated boat, and he labored harder at the oar than I could bear to see without noting his exertion to him. This was fatal; instantly he owned that I was right, and he confessed, moreover, that he was the father of a family, and that some of his children were then suffering from sickness as well as want. What could one do but make the fare up to the first demand of three francs after having got the price down to one and a half? At the time it seemed to me that I was somehow by this means getting the better of the cabman who had obliged me to pay a franc more than his stipulated extortion, but I do not now hope to make it appear so to the reader.

IV

NAPLES AND HER JOYFUL NOISE

We heard the joyful noise of Naples as soon as our steamer came to anchor within the moles whose rigid lines perhaps disfigure her famous bay, while they render her harbor so secure. The noise first rose to us, hanging over the guard, and trying to get phrases for the glory of her sea and sky and mountains and monuments, from a boat which seemed to have been keeping abreast of us ever since we had slowed up. It was not a largo boat, but it managed to contain two men with mandolins, a mother of a family with a guitar, and a young girl with an alternate tambourine and umbrella. The last instrument was inverted to catch the coins, such as they were, which the passengers flung down to the minstrels for their repetitions of "Santa Lucia," "Funicoli-Funicola," "Il Cacciatore," and other popular Neapolitan airs, such as "John Brown's Body" and "In the Bowery." To the songs that had a waltz movement the mother of a family performed a restricted dance, at some risk of falling overboard, while she smiled radiantly up at us, as, in fact, they all did, except the young girl, who had to play simultaneously on her tambourine and her inverted umbrella, and seemed careworn. Her anxiety visibly deepened to despair when she missed a shilling, which must have looked as large to her as a full moon as it sank slowly down into the sea.

W. D. Howells

But her despair did not last long; nothing lasts long in Naples except the joyful noise, which is incessant and perpetual, and which seems the expression of the universal temperament in both man and beast. Our good-fortune placed us in a hotel fronting the famous Castel dell' Ovo, across a little space of land and water, and we could hear, late and early, the cackling and crowing of the chickens which have replaced the hapless prisoners of other days in that fortress. At times the voices of the hens were lifted in a choral of self-praise, as if they had among them just laid the mighty structure which takes its name from its resemblance to the egg they ordinarily produce. In other lands the peculiar note of the donkey is not thought very melodious, but in Naples before it can fade away it is caught up in the general orchestration and ceases in music. The cabmen at our corner, lying in wait by scores for the strangers whom it is their convention to suppose ignorant of their want of a carriage, quarrelled rhythmically with one another; the mendicants, lying every-where in wait for charity, murmured a modulated appeal; if you heard shouts or yells afar off they died upon your ear in a strain of melody at the moment when they were lifted highest. I am aware of seeming to burlesque the operatic fact which every one must have noticed in Naples; and I will not say that the neglected or affronted babe, or the trodden dog, is as tuneful as the midnight cat there, but only that they approach it in the prevailing tendency of all the local discords to soften and lose themselves in the general unison. This embraces the clatter of the cabs, which are seldom less than fifty years old, and of a looseness in all their joints responsive to their effect of dusty decrepitude. Their clatter penetrates the volumed tread of the myriad feet in a city where, if you did not see all sorts of people driving, you would say the whole population walked. Above the manifold noises gayly springing to the sky spreads and swims the clangor of the church-bells and holds the terrestrial uproar in immeasurable solution. It would be rash to say that the whole population of Naples is always in the street, for if you look into the shops or cafes, or, I dare say, the houses, you will find them quite full; but the general statement verifies itself almost tiresomely in its agreement with what everybody has always said of Naples. It is so quite what you expect that if you could you would turn away in satiety, especially from the swarming life of the poor, which seems to have no concealments from the public, but frankly works at all the trades and arts that can be carried on out-of-doors; cooks, eats, laughs, cries, sleeps, wakes, makes love, quarrels, scolds, does everything but wash itself—clothes enough it washes for other people's life. There is a reason for this in the fact that in bad weather at Naples it is cold and dark and damp in-doors, and in fine so bright and warm and charming without that there is really no choice. Then there is the expansive temperament, which if it were shut up would probably be much more explosive than it is now. As it is, it vents itself in volleyed detonations and scattered shots which language can give no sense of.

For the true sense of it you must go to Naples, and then you will never lose the sense of it. I had not been there since 1864, but when I woke up the morning after my arrival, and heard the chickens cackling in the Castel dell' Ovo, and the donkeys braying, and the cab-drivers quarrelling, and the cries of the street vendors, and the dogs barking, and the children wailing, and their mothers scolding, and the clatter of wheels and hoops and feet, and all that mighty harmony of the joyful Neapolitan noises, it seemed to me that it was the first morning after my first arrival, and I was still only twenty-seven years old. As soon as possible, when the short but sweet Vincenzo had brought up my breakfast of tea and bread-and-butter and honey (to which my appetite turned from the gross superabundance of the steamer's breakfasts with instant acquiescence), and announced with a smile as liberal as the sunshine that it was a fine day, I went out for those impressions which I had better make over to the reader in their original disorder. Vesuvius, which was silver veiled the day before, was now of a soft, smoky white, and the sea, of a milky blue, swam round the shore and out to every dim island and low cape and cliffy promontory. The street was full of people on foot and in trolleys and cabs and donkey pleasure-carts, and the familiar teasing of cabmen and peddlers and beggars began with my first steps toward what I remembered as the Toledo, but what now called itself, with the moderner Italian patriotism, the Via Roma. The sole poetic novelty of my experience was in my being offered loaves of bread which, when I bought them, would be given to the poor, in honor of what saint's day I did not learn. But it was all charming; even the inattention of the young woman over the book-counter was charming, since it was a condition of her flirtation with the far younger man beside me who wanted something far more interesting from her than any brief sketch of the history of Naples, in either English or Italian or French or, at the worst, German. She was very pretty, though rather powdered, and when the young man went away she was sympathetically regretful to me that there was no such sketch, in place of which she offered me several large histories in more or less volumes. But why should I have wanted a history of Naples when I had Naples itself? It was like wanting a photograph when you have the original. Had I not just come through the splendid Piazza San Ferdinando, with the nobly arcaded church on one hand and the many-statued royal palace on the other, and between them a lake of mellow sunshine, as warm as ours in June

What I found Naples and the Neapolitans in 1908 I had found them in 1864, and Mr. Gray (as he of the "Elegy" used to be called on his title-pages) found them in 1740. "The streets," he wrote home to his mother, "are one continued market, and thronged with populace so much that a coach can hardly pass. The common sort are a jolly, lively kind of animals, more industrious than Italians usually are; they work till evening; then they take their lute or guitar (for they all play) and walk about the city or upon the seashore with it, to enjoy the fresco." There was, in fact, a bold gayety in the aspect of the city, without the refinement which you do not begin to feel till you get into North Italy. When I came upon church after church, with its facade of Spanish baroque, I lamented the want of Gothic delicacy and beauty, but I was consoled abundantly later in the churches antedating the Spanish domination. I had no reason, such as travellers give for hating places, to be dissatisfied with Naples in any way. I had been warned that the customs officers were terrible there, and that I might be kept hours with my baggage. But the inspector, after the politest demand for a declaration of tobacco, ordered only a small valise, the Benjamin of its tribe, opened and then closed untouched; and his courteous forbearance, acknowledged later through the hotel porter, cost me but a dollar. The hotel itself was inexpressibly better in lighting, heating, service, and table than any New York hotel at twice the money—in fact, no money could buy the like with us at any hotel I know of; but this is a theme which I hope to treat more fully hereafter. It is true that the streets of Naples are very long and rather narrow and pretty crooked, and full of a damp cold that no sunlight seems ever to hunt out of them; but then they are seldom ironed down with trolley-tracks; the cabs feel their way among the swarming crowds with warning voices and smacking whips; even the prepotent automobile shows some tenderness for human life and limb, and proceeds still more cautiously than the cabs and carts—in fact, I thought I saw recurrent proofs of that respect for the average man which seems the characteristic note of Italian liberty; and this belief of mine, bred of my first observations in Naples, did not, after twelve weeks in Italy, prove an illusion. If it is not the equality we fancy ourselves having, it is rather more fraternity in effect.

The failure of other researches for that sketch of Neapolitan history left me in the final ignorance which I must share with the reader; but my inquiries brought me prompt knowledge of one of those charming features in which the Italian cities excel, if they are not unique. I remember too vaguely the Galleria, as they call the beautiful glazed arcade of Milan, to be sure that it is finer than the Galleria at Naples, but I am sure this is finer than that at Genoa, with which, however, I know nothing in other cities to compare. The Neapolitan gallery, wider than any avenue of the place, branching in the form of a Greek cross to four principal streets, is lighted by its roof of glass, and a hundred brilliant shops and cafes spread their business and leisure over its marble floor. Nothing could be architecturally more cheerful, and, if it were not too hot in summer, there could be no doubt of its adaptation to our year, for it could be easily closed against the winter by great portals, and at other seasons would give that out-door expansion which in Latin countries hospitably offers the spectacle of pleasant eating and drinking to people who have nothing to eat and drink. These spectators could be kept at a distance with us by porters at the entrances, while they would not be altogether deprived of the gratifying glimpses.

I do not know whether poverty avails itself of its privileges by visiting the Neapolitan gallery; but probably, like poverty elsewhere, it is too much interested by the drama of life in its own quarter ever willingly to leave it. Poverty is very conservative, for reasons more than one; its quarter in Naples is the oldest, and was the most responsive to our recollections of the Naples of 1864. Overhead the houses tower and beetle with their balconies and bulging casements, shutting the sun, except at noon, from the squalor below, where the varied dwellers bargain and battle and ply their different trades, bringing their work from the dusk of cavernous shops to their doorways for the advantage of the prevailing twilight. Carpentry and tailoring and painting and plumbing, locksmithing and copper-smithing go on there, touching elbows with frying and feeding, and the vending of all the strange and hideous forms of flesh, fish, and fowl. If you wish to know how much the tentacle of a small polyp is worth you may chance to see a cent pass for it from the crone who buys to the boy who sells it smoking from the kettle; but the price of cooked cabbage or pumpkin must remain a mystery, along with that of many raw vegetables and the more revolting viscera of the less-recognizable animals.

The poor people worming in and out around your cab are very patient of your progress over the terrible floor of their crooked thoroughfare, perhaps because they reciprocate your curiosity, and perhaps because they are very amiable and not very sensitive. They are not always crowded into these dismal chasms; their quarter expands here and there into market-plates, like the fish-market where the uprising of the fisherman Masaniello against the Spaniards fitly took place; and the Jewish market-place, where the poor young Corradino, last of the imperial Hohenstaufen line, was less appropriately beheaded by the Angevines. The open spaces are not less loathsome than the reeking alleys, but if you have the intelligent guide we had you approach them through the triumphal arch by which Charles V. entered Naples, and that is something. Yet we will now talk less of the emperor than of the guide, who appealed more to my sympathy.

He had been six years in America, which he adored, because, he said, he had got work and earned his living there the very day he landed. That was in Boston, where he turned his hand first to one thing and then another, and came away at last through some call home, honoring and loving the Americans as the kindest, the noblest, the friendliest people in the world. I tried, politely, to persuade him that we were not all of us all he thought us, but he would not yield, and at one place he generously claimed a pre-eminence in wickedness for his fellow-Neapolitans. That was when we came to a vast, sorrowful prison, from which an iron cage projected into the street. Around this cage wretched women and children and old men clustered till the prisoners dear to them were let into it from the jail and allowed to speak with them. The scene was as public as all of life and death is in Naples, and the publicity seemed to give it peculiar sadness, which I noted to our guide. He owned its pathos; "but," he said, "you know we have a terrible class of people here in Naples." I protested that there were terrible classes of people everywhere, even in America. He would not consent entirely, but in partly convincing each other we became better friends. He had a large black mustache and gentle black eyes, and he spoke very fair English, which, when he wished to be most impressive, he dropped and used a very literary Italian instead. He showed us where he lived, on a hill-top back of our gardened quay, and said that he paid twelve dollars a month for a tenement of five rooms there. Schooling is compulsory in Naples, but he sends his boy willingly, and has him especially study English as the best provision he can make for him—as heir of his own calling of cicerone, perhaps. He has a little farm at Bavello, which he tills when it is past the season for cultivating foreigners in Naples; he expects to spend his old age there; and I thought it not a bad lookout. He was perfectly well-mannered, and at a hotel where we stopped for tea he took his coffee at our table unbidden, like any American fellow-man. He and the landlord had their joke together, the landlord warning me against him in English as "very bad man," and clapping him affectionately on the shoulder to emphasize the irony. We did not demand too much social information of him; all the more we valued the gratuitous fact that the Neapolitan nobles were now rather poor, because they preferred a life of pleasure to a life of business. I could have told him that the American nobles were increasingly like them in their love of pleasure, but I would not have known how to explain that they were not poor also. He was himself a moderate in politics, but he told us, what seems to be the fact everywhere in Italy, that singly the largest party in Naples is the Socialist party.

He went with me first one day to the beautiful old Church of Santa Chiara, to show me the Angevine tombs there, in which I satisfied a secret, lingering love for the Gothic; and then to the cathedral, where the sacristan showed us everything but the blood of St. Jannarius, perhaps because it was not then in the act of liquefying; but I am thankful to say I saw one of his finger-bones. My guide had made me observe how several of the churches on the way to this were built on the sites and of the remnants of pagan temples, and he summoned the world-old sacristan of St. Januarius to show us evidences of a rival antiquity in the crypt; for it had begun as a temple of Neptune. The sacristan practically lived in those depths and the chill sanctuary above them, and-he was so full of rheumatism that you could almost hear it creak as he walked; yet he was a cheerful sage, and satisfied with the fee which my guide gave him and which he made small, as he explained, that the sacristan might not be discontented with future largesse. I need not say that each church we visited had its tutelary beggar, and that my happy youth came back to me in the blindness of one, or the mutilation of another, or the haggish wrinkles of a third. At Santa Chiara I could not at first make out what it was which caused my heart to rejoice so; but then I found that it was because the church was closed, and we had to go and dig a torpid monk out of his crevice in a cold, many-storied cliff near by, and get him to come and open it, just as I used, with the help of neighbors, to do in the past.

Our day ended at sunset—a sunset of watermelon red—with a visit to the Castel Nuovo, where my guide found himself at

W. D. Howells

home with the garrison, because, as he explained, he had served his term as a soldier. He was the born friend of the custodian of the castle church, which was the most comfortable church for warmth we had visited, and to which we entered by the bronze gates of the triumphal arch raised in honor of the Aragonese victory over the Angevines in 1442, when this New Castle was newer than it is now. The bronze gates record in bas-relief the battles between the French and Spanish powers in their quarrel over the people one or other must make its prey; but whether it was to the greater advantage of the Neapolitans to be battened on by the house of Aragon and then that of Bourbon for the next six hundred years after the Angevines had retired from the banquet is problematical. History is a very baffling study, and one may be well content to know little or nothing about it. I knew so little or had forgotten so much that I scarcely deserved to be taken down into the crypt of this church and shown the skeletons of four conspirators for Anjou whom Aragon had put to death—two laymen and an archbishop by beheading, and a woman by dividing crosswise into thirds. The skeletons lay in their tattered and dusty shrouds, and I suppose were authentic enough; but I had met them, poor things, too late in my life to Avish for their further acquaintance. Once I could have exulted to search out their story and make much of it; but now I must leave it to the reader's imagination, along with most other facts of my observation in Naples.

I was at some pains to look up the traces of my lost youth there, and if I could have found more of them no doubt I should have been more interested in these skeletons. Eor forty-odd years I had remembered the prodigious pictures-queness of certain streets branching from a busy avenue and ascending to uplands above by stately successions of steps. When I demanded these of my guide, he promptly satisfied me, and in a few moments, there in the Chiaja, we stood at the foot of such a public staircase. I had no wish to climb it, but I found it more charming even than I remembered. All the way to the top it was banked on either side with glowing masses of flowers and fruits and the spectacular vegetables of the South, and between these there were series of people, whom I tacitly delegated to make the ascent for me, passing the groups bargaining at the stalls. Nothing could have been better; nothing that I think of is half so well in New York, where the markets are on that dead level which in the social structure those above it abhor; though there are places on the East River where we might easily have inclined markets.

Other associations of that far past awoke with my identification of the hotel where we had stayed at the end of the Villa Nazionale. In those days the hotel was called, in appeal to our patriotism, more flattered then than now in Europe, Hotel Washington; but it is to-day a mere pension, though it looks over the same length of palm-shaded, statue-peopled garden. The palms were larger than I remembered them, and the statues had grown up and seemed to have had large families since my day; but the lovely sea was the same, with all the mural decorations of the skyey horizons beyond, dim precipices and dreamy island tops, and the dozing Vesuvius mistakable for any of them. At one place there was a file of fishermen, including a fisherwoman, drawing their net by means of a rope carried across the carriage-way from the seawall, with a splendid show of their black eyes and white teeth and swarthy, bare legs, and always there were beggars, both of those who frankly begged and those who importuned with postal-cards. This terrible traffic pervades all southern Europe, and everywhere pesters the meeting traveller with undesired bargains. In its presence it is almost impossible to fit a scene with the apposite phrase; and yet one must own that it has its rights. What would those boys do if they did not sell, or fail to sell, postal-cards. It is another aspect of the labor problem, so many-faced in our time. Would it be better

W. D. Howells

that they should take to open mendicancy, or try to win the soft American heart with such acquired slang as "Skiddoo to twenty-three"? One who had no postal-cards had English enough to say he would go away for a penny; it was his price, and I did not see how he could take less; when he was reproached by a citizen of uncommon austerity for his shameless annoyance of strangers, I could not see that he looked abashed—in fact, he went away singing. He did not take with him the divine beauty of the afternoon light on the sea and mountains; and, if he was satisfied, we were content with our bargain.

In fact, it would be impossible to exaggerate in the praise of that incomparable environment. At every hour of the day, and, for all I know, the night, it had a varying beauty and a constant loveliness. Six days out of the week of our stay the sunshine was glorious, and five days of at least a May or September warmth; and though one day was shrill and stiff with the *tramontana,* it was of as glorious sunshine as the rest. The gale had blown my window open and chilled my room, but with that sun blazing outside I could not believe in the hurricane which seemed to blow our car up the funicular railway when we mounted to the height where the famous old Convent of San Martino stands, and then blew us all about the dust-clouded streets of that upland in our search for the right way to the monastery. It was worth more than we suffered in finding it; for the museum is a record of the most significant events of Neapolitan history from the time of the Spanish domination down to that of the Garibaldian invasion; and the church and corridors through which the wind hustled us abound in paintings and frescos such as one would be willing to give a whole week of quiet weather to. I do not know but I should like to walk always in the convent garden, or merely look into it from my window in the cloister wall, and gossip with my fellow-friars at their windows. We should all be ghosts, of course, but the more easily could the sun warm us through in spite of the *tramontana*.

I do not know that Naples is very beautiful in certain phases in which Venice and Genoa are excellent. Those cities were adorned by their sons with palaces of an outlook worthy of their splendor. But in the other Italian cities the homes of her patricians were crowded into the narrow streets where their architecture fails of its due effect. It is so with them in Naples, and even along the Villa Nazionale, where many palatial villas are set, they seclude themselves in gardens where one fancies rather than sees them. These are, in fact, sometimes the houses of the richest bourgeoisie—bankers and financiers—and the houses which have names conspicuous in the mainly inglorious turmoil of Neapolitan history help unnoted to darken the narrow and winding ways of the old city. A glimpse of a deep court or of a towering facade is what you get in passing, but it is to be said of the sunless streets over which they gloom that they are kept in a modern neatness beside which the dirt of New York is mediaeval. It is so with most other streets in Naples, except those poorest ones where the out-door life insists upon the most intimate domestic expression. Even such streets are no worse than our worst streets, and the good streets are all better kept than our best.

I am not sure that there are even more beggars in Naples than in New York, though I will own that I kept no count. In both cities beggary is common enough, and I am not noting it with disfavor in either, for it is one of my heresies that comfort should be constantly reminded of misery by the sight of it—comfort is so forgetful. Besides, in Italy charity costs so little; a cent of our money pays a man for the loss of a leg or an arm; two cents is the compensation for total blindness; a sick mother with a brood of starving children is richly rewarded for her pains with a nickel worth four cents.

W. D. Howells

Organized charity is not absent in the midst of such volunteers of poverty; one day, when we thought we had passed the last outpost of want in our drive, two Sisters of Charity suddenly appeared with out-stretched tin cups. Our driver did not imagine our inexhaustible benovelence; he drove on, and before we could bring him to a halt the Sisters of Charity ran us down, their black robes flying abroad and their sweet faces flushed with the pursuit. Upon the whole it was very humiliating; we could have wished to offer our excuses and regrets; but our silver seemed enough, and the gentle sisters fell back when we had given it.

That was while we were driving toward Posilipo for the beauty of the prospect along the sea and shore, and for a sense of which any colored postal-card will suffice better than the most hectic word-painting. The worst of Italy is the superabundance of the riches it offers ear and eye and nose—offers every sense—ending in a glut of pleasure. At the point where we descended from our carriage to look from the upland out over the vast hollow of land and sea toward Pozzuoli, which is so interesting as the scene of Jove's memorable struggle with the Titans, and just when we were really beginning to feel equal to it, a company of minstrels suddenly burst upon us with guitars and mandolins and comic songs much dramatized, while the immediate natives offered us violets and other distracting flowers. In the effect, art and nature combined to neutralize each other, as they do with us, for instance, in those restaurants where they have music during dinner, and where you do not know whether you are eating the *chef-d'oeuvre* of a cook or a composer.

It was at the new hotel which is evolving itself through the repair of the never-finished and long-ruined Palace of Donn' Anna, wife of a Spanish viceroy in the seventeenth century, that our guide stopped with us for that cup of tea already mentioned. We had to climb four nights of stairs for it to the magnificent salon overlooking the finest postal-card prospect in all Naples. We lingered long upon it, in the balcony from which we could have dropped into the sunset sea any coin which we could have brought ourselves to part with; but we had none of the bad money which had been so easily passed off upon us. This sort rather abounds in Naples, and the traveller should watch not only for false francs, but for francs of an obsolete coinage which you can know by the king's head having a longer neck than in the current pieces. At the bookseller's they would not take a perfectly good five-franc piece because it was so old as 1815; and what becomes of all the bad money one innocently takes for good? One fraudulent franc I made a virtue of throwing away; but I do not know what I did with a copper refused by a trolley conductor as counterfeit. I could not take the affair seriously, and perhaps I gave that copper in charity.

As we drove hotehvard through the pink twilight we met many carriages of people who looked rich and noble, but whether they were so I do not know. I only know that old ladies who regard the world severely from their coaches behind the backs of their perfectly appointed coachmen and footmen ought to be both, and that old gentlemen who frown over their white mustaches have no right to their looks if they are neither. It was, at any rate, the hour of the fashionable drive, which included a pause midway of the Villa Nazionale for the music of the military band.

The band plays near the Aquarium, which I hope the reader will visit at the earlier hours of the day. Then, if he has a passion for polyps, and wishes to imagine how they could ingulf good-sized ships in the ages of fable, he can see one of the hideous things float from its torpor in the bottom of its tank, and seize Avith its hungry tentacles the food lowered to it by a string. Still awfuller is it to see it rise and reach with those prehensile members, as with the tails of a

W. D. Howells

multi-caudate ape, some rocky projection of its walls and lurk fearsomely into the hollow, and vanish there in a loathly quiescence. The carnivorous spray and bloom of the deep-sea flowers amid which drowned men's "bones are coral made" seem of one temperament with the polyps as they slowly, slowly wave their tendrils and petals; but there is amusement if not pleasure in store for the traveller who turns from them to the company of shad softly and continuously circling in their tank, and regarding the spectators with a surly dignity becoming to people in better society than others. One large shad, imaginably of very old family and independent property, sails at the head of several smaller shad, his flatterers and toadies, who try to look like him. Mostly his expression is very severe; but in milder moments he offers a perverse resemblance to some portraits of Washington.

All our days in Naples died like dolphins to the music which I have tried to impart the sense of. The joyful noises which it was made up of culminated for us on that evening when a company of the street and boat musicians came into the hotel and danced and sang and played the tarantella. They were of all ages, sexes, and bulks, and of divers operatic costumes, but they were of one temperament only, which was glad and childlike. They went through their repertory, which included a great deal more than the tarantella, and which we applauded with an enthusiasm attested by our contributions when the tambourine went round. Then they repeated their selections, and at the second collection we guests of the hotel repeated our contributions, but in a more guarded spirit. After the second repetition the prettiest girl came round with her photographs and sold them at prices out of all reason. Then we became very melancholy, and began to steal out one by one. I myself did not stay for the fourth collection, and I cannot report how the different points of view, the Southern and the Northern, were reconciled in the event which I am not sure was final. But I am sure that unless you can make allowance for a world-wide difference in the Neapolitans from yourself you can never understand them. Perhaps you cannot, even then.

W. D. Howells

V

POMPEII REVISITED

Because I felt very happy in going back to Pompeii after a generation, and being alive to do so in the body, I resolved to behave handsomely by the cabman who drove me from my hotel to the station. I said to myself that I would do something that would surprise him, and I gave him his fee and nearly a franc over; but it was I who was surprised, for he ran after me into the station, as I supposed, to extort more. He was holding out a franc toward me, and I asked the guide who was bothering me to take him to Pompeii (where there are swarms of guides always on the grounds) what the matter was. "It is false," he explained, and this proved true, though whether the franc was the one I had given the driver or whether it was one which he had thoughtfully substituted for it to make good an earlier loss I shall now never know. I put it into my pocket, wondering what I should do with it; the question what you shall do with counterfeit money in Italy is one which is apt to recur as I have hinted, and in despair of solving it at the moment I threw the false franc out of the car-window; it was the false franc I have already boasted of throwing away.

This was, of course, after I got into the car, and after I had suffered another wrong, and was resolved at least to be good myself. I had taken first-class tickets, but, when we had followed several conductors up and down the train, the last of them said there were no first-class places left, though I shall always doubt this. I asked what we should do, and he shrugged. I had heard that if you will stand upon your rights in such a matter the company will have to put on another car for you. But I was now dealing with the Italian government, which has nationalized the railroads, but has apparently not yet repleted the rolling stock; and when the conductor found us places in a second-class carriage, rather than quarrel with a government which had troubles enough already I got aboard. I suppose really that I have not much public spirit, and that the little I have I commonly leave at home; in travelling it is burdensome. Besides, the second-class carriage would have been comfortable enough if it had not been so dirty; it looked as if it had not been washed since it was flooded with liquid ashes at the destruction of Pompeii, though they seemed to be cigar ashes.

The country through which we made the hour's run was sympathetically squalid. We had, to be sure, the sea on one side, and that was clean enough; but the day was gray, and the sea was responsively gray; while the earth on the other side was torn and ragged, with people digging manure into the patches of broccoli, and gardening away as if it had been April instead of January. There were shabby villas, with stone-pines and cypresses herding about the houses, and tatters of life-plant overhanging their shabby walls; there were stucco shanties which the men and women working in the fields would lurk in at nightfall. At places there was some cheerful boat building, and at one place there was a large macaroni manufactory, with far stretches of the product dangling in hanks and skeins from rows of trellises. We passed through towns where women and children swarmed, working at doorways and playing in the dim, cold streets; from the balconies everywhere winter melons hung in nets,

　　　　W. D. Howells

dozens and scores of them, such as you can buy at the Italian fruiterers' in New York, and will keep buying when once you know how good they are. In Naples they sell them by the slice in the street, the fruiterer carrying a board on his head with the slices arranged in an upright coronal like the rich, barbaric head-dress of some savage prince.

Our train was slow and our car was foul, but nothing could keep us from arriving at Pompeii in very good spirits. The entrance to the dead city is gardened about with a cemeterial prettiness of evergreens; but, after you have bought your ticket and been assigned your guide, you pass through this decorative zone and find yourself in the first of streets where the past makes no such terms with the present. If some of the houses of an ampler plan had little spaces beyond the atrium planted with such flowers as probably grew there two thousand years ago, and stuck round with tiny figurines, it was to the advantage of the people's fancy; but it did not appeal so much to the imagination as the mould and moss, and the small, weedy network that covered the ground in the roofless chambers and temples and basilicas, where the broken columns and walls started from the floors which this unmeditated verdure painted in the favorite hue of ruin.

Most of the places I re-entered through my recollection of them, but to this subjective experience there was added that of seeing much newer and vaster things than I remembered. That sad population of the victims of the disaster, restored to the semhlance of life, or perhaps rather of death, in plaster casts taken from the moulds their decay had left in the hardening ashes, had much increased in the melancholy museum where one visits them the first thing within the city gates. But their effect was not cumulative; there were more writhing women and more contorted men; but they did not make their tragedy more evident than it had been when I saw them, fewer but not less affecting, all those years ago. It was the same with the city itself; Pompeii had grown, like the rest of the world in the interval, and, although it had been dug tip instead of built up, a good third had been added to the count of its streets and houses. There were not, so far as I could see, more ruts from chariot-wheels in the lava blocks of the thoroughfares, but some convincingly two-storied dwellings had been exhumed, and others with ceilings in better condition than those of the earlier excavations; there were more all-but-unbroken walls and columns; some mosaic floors were almost as perfect as when their dwellers fled over them out of the stifling city. But upon the whole the result was a greater monotony; the revelation of house after house, nearly the same in design, did not gain impressiveness from their repetition; just as the case would be if the dwellings of an old-fashioned cross-town street in New York were dug out two thousand years after their submergence by an eruption of Orange Mountain. The identity of each of the public edifices is easily attested to the archaeologist, but the generally intelligent, as the generally unintelligent, visitor must take the archaeologist's word for the fact. One temple is much like another in its stumps of columns and vague foundations and broken altars. Among the later discoveries certain of the public baths are in the best repair, both structurally and decoratively, and in these one could replace the antique life with the least wear and tear of the imagination.

I could not tell which the several private houses were; but the guide-books can, and there I leave the specific knowledge of them; their names would say nothing to the reader if they said nothing to me. In Pompeii, where all the houses were rather small, some of the new ones were rather large, though not larger than a few of the older ones. Not more recognizably than these, they had been devoted to the varied uses known to advanced civilization in all ages: there were dwellings, and taverns and drinking-houses and eating-houses, and there were those houses where the feet of them that abide therein and of those that frequent them alike take hold on hell. In these the guide stays the men of his party to prove the character of the places to them from the frescos and statues; but it may be questioned if the visitors so indulged had not better taken the guide's word for the fact. There can be no doubt that at the heart of paganism the same plague festered which poisons Christian life, and which, while the social conditions remain the same from age to age, will poison life forever.

The pictures on the walls of the newly excavated houses are not strikingly better than those I had not forgotten; but of late it has been the purpose to leave as many of the ornaments and utensils in position as possible. The best are, as they ought to be, gathered into the National Museum at Naples, but those which remain impart a more living sense of the past than such wisely ordered accumulations; for it is the Pompeian paradox that in the image of death it can best recall life. It is a grave which has been laid bare, and it were best to leave its ghastly memories unhindered by other companionship. One feels that one ought to be there alone in order to see it aright. One should not perhaps

"Go visit it by the pale moonlight,"

but if one could have it all to one's self by day, such a gray day as we had for it, there is no telling what might happen. One thing only would certainly happen: one would get lost. It never was a town of large area; and, like all spaces that have been ruined over, it looked smaller than it would have looked if all its walls were standing with all their roofs upon them. Still, it was a mesh of streets, out of which you would in vain have sought your way if you had been caught in it alone; though it is mostly so level that if you had mounted a truncated column almost anywhere you could have looked over the labyrinth to its verge.

It was not much crowded by visitors; though there were strings of them at the heels of the respective guides, with, I thought, a prevalence of the Germans, who are now over-running Italy; I am sorry to say they are not able to keep it cheap, at least for other nationalities. Among these I noted two little smiling, shining, twinkling Japs, who carried kodaks for the capture of that classical antiquity which could never really belong to them. Their want of a pagan past in common with us may be what keeps us alien even more than the want of a common Christian tradition.

"The glory that was Greece
And the grandeur that was Rome"

could never mean to our brown companions what they meant to us; but they put on a polite air of being interested in the Graeco-Roman ruin, and were so gentle and friendly that one could almost feel they were fellow-men. Very likely they were; at any rate, until we are at war with them I shall believe so.

Our guide, whom we had really bought the whole use of at the gate, thriftily took on another party, with our leave, and it was pleasant to find that the American type from Utah was the same as from Ohio or Massachusetts; with all our differences we are the most homogeneous people under the sun, and likest a large family. We all frankly got tired at about the same time at the same place, and agreed that we had, without the amphitheatre, had enough when we ended at the Street of Tombs, where the tombs are in so much better repair than the houses. For myself, I remembered the amphitheatre so perfectly from 1864 that I did not see how I could add a single emotion there in 1908 to those I had already turned into literature; and though Pompeii is but

W. D. Howells

small, the amphitheatre is practically as far from the Street of Tombs, after you have walked about the place for two hours, as the Battery is from High Bridge. There is no Elevated or Subway at Pompeii, and even the lines of public chariots, if such they were, which left those ruts in the lava pavements seem to have been permanently suspended after the final destruction in the year 79.

We were not only very tired, but very hungry, and we asked our guide to take us back the shortest way. I suggested a cross-cut at one point, and he caught at the word eagerly, and wrote it in his note-book for future use. He also acted upon it instantly, and we cut across the back yards and over the kitchen areas of several absent citizens on our way back. Our guide was as good and true as it is in the nature of guides to be, but absolute goodness and truth are rather the attributes of American travellers; and you will not escape the small graft which the guides are so rigorously forbidden to practise. Pompeii is no longer in the keeping of the Italian army; with the Italian instinct of decentralization the place has claimed the right of self-government, and now the guides are civilians, and not soldiers, as they were in my far day. They do not accept fees, but still they take them; and our guide said that he had a brother-in-law who had the best restaurant outside the gate, where we could get luncheon for two francs. As soon as we were in the hands of the runner for that restaurant the price augmented itself to two francs and a half; when we mounted to the threshold, lured on by the fascinating mystery of this increase, it became three francs, without wine. But as the waiter justly noted, in hovering about us with the cutlery and napery while he laid the table, a two-fifty luncheon was unworthy such lords as we. When he began to bring on the delicious omelette, the admirable fish, the excellent cutlets, he made us observe that if we paid three francs we ought to eat a great deal; and there seemed reason in this; at any rate, we did so. The truth is, that luncheon was worth the money, and more; as for the Vesuvian wine, it had the rich red blood of the volcano in it, and it could not be bought in New York for half a franc the bottle, if at all; at thrice that sum in Naples it was not a third as good.

If there had been anything to do after lunch except go to the train, we could not have done it, we were so spent with our two hours' walk through Pompeii, though the gray day had been rather invigorating. Certainly it was not so exhausting as that white-hot day forty-three years before when I had broiled over the same ground under the blazing sun of a Pompeian November. Yet the difference in the muscles and emotions of twenty-seven as against those of seventy told in favor of the white-hot day; and, besides that, in the time that had elapsed a much greater burden of antiquity had been added to the city than had accumulated in its history between the year 79 and the year 1864. During most of those centuries Pompeii had been dreamlessly sleeping under its ashes, but in the ensuing less than half a century it had wakefully, however unwillingly, witnessed such events as the failure of secession and the abolition of slavery, the unification of Italy and Germany, the fall of the Second Empire, the liberation of Cuba, and the acquisition of the Philippines, the exile of Richard Croker, the destruction of the Boer Republic, the rise and spread of the trusts, the purification of municipal politics, the invention of wireless telegraphy, and the general adoption of automobiling. These things, and others like them, had perhaps not aged Pompeii so much as they had aged me, but their subjective effect was the same, and upon the whole I was not altogether sorry to have added scarcely a new impression of the place to those I had been carrying for more than a generation. Quantitatively there were plenty of new impressions to be had; impressions of more roofs, gardens, columns, houses, temples, walls, frescos; but qualitatively the Greater Pompeii was now not different from the lesser which I remembered so well.

W. D. Howells

This, at least, was what I said to myself on the ground and afterward in the National Museum at Naples, where most of the precious Pompeian things, new and old, are heaped up. They still make but a poor show there beside the treasures of Herculaneum, where the excavation of a few streets and houses has yielded costlier and lovelier things than all the lengths and breadths of Pompeii. But not for this would I turn against Pompeii at the last moment, as it were, though my second visit had not aesthetically enriched me beyond my first. I keep the vision of it under that gray January sky, with Vesuvius smokeless in the background, and the plan of the dead city, opener to the eye than ever it could have been in life, inscribed upon the broadly opened area of the gentle slopes within its gates. Whether one had not better known it dead than alive, one might not wish perhaps to say; but the place itself is curiously without pathos; Newport in ruins might not be touching; possibly all skeletons or even mummies are without pathos; and Pompeii is a skeleton, or at the most a mummy, of the past.

Seeing what antiquity so largely was, however, one might be not only resigned but cheerful in the ef-facement of any particular piece of it; and for a help to this at Pompeii I may advise the reader to take with him a certain little guide-book, written in English by a very courageous Italian, which I chanced to find in Naples. Though it treats of the tragical facts with seriousness, it is not with equal gravity that one reads that sixteen years before the Vesuvian eruption "the region had been shaken by strong sismic movements, which induced Pompei inhabitants to forsake precipitately their habitations. But being the amazement up, they got one's home again as soon as the earth was quiet and all fear and sadness went off by memory." Signs of the final disaster to follow were not wanting; the wells failed, the water-courses were crossed by currents of carbonic acid; "the domestic animals were also very sensible of the approaching of the scourge; they lost the habitual vivacity, and having the food in disgust, had from time to time to complain with mournful wailings, without justified reasons. . . . The sky became of a thick darkness, . . . interrupted only by flashes of light which the lava riverberated, by the bloody gliding of the thunderbolts, by the incandescence of enormous projectiles, thrown to an incommensurable highness. . . . Death surprised the charming town; houses and streets became the tombs of the unhappies hit by an atrocious torture."

The author's study of the life of Pompeii is notable for diction which, if there were logic in language, would be admirable English, for while yet in his mind it must have been "very choice Italian." He tells us that "Pompei's dwellings are surprising by their specific littleness," and explains that "Pompei inhabitants, for the habitudes of the climate could allow, lived almost always to the open sky," just as the Naples inhabitants do now. "They got home only to rest a little, to fulfill life wants, to be protected by bad weather. They spent much time during the day in forum, temples, thermes, tennis-court, or intervened to public sports, religious functions and meetings. . . . Few houses only had windows. The sunlight and ventilation to the ancients was given through empty spaces in the roofs. . . . Hoofs knocked under the weight of materials thrown out by Vesuvius; it is undoubted, however, that roofs were provided with covers or supported terraces. In the middle of the roofs was cut an ouerture through which air and light brought their benefits to the underlaid ambients. . . . Proprietor disposed the locals according to his own delight. . . . So that, there were bed, bath, dining, talking and game rooms." In the peristyle "the ground was gardened, the area shared in flower beds, had narrow paths; herbs, flowers, shrubs were put with art well in order on flower beds, delighted from time to time by statues of various subjects," as may be noted in the actual restorations of some of the Pompeian houses,

As for their spiritual life, "Pompeian's religion, like by Roman people, was the Paganism. Deities were worshipped in the temples with prayers, sagrifices, vows, and festivities. . . . Banquets to the Deity were joined to prayers. In fact, dining tables were dressed near the altars, and all around them on dining beds, *tricli-nari,* placed Divinities statues as these were assembled to own account to the joyous banquest." Auspices or auguries "gave interpretation to thunders, lightnings, winds, rain crashes, comets, or to bird songs and flights. . . . Horuspices inquired the divine will on the animal bowels, sacrificed to the altar; they took out further indications by fleshes and bowels flames when burnt on the altar."

An important feature of Pompeian social life was the bath, which "was one of the hospitality duty, and very often required in several religious functions. . . . Large and colossal edifices were quite furnished with all the necessary for care and sport. Besides localities for all kind of bath—cold, warm, steam bath—didn't want parks, alleys, and porticos in order to walk; lists rings for gymnastic exercises, conversation and reading rooms, localities for theatrical representations, swimming stations, localities for scientific disquisitions, moral and religious teachings. The most splendid art works adorned the ambient."

When we pass to the popular amusements we are presented with the materials of pictures vividly realized in *The Last Days of Pompeii,* but somewhat faded since. "In the beginning gladiators' rank was made by condemned to death slaves and war prisoners. Later also thoughtless young men, who had never learned an advantageous trade, became gladiators." In the arena they engaged in sham fights till the spectators demanded blood. Then, "sometimes one provided one's self nets for wrapping up the adversary, who, hit by a trident much, frequently die. When the gladiator was deadly wounded, forsaking the arm, struck down and stretching the index, asked the people grace of life. The spectators decided up his destiny, turning the thumb to the breast, or toward the ground. The thumb turned toward the ground was the unlucky's death doom, and he had without fail the throat cut off."

Such, dimly but unmistakably seen through our Italian author's well-reasoned English, were the ancient Pompeians; and, upon the whole, the visitor to their city could not wish them back in it. I preferred even those modern Pompeians who followed us so molestively to the train with bargains in postal-cards and coral. They are very alert, the modern Pompeians, to catch the note of national character, and I saw one of them pursuing an elderly American with a spread of hat-pins, primarily two francs each, and with the appeal, evidently studied from some fair American girl: "Buy it, Poppa! Six for one franc. Oh, Poppa, buy it!"

I had again lavished my substance upon first-class tickets, and so had my Utah friend, who expounded his philosophy of travel as we managed to secure a first-class carriage. "When I can't go first-class in Italy, I'll go home." I promptly and proudly agreed with him, but I concealed my morning's experience of the fact that in Italy you may sometimes go second class when you have paid first. I agreed with him, however, in not minding the plunder of Italian travel, since, with all the extortions, it would come to a third less than you expected to spend. His was the true American spirit.

VI

ROMAN HOLIDAYS

I. HOTELS, PENSIONS, AND APARTMENTS

"Shall I not take mine ease in mine inn?" the traveller asks rather anxiously than defiantly when he finds himself a stranger in a strange place, and he is apt to add, if he has not written or wired ahead to some specific hotel, "Which of mine inns shall I take mine ease in?" He is the more puzzled to choose the more inns there are to choose from, and his difficulty is enhanced if he has not considered that some of his inns may be full or may be too dear, and yet others undesirable.

The run from Naples in four hours and a half had been so flattering fair an experience to people who had last made it in eight that they arrived in Rome on a sunny afternoon of January preoccupied with expectations of an instant ease in their inn which seemed the measure of their merit. They indeed found their inn, and it was with a painful surprise that they did not find the rooms in it which they wanted. There were neither rooms full south, nor over the garden, nor off the tram, and in these circumstances there was nothing for it but to drive to some one else's inn and try for better quarters there. They, in fact, drove to half a dozen such, their demands rising for more rooms and sunnier and quieter and cheaper, the fewer and darker and noisier and dearer were those they found.

The trouble was that they found in the very first alien hotel where they applied an apartment so exactly what they wanted, with its four rooms and bath, all more or less full south, though mostly veering west and north, that they carried the fatal norm in their consciousness and tested all other apartments by it, the earlier notion of single rooms being promptly rejected after the sight of it. The reader will therefore not be so much, astonished as these travellers were to learn that there was nothing else in Rome (where there must be about five hundred hotels, *hotels garnis,* and pensions) that one could comparatively stay even overnight in, and that they settled in that alluring apartment provisionally, the next day being Sunday, and the crystalline Saturday of their arrival being well worn away toward its topaz and ruby sunset. Of course, they continued their search for several days afterward, zealously but hopelessly, yet not fruitlessly, for it resulted in an acquaintance with Roman hotels which they might otherwise never have made, and for one of them in literary material of interest to every one hoping to come to Rome or despairing of it. The psychology of the matter was very curious, and involved the sort of pleasing self-illusion by which people so often get themselves over questionable passes in life and come out with a good conscience, or a dead one, which is practically the same thing. These particular people had come to Rome with reminiscences of in-expensiveness and had intended to recoup themselves for the cost of several previous winters in New York hotels by the saving they would make in their Roman sojourn. When it appeared, after all the negotiation and consequent abatement, that their Roman hotel apartment would cost them hardly a fifth less than they had last paid in

W. D. Howells

New York, they took a guilty refuge in the fact that they were getting for less money something which no money could buy in New York. Gradually all sense of guilt wore off, and they boldly, or even impudently, said to themselves that they ought to have what they could pay for, and that there were reasons, which they were not obliged to render in their frankest soliloquies, why they should do just what they chose in the matter.

The truth is that the modern Roman hotel is far better in every way than the hotel of far higher class, or of the highest class, in New York. In the first place, the managers are in the precious secret, which our managers have lost, of making you believe that they want you; and, having you, they know how to look after your pleasure and welfare. The table is always of more real variety, though vastly less stupid profusion than ours. The materials are wholesomer and fresher and are without the proofs, always present in our hotel viands, of a probationary period in cold storage. As for the cooking, there is no comparison, whether the things are simply or complexly treated; and the service is of that neatness and promptness which ours is so ignorant of.

Your agreement is usually for meals as well as rooms; the European plan is preferably ignored in Europe; and the *table d'hote* luncheon and dinner are served at small, separate tables; your breakfast is brought to your room. Being old-fashioned, myself, I am rather sorry for the small, separate tables. I liked the one large, long table, where you made talk with your neighbors; but it is gone, and much facile friendliness with it, on either hand and across the board. The rooms are tastefully furnished, and the beds are unquestionable; the carpets warmly cover tho floor if stone, or amply rug it if of wood. The steam-heating is generous and performs its office of "roasting you out of the house" without the sizzling and crackling which accompany its efforts at home. The electricity really illuminates, and there is always an electric lamp at your bed-head for those long hours when your remorse or your digestion will not let you sleep, and you must substitute some other's waking dreams for those of your own slumbers. Above all, there is a lift, or elevator, not enthusiastically active or convulsively swift, but entirely practicable and efficient. It will hold from four to eight persons, and will take up at least six without reluctance.

It must be clearly understood that the ideal of American comfort is fully and faithfully realized, and if the English have reformed the Italian hotels in respect of cleanliness, it is we who have brought them quite to our domestic level in regard to heat and light. But if we want these things in Rome, we must pay for them as we do at home, though still we do not pay so much as we pay at home. The tips are about half our average, but whether they are given currently or ultimately I do not know. Who, indeed, knows about others' tips anywhere in the world? I asked an experienced fellow-citizen what the custom was, and he said that he believed the English gave in going away, but he thought the spirits of the helpers drooped under the strain of hope deferred, and he preferred to give every week. The donations, I understood, were pooled by the dining-room waiters and then equally divided; but gifts bestowed above stairs were for the sole behoof of him or her who took them. Germans are said to give less than Anglo-Saxons, and it is said that Italians in some cases do not give at all. But, again, who knows? The Italians are said never to give drink money to the cabmen, but to pay only the letter of the tariff. If I had done that in driving about to look up worse hotels than the one I chose first and last, I should now be a richer man, but I doubt if a happier. Two cents seems to satisfy a Roman cabman; five cents has for him the witchery of money found in the road; but I must not leave the subject of hotels for that of cabs, however alluringly it beckons.

W. D. Howells

The reader who knows Italy only from the past should clear his mind of his old impressions of the hotels. There is no longer that rivalry between the coming guest and the manager to see how few or many candles can be lighted in his room and charged in the bill; there are no longer candles, but only electricity. There is no longer an extortion for hearth-fires which send all the heat up the chimney; there are steam radiators in every room. There is no longer a tedious bargaining for rooms; the price is fixed and cannot be abated except for a sojourn of weeks or months. But the price is much greater than it used to be—twice as great almost; for the taxes are heavy and provisions are dear, and coal and electricity are costly, and you must share the expense with the landlord. He is not there for his health, and, if for your comfort, you are not his invited guest. As I have intimated, an apartment of four rooms with a bath will cost almost as much, with board, as the same quarters in New York, but you will get far more for your money in Rome. If you take a single room, even to the south, in many first-class Roman hotels it will cost you for room and board only two dollars or two and a half a day, which is what you pay for a far meaner and smaller room alone in New York; and the Roman board is such, as you can get at none but our most expensive houses for twice the money. Generally you cannot get a single room and bath, but at present a very exclusive hotel is going up in a good quarter which promises, with huge English signs, a bath with every room and every room full south. One does not see just how the universal sunny exposure is to be managed, but there can be no question of the baths; and, with the steam radiators everywhere, the northernmost room might well imagine itself full south.

Nearly all the hotels have a pleasant tea-room, which is called a winter garden, because of a pair of palm-trees set under the centre of its glass roof and the painted bamboo chairs and tables set about. This sort of garden is found even in the hotels which are almost of the grade of pensions and of their prices; but generally the pensions proper are without it. Their rates are much lower, but quite as good people frequent them, and they are often found in good streets and sometimes open into or overlook charming gardens; the English especially seem to like the pensions, which are managed like hotels. They are commonly without steam-heat, which might account for their being less frequented by Americans.

There are two supreme hotels in Rome—one in the Ludovisi quarter, as it is called, and the other near the Baths of Diocletian, which Americans frequent to their cost, for the rates approach a New York or London magnificence. The first is rather the more spectacular of the two and is the resort of all the finer sort of afternoon tea-drinkers, who find themselves the observed of observers of all nationalities; there is music and dress, and there are titles of every degree, with as much informality as people choose, if they go to look, or as much state if they go to be looked at; these things are much less cumbrously contrived than with us. The other hotel, I have the somewhat unauthorized fancy, is rather more addicted to very elect dinner-parties and suppers. Below these two are an endless variety of first-rate and second-rate houses, both in the newer quarter of the city, where the villa paths have been turned into streets, and in the old town on all the pleasant squares and avenues. There is a tradition of unhealth concerning the old town which the modern death-rate of Rome shows to be unjust; at the worst these places have more dark and damp, and the hotels are not steam-heated.

It has seemed to me that there are not so many *hotels garnis* in Rome as there used to be in Italian cities, but they, too, abound in pleasant streets, and the stranger who has a fancy for lodgings with breakfast in his rooms, and likes to browse about for his luncheon and dinner, will easily suit himself. If it comes to taking a furnished apartment for the season, there is much range in price and much choice in place. The agents who have them to let will begin, rather dismayingly, "Oh, apartments in Rome are very dear." But you learn on inquiry that a furnished flat in the Ludovisi region, in a house with a lift and full sun, may be had for two hundred dollars a month. From this height the rents of palatial apartments soar to such lonely peaks as eight hundred and sink to such levels as a hundred and twenty or a hundred; and for this you have linen and silver and all the movables and utensils you want, as well as several vast rooms opening wastefully from one to another till you reach the salon. The rents of the like flats, if vacant, would be a quarter or a third less, though again the agents begin by telling you that there is very little difference between the rents of furnished and unfurnished flats. The flats are in every part of the old town and the new; and some are in noble sixteenth and seventeenth century palaces, such as we are accustomed to at home only in the theatre. My own experience is that everybody, especially in houses where there are no lifts, lives on the top floor. You pass many other floors in going up, but you are left to believe that nobody lives on them. When you reach the inhabited levels, you find them charming inside for their state and beauty, and outside for their magnificent view, which may be pretty confidently relied upon to command the dome of St. Peter's. That magnificent stone bubble seems to blow all round the horizon.

When you have taken your furnished flat, the same agency will provide you a cook at ten or twelve dollars a month, a maid at seven dollars, a lady's maid at eight or nine dollars, and so on; the cook will prefer to sleep out of the house. Then will come the question of provisions, and these seem really to be dear in Rome. Meats and vegetables both are dear, and game and poultry. Beef will be forty cents a pound, and veal and mutton in proportion; a chicken which has been banting for the table from its birth will be forty cents; eggs which have not yet taken active shape are twenty-five and thirty cents throughout winters so bland that a hen of any heart can hardly keep from laying every day. I am afraid I am no authority on butter and milk, and groceries I do not know the prices of; but coffee ought to be cheap, for nobody drinks anything but substitutes more or less unabashed.

For the passing stranger, or even the protracted so-journer, whose time and money are not too much at odds, a hotel is best, and a hotel in the new quarter is pleasanter than one in the old quarters. Ours, at any rate, was in a wide, sunny, and (if I must own it) dusty street, laid out in a line of beauty on the borders of the former Villa Ludovisi, where the aging or middle-aging reader used to come to see Guercino's "Aurora" in the roof of the casino. Now all trace of the garden is hidden under vast and vaster hotels and great blond apartment-houses, and ironed down with trolley-rails; but the Guercino has been spared, though it is no longer so accessible to the public. Still, there is a garden left, and our hotel, with others, looks across the sun and dust of its street into the useful vegetation of the famous old Capuchin convent, with the church, to which I came so eagerly so long ago to revere Guido's "St. Michael and the Dragon" and the decorative bones of the good brothers braided on the walls and roofs of the crypt in the indissoluble community of floral and geometric designs.

All through the months of February and March I woke to the bell that woke the brothers to their prayers before daybreak and burst the beauty-sleep of the hotel-dwellers, who have so far outnumbered the monks since the obliteration of the once neighboring villa. This was, of course, a hardship, and one thought things of that bell which the monks were too good to say; but being awake, and while one was reading one's self to

W. D. Howells

sleep again, one could hear the beginning of the bird singing in the modern garden in the rear which followed upon the bell-ringing. I do not know what make or manner of bird it was that mostly sang among the palms and laurels and statues, but it had a note of liquid gold, which it poured till a certain flageolettist, whom I never saw, came to the corner under the villa wall and blew his soul into one end of his instrument and out of the other in the despondent breathings of most melancholy music. Then, having attuned the spirits of his involuntary listeners to a pensive sympathy, he closed with that international hymn which does not rightly know whether it is "My Country, 'tis of Thee," or "God Save the King," but serves equally for the patriotism of any English or Americans in hearing. I do not know why this harmless hymn, which the flageolettist gave extremely well, should always have seemed to provoke the derision of the donkey which apparently dwelt in harmony with the birds in that garden, but the flageolettist had no sooner ended than the donkey burst into a bray, loud, long, and full of mockery, with a close of ironical whistling and most insolent hissing; you would think that some arch-enemy of the Anglo-Saxon race was laughing the new-felt unity of the English and Americans to scorn. Later, but still before daylight, came the wild cry of a boy, somewhere out of perdition, following the deep bass invitation of his father's lost spirit to buy his wares, whatever they were. We never knew, but we liked that boy's despairing wail, and would not have missed it for ever so much extra slumber. When all hope of more sleep was past there was no question of the desirability of the boy who visibly arranged his store of oranges on the curbstone under the villa wall, and seemed to think that they had a peculiar attraction from being offered for sale in pairs. His cry filled the rest of the forenoon.

The Italian spring comes on slowly everywhere, with successive snubs in its early ardor from the snows on the mountains, which regulate the climate from north to south. We could not see that it made more speed behind the sheltering walls of the Capuchin convent garden than in other places. The old gardener whom we saw pottering about in it seemed to potter no more actively at the end of March than at the beginning of February; on the first days of April a heap of old leaves and stalks was sending up the ruddy flame and pleasant smell that the like burning heaps do with us at the like hour of spring—in fact, vegetation had much more reason to be cheerful throughout February than at any time in March. Those February days were really incomparable. They had not the melting heat of the warm spells that sometimes come in our Februaries; but their suns were golden, and their skies unutterably blue, and their airs mild, yet fresh. You always wanted a heavy coat for driving or for the shade in walking; otherwise the temperature was that of a New England April which was resolved to begin as it could carry out. But March came with cold rains of whole days, and with suns that might overheat but could not be trusted to warm you. The last Sunday of January I found ice in the Colosseum; but that was the only time I saw ice anywhere in Rome. In March, however, in a moment of great exasperation from the mountains, it almost snowed. Yet that month would in our climate have been remembered for its beauty and for a prevailing kindness of temperature. The worst you could say of it was that it left the spring in the Capuchin garden where it found it. But possibly, since the temporal power was overthrown, the seasons are neglected and indifferent. Certainly man seems so in the case of the Capuchin convent. Great stretches of the poor old plain edifice look vacant, and the high wall which encloses it is plastered and painted with huge advertisements of clothiers and hotels and druggists, and announcements of races and other events out of keeping with its character and tradition.

The sentimentalists who overrun Rome from all the Northern

lands will tell you that this is of a piece with all the Newer Rome which has sprung into existence since the Italian occupation. Their griefs with the thing that is are loud and they are long; but I, who am a sentimentalist too, though of another make, do not share them. No doubt the Newer Rome has made mistakes, but, without defending her indiscriminately, I am a Newer-Roman to the core, perhaps because I knew the Older Rome and what it was like; and not all my brother and sister sentimentalists can say as much.

II. A PRAISE OF NEW ROME

Rome and I had both grown older since I had seen her last, but she seemed not to show so much as I the forty-three years that had passed. Naturally a city that was already twenty-seven centuries of age (and no one knows how much more) would not betray the lapse of time since 1864 as a man must who was then only twenty-seven years of age. In fact, I should say that Rome looked, if anything, younger at our second meeting, in 1908, or, at any rate, newer; and I am so warm a friend of youth (in others) that I was not sorry to find Rome young, or merely new, in so many good things. At the same time I must own that I heard no other foreigner praising her for her newness except a fellow-septuagenarian, who had seen Rome earlier even than I, and who thought it well that the Ghetto should have been cleared away, though some visitors, who had perhaps never lived in a Ghetto, thought it a pity if not a shame, and an incalculable loss to the picturesque. These also thought the Tiber Embankments a wicked sacrifice to the commonplace, though the mud-banks of other days invited the torrent to an easy overflow of whole quarters of the town, which were left reeking with the filth of the flood that overlay the filth of the streets, and combined with it to an effect of disease and of discomfort not always personally unknown to the lover of the picturesque. There used to be a particular type of typhoid known as Roman fever, but now quite unknown, thanks to the Tiber Embankments and to the light and air let into the purlieus of that mediaeval Rome for which the injudicious grieve so loudly. The perfect municipal housekeeping of our time leaves no darkest and narrowest lane or alley unswept; every morning the shovel and broom go over the surfaces formerly almost impassable to the foot and quite impossible to the nose.

W. D. Howells

I am speaking literally as well as frankly, and though I can understand why some envious New-Yorker, remembering our blackguard streets and avenues, should look askance at the decency of the newer Rome and feign it an offence against beauty and poetry, I do not see why a Londoner, who himself lives in a well-kept town, should join with any of my fellow-barbarians in hypocritically deploring the modern spirit which has so happily invaded the Eternal City. The Londoner should rather entreat us not to be humbugs and should invite us to join him in rejoicing that the death-rate of Rome, once the highest in the civilized world, is now almost the lowest. But the language of Shakespeare and Milton is too often internationally employed in deploring the modernity which has housed us aliens there in such perfect comfort and safety. One must confine one's self to instances, and one may take that of the Ludovisi Quarter, as it is called, where I dwelt in so much peace and pleasure except when I was reminded that it was formed by plotting the lovely Villa Ludovisi in house lots and building it up in attractive hotels and apartment-houses. Even then I did not suffer so keenly as some younger people, who had never seen the villa, seemed to do, though there are still villas to burn in and about Rome, and they could not really miss the Ludovisi. It was a pretty place, but not beyond praise, and the quarter also is pretty, though also not beyond praise. The villa was for the pleasure and pride of one family, but it signified, even in its beauty, nothing but patrician splendor, which is a poor thing at best; and the quarter is now for the pleasure and pride of great numbers of tourists, mostly of that plutocracy from which a final democracy is inevitably to evolve itself. I could see no cause to beat the breast in this; and in humbler instances, even to very humble, I could not find that things were nearly as bad in Rome as they have been painted.

There is no doubt but at one time, directly after the coming of the capital, Rome was badly overbuilt. There is no doubt, also, that Rome has grown up to these rash provisions for her growth, and that she now "stuffs out her vacant garments with her form" pretty fully. One must not say that all the flats in all the houses are occupied, but most of them are; and if now the property of the speculators is the property of the banks, the banks are no bad landlords, and the law does not spare them the least of their duties to their tenants; or so, at least, it is said.

Another typical wrong to the old Rome, or rather to the not-yet Rome, was the building-up, beyond the Tiber, of the Quarter of the Fields, so called, where Zola in his novel of *Rome* has placed most of the squalor which he so lavishly employs in its contrasts. In these he shows himself the romanticist that he always frankly owned he was in spite of himself; but after I had read his book I made it my affair to visit the scenes of poverty and misery in the Quartiere dei Prati. When I did so I found that I had already passed through the quarter without noting anything especially poor or specifically miserable, and I went a third time to make sure that I had not overlooked something impressively lamentable. But I did not see above three tenement-houses with the wash hung from the windows, and with the broken shutters of poverty and misery, in a space where on the East Side or the North Side in New York I could have counted such houses by the score, almost the hundred. In this quarter the streets were swept every morning as they are everywhere in Rome, and though toward noon they were beginning to look as slovenly as our streets look when they have just been "cleaned," I knew that the next morning these worst avenues of Rome would be swept as our best never have been since the days of Waring.

Beyond the tenements the generous breadth of the new streets has been bordered by pleasant stucco houses of the pretty Italian type, fleetingly touched but not spoiled by the taste of the *art nouveau,* standing in their own grounds, and not so high-fenced but one could look over their garden-walls into the shrubs and flowers about them. Like suburban effects are characteristic of the new wide residential streets on the hither side of the Tiber, and on both shores the streets expand from time to time into squares, with more or less tolerable new monuments—say, of the Boston average—in them. The business streets where they bear the lines of the frequently recurrent trams are spacious and straight, and though they are not the Corso, the Corso itself, it must be remembered, is only a street of shops by no means impressive, and is mostly dim under the overtowering walls of palaces which have no space to be dignified in. Now and then their open portals betray a glimpse of a fountained or foliaged court, but whether these palaces are outwardly beautiful or not no one can tell from what sight one can get of them; no, not even the most besotted sentimentalist of those who bewail the loss of mediaeval Rome when they mean Rome of the Renaissance. How much of that Rome has been erased by modern Rome I do not know, but I think not so much as people pretend. Some of the ugly baroque churches have been pulled down to allow the excavation of imperial Rome, but there are plenty of ugly baroque churches left. It is said the princely proprietors of the old palaces which are let in apartments along the different Corsos (for the Corso is several) are going to pull them down and put up modern houses, with the hope of modern rents, but again I do not know. More than once the fortuities of hospitality found one the guest of dwellers in such stately domiciles, and I could honestly share the anxiety with which they spoke of these rumors; but there are a great many vast edifices of the sort, and I should not be surprised if I went back to Rome after another forty-three years to find most of them standing in 1951 where they now stand in 1908. Rome was not built in a day, and it will not be unbuilt or rebuilt within the brief period that will make me one hundred and fourteen years old. By that time I shall have outlived most of the medievalists, and I can say to the few survivors: "There, you see that new Rome never went half so far as you expected."

But no doubt it will go further than it has yet gone, in the way that is for the good and comfort of mankind. In one of the newer quarters, of which the Baths of Diocletian form the imperial centre, my just American pride was flattered by tho sign on a handsome apartment-house going up in gardened grounds, which advertised that it was to be finished with a lift and steam-heating. Many of the newer houses are already supplied with lifts, but central heating is as yet only beginning to spread from the hotels, where steam has been installed in compliance with the impassioned American demand to be warm all round when one is in-doors. New Rome is not going so fast and so far but that it will keep, to whatever end it reaches, one of the characteristic charms of the old and older Rome. I shall expect to see when I come back in 1951 the same or the like corners of garden walls, with the tops of shining foliage peering over them, that now enchant the passer in the street; from the windows of my electric-ele-vatored, steam-heated apartment I shall look down into the seclusion of gardens, with the golden globes of orange espaliers mellowing against the walls, and the fountain in the midst of oleanders and of laurels

"Shaking its loosened silver in the sun."

Slim cypresses will then as now blacken through the delicate air against the blue sky, and a stone-pine will spread its umbrella over some sequestered nook. By that time the craze for the eucalyptus which now possesses all Italy will be over, and every palm-tree will be cut down, while the ilex will darken in its place and help the eternal youth of the marbles to a greener old age of moss and mould in the gloom of its

W. D. Howells

spreading shade. All these things beautifully abound in Rome now, as they always have abounded, and there is no reason to fear that they will cease to abound.

Rome grows, and as Italy prospers it will grow more and more, for there must forever be a great and famous capital where there has always been one. The place is so perfectly the seat of an eternal city that it might well seem to have been divinely chosen because of the earth and heaven which are more in sympathy there than anywhere else in the world. The climate is beyond praise for a winter which is mild without being weak; there is a summer of tolerable noonday heat, and of nights deliciously cool; the spring is scarcely earlier than in our latitudes, but the fall is a long, slow decline from the temperature of October to the lowest level of January without the vicissitudes of other autumns. The embrowning or reddening or yellowing leaves turn sere, but drop or cling to their parent boughs as they choose, for there is seldom a frost to loosen their hold, and seldom a storm to tear them away.

So it is said by those who profess a more intimate acquaintance with the Roman meteorology than I can boast, but from the little I know I can believe anything of it that is of good report. Everywhere the prevalence of the ilex, the orange, the laurel, the pine, flatters January with an illusion of June, and under our hotel windows I was witness of the success of the sycamore leaves in keeping a grip of their native twigs even after the new buds came to push them away. In the last days of March a plum-tree hung its robe of white blossoms over the wall of the Capuchin convent from the garden within; but the almond-trees had been in bloom for six weeks before, and the deeper pink of the peach had more warmly flushed the suburbs for fully a fortnight.

Still, a mild winter and an endurable summer will not of

themselves make a great capital, and it was probably the Romans themselves who in the past made Rome the capital of the world, first politically and then religiously. Whether they will make it so hereafter remains to be seen. In the sense of all the Italians being Romans, I believe, with my profound faith in the race, that they are very capable of doing it; and they will have the help of the whole world in the work, or what is most liberal and enlightened in the whole world. As it is, Rome has a pull with Occidental civilization which forever constitutes her its head city. The only European capitals comparable with her are London, Paris, and Berlin; one cannot take account of New York, which is merely the commercial metropolis of America, with a possibility of becoming the business centre of both hemispheres. Washington is still in its nonage and of a numerical unimportance in which it must long remain almost ludicrously inferior to other capitals, not to dwell upon its want of anything like artistic, literary, scientific, and historical primacy. It is the voluntary political centre of the greatest republic of any time and of a nation which is already unrivalled in its claim upon the future. But it is not of the involuntary and unconscious growth of a capital like London, which is the centre of a mighty state, deep-rooted in the past, and the capital of that Anglo-Saxon race of which we are ourselves a condition, and of a colonial empire without a present equal. Paris is France in the sense of representing the intense life of a nation unsurpassed in the things which enlighten and ennoble the human intellect and advance mankind. Berlin is the concentration of the strong will of a state which has made itself great out of the weak will of sundry inferior states, homogeneous in their disunity more than in any positive quality, and which stands for a political ideal more nearly reactionary, more nearly mediaeval, than any other modern state. Berlin is not German as Paris is French, and Rome is not so exclusively Italian. In fact, her greatness, accomplished and destined, lies

W. D. Howells

in just the fact that she is not and never can be exclusively Italian. Human interests too universal and imperative for the control of a single race, even so brilliant and so gifted as the Italian race, which is naturally and necessarily in possession, centre about her through history, religion, art, and make every one at home in the city which is the capital of Christendom. Now and then I saw some shining and twinkling Japs going about with Baedekers, and I imagined them giving a modest and unprejudiced mind to Rome without claiming, tacitly or explicitly, the right to dispute the Italian theory and practice in its control. But every Occidental stranger (if any one of European blood is a stranger in the home of Christianity) I knew to be there in a mood more or less critical, and in a disposition to find fault with the Rome which is now making, or making over.

We journeyers or sojourners can do this without expense or inconvenience to ourselves, and we can easily blame the Italian conception of the future city which, to name but one fact, has made it possible for us to visit her in comfort at every season and to come away without having come down with the Roman fever. In spite of the sort of motherly, or at the worst step-motherly, welcome which she gives to all us closely or distantly related children of hers; in spite of her immemorial fame and her immortal beauty; in spite of her admirable housekeeping, in which she rises every morning at daybreak and sweeps clean every hole and corner of her dwelling; in spite of her wonderful sky, her life-giving air; in spite of the level head she keeps in her political affairs, and the miraculous poise she maintains between the antagonism of State and Church; in spite of her wise eclecticism in modern improvements; in spite of her admirable hygiene, which has constituted her one of the healthiest, if not the healthiest city in Europe; in spite of the solvency which she preserves amid expenses to which the vast scale of antiquity obliges her in all her public enterprises (a thing to be hereafter studied), we, the ungracious offspring of her youth, come from our North and West and censure and criticise and carp. I have seldom conversed with any fellow-visitor in Rome who could not improve her in some phase or other, who could not usefully advise her, who, at the best, did not patronize her. I offer myself as almost the sole example of a stranger who was contented with her as she is, or as she is going to be without his help; and I am the more confident, therefore, in suggesting to Rome an expedient by which she can repair the finances which her visitors say are so foolishly and wastefully mismanaged in her civic schemes. A good round tax, such as Carlsbad levies upon all sojourners, if laid upon the multitudinous tourists joining in such a chorus of criticism of Rome would give them the indefeasible right to their opinions and would help to replete a treasury which they believe is always in danger of being exhausted.

W. D. Howells

III. THE COLOSSEUM AND THE FORUM

As I have told, the first visit I paid to the antique world in Rome was at the Colosseum the day after our arrival. For some unknown reason I was going to begin with the Baths of Caracalla, but, as it happened, these were the very last ruins we visited in Rome; and I do not know just what accident diverted us to the Colosseum; perhaps we stopped because it was on the way to the Baths and looked an easier conquest. At any rate, I shall never regret that we began with it.

After twoscore years and three it was all strangely familiar. I do not say that in 1864 there was a horde of boys at the entrance wishing to sell me postcards—these are a much later invention of the Enemy—but I am sure of the men with trays full of mosaic pins and brooches, and looking, they and their wares, just as they used to look. The Colosseum itself looked unchanged, though I had read that a minion of the wicked Italian government had once scraped its flowers and weeds away and cleaned it up so that it was perfectly spoiled. But it would take a good deal more than that to spoil the Colosseum, for neither the rapine of the mediaeval nobles, who quarried their palaces from it, nor the industrial enterprise of some of the popes, who wished to turn it into workshops, nor the archeology of United Italy had sufficed to weaken in it that hold upon the interest proper to the scene of the most stupendous variety shows that the world has yet witnessed. The terrible stunts in which men fought one another for the delight of other men in every manner of murder, and wild beasts tore the limbs of those glad to perish for their faith, can be as easily imagined there as ever, and the traveller who visits the place has the assistance of increasing hordes of other tourists in imagining them.

I will not be the one to speak slight of that enterprise which marshals troops of the personally conducted through the place and instructs them in divers languages concerning it. Save your time and money so, if you have not too much of either, and be one of an English, French, or German party, rather than try to puzzle the facts out for yourself, with one contorted eye on your Baedeker and the other on the object in question. In such parties a sort of domestic relation seems to grow up through their associated pleasures in sight-seeing, and they are like family parties, though politer and patienter among themselves than real family parties. They are commonly very serious, though they doubtless all have their moments of gayety; and in the Colosseum I saw a French party grouped for photography by a young woman of their number, who ran up and down before them with a kodak and coquet-tishly hustled them into position with pretty, bird-like chirpings of appeal and reproach, and much graceful self-evidencing. I do not censure her behavior, though doubtless there were ladies among the photographed who thought it overbold; if the reader had been young and blond and *svelte,* in a Parisian gown and hat, with narrow russet shoes, not too high-heeled for good taste, I do not believe he would have been any better; or, if he would, I should not have liked him so well.

On the earlier day which I began speaking of I found that I was insensibly attaching myself to an English-hearing party of the personally conducted, in the dearth of my own recollections of the local history, but I quickly detached myself for shame and went back and meekly hired the help of a guide who had already offered his services in English, and whom I had haughtily spurned in his own tongue. His English, though queer, was voluminous; but I am not going to drag the reader at our heels laden with lore which can be applied only on the spot or in the presence of postal-card views of the Colosseum. It is enough that before my guide released us we knew where was the box of Caesar, whom those about to die saluted, and where the box of the Vestals whose fatal thumbs gave the signal of life or death for the unsuccessful performer; where the wild beasts were kept, and where the Christians; where were the green-rooms of the gladiators, who waited chatting for their turn to go on and kill one another. One must make light of such things or sink under them; and if I am trying to be a little gay, it is for the readers' sake, whom I would not have perish of their realization. Our guide spared us nothing, such was his conscience or his science, and I wish I could remember his name, for I could commend him as most intelligent, even, when least intelligible. However, the traveller will know him by the winning smile of his rosy-faced little son, who follows him round and is doubtless bringing himself up as the guide of coming generations of tourists. There had been a full pour of forenoon sunshine on the white dust of the street before our hotel, but the cold of the early morning, though it had not been too much for the birds that sang in the garden back of us, had left a skim of ice in damp spots, and now, in the late gray of the afternoon, the ice was visible and palpable underfoot in the Colosseum, where crowds of people wandered severally or collectively about in the half-frozen mud. They were, indeed, all over the place, up and down, in every variety of costume and aspect, but none were so picturesque as a little group of monks who had climbed to a higher tier of the arches and stood looking down into the depths where we looked up at them, denned against the sky in their black robes, which opened to show their under robes of white. They were picturesque, but they were not so monumental as an old, unmistakable American in high-hat, with long, drooping side-whiskers, not above a purple suspicion of dye, who sat on a broken column and vainly endeavored to collect his family for departure. Whenever he had gathered two or three about him they strayed off as the others came up, and we left him sardonically patient of their adhesions and defections, which seemed destined to continue indefinitely, while we struggled out through the postal-card boys and mosaic-pin men to our carriage. Then we drove away through the quarter of somewhat jerry-built apartment-houses which neighbor the Colosseum, and on into the salmon sunset which, after the gray of the afternoon, we found waiting us at our hotel, with the statues on the balustrated wall of the villa garden behind it effectively posed in the tender light, together with the eidolons of those picturesque monks and that monumental American.

We could safely have stayed longer, for the evening damp no longer brings danger of Roman fever, which people used to take in the Colosseum, unless I am thinking of the signal case of Daisy Miller. She, indeed, I believe, got it there by moonlight; but now people visit the place by moonlight in safety; and there are even certain nights of the season advertised when you may see it by the varicolored lights of the fireworks set off in it. My impression of it was quite vivid enough without that, and the vision of the Colosseum remained, and still remains, the immense skeleton of the stupendous form stripped of all integumental charm and broken down half one side of its vast oval, so that wellnigh a quarter of the structural bones are gone.

With its image there persisted and persists the question constantly recurrent in the presence of all the imperial ruins, whether imperial Rome was not rather ugly than otherwise. The idea of those world-conquerors was first immensity and then beauty, as much as could survive consistently with getting immensity into a given space. The question is most of all poignant in the Forum, which I let wait a full fortnight before moving against it in the warm sun of an amiable February morning. On my first visit to Rome I could hardly wait for day to dawn after my arrival before rushing to the Cow Field, as it was then called, and seeing the wide-horned cattle chewing the cud among the broken monuments now so carefully cherished and, as it were, sedulously cultivated. It is doubtful whether all that has since been done, and which could not but have been done, by the eager science as much involuntarily as voluntarily applied to the task, has resulted in a more potent suggestion of what the Forum was in the republican or imperial day than what that simple, old, unassuming Cow Field afforded. There were then as now the beautiful arches; there were the fragments of the temple porches, with their pillars; there was the "unknown column with the buried base"; there were all the elements of emotion and meditation; and it is possible that sentiment has only been cumbered Avith the riches which archasology has dug up for it by lowering the surface of the Cow Field fifteen or twenty feet; by scraping clean the buried pavements; by identifying the storied points; by multiplying the fragments of basal or columnar marbles and revealing the plans of temples and palaces and courts and tracing the Sacred Way on which the magnificence of the past went to dusty death. After all, the imagination is very childlike, and it prefers the elements of its pleasures simple and few; if the materials are very abundant or complex, it can make little out of them; they embarrass it, and it turns critical in self-defence. The grandeur that was Rome as visioned from the Cow Field becomes in the mind's eye the kaleidoscopic clutter which the resurrection of the Forum Romanum must more and more realize.

If the visitor would have some rash notion of what the ugliness of the place was like when it was in its glory, he may go look at the plastic reconstruction of it, indefinitely reduced, in the modest building across the way from the official entrance to the Forum. One cannot say but this is intensely interesting, and it affords the consolation which the humble (but not too humble) spirit may gather from witness of the past, that the fashion of this world and the pride of the eyes and all ruthless vainglory defeated themselves in ancient Rome, as they must everywhere when they can work their will. If one had thought that in magnitude and multitude some entire effect of beauty was latent, one had but to look at that huddle of warring forms, each with beauty in it, but beauty lost in the crazy agglomeration of temples and basilicas and columns and arches and statues and palaces, incredibly painted and gilded, and huddled into spaces too little for the least, and crowding severally upon one another, without relation or proportion. Their mass is supremely tasteless, almost senseless; that mob of architectural incongruities was not only without collective beauty, but it was without that far commoner and cheaper thing which we call picturesqueness. This has come to it through ruin, and we must give a new meaning to the word vandalism if we would appreciate what the barbarians did for Rome in tumbling her tawdry splendor into the heaps which are now at least paint-able. Imperial Rome as it stood was not paintable; I doubt if it would have been even photographable to anything but a picture post-card effect.

But as yet I wandered in the Forum safe from the realization of its ugliness when it was in its glory. I cannot say that even now it is picturesque, but it is paintable, and certainly it is pathetic. Stumps of columns, high and low, stand about in the places where they stood in their unbroken pride, and though it seems a hardship that they should not have been left lying in the kindly earth or on it instead of being pulled up and set on end, it must be owned that they are scarcely overworked in their present postures. More touching are those inarticulate heaps, cairns of sculptured fragments, piled here and there together and waiting the knowledge which is some time to assort them and translate them into some measure of coherent meaning. But it must always be remembered that when they were coherent they were only beautiful parts of a whole that was brutally unbeautiful. We have but to use the little common-sense which Heaven has

W. D. Howells

vouchsafed some of us in order to realize that Rome, either republican or imperial, was a state for which we can have no genuine reverence, and that mostly the ruins of her past can stir in us no finer emotion than wonder. But necessarily, for the sake of knowledge, and of ascertaining just what quantity and quality of human interest the material records of Roman antiquity embody, archaeology must devote itself with all possible piety to their recovery. The removal, handful by handful, of the earth from the grave of the past which the whole Forum is, tomb upon tomb, is as dramatic a spectacle as anything one can well witness; for that soil is richer than any gold-mine in its potentiality of treasure, and it must be strictly scrutinized, almost by particles, lest some gem of art should be cast aside with the accumulated rubbish of centuries. Yet this drama, poignantly suggestive as it always must be, was the least incident of that morning in the Forum which it was my fortune to pass there with other better if not older tourists as guest of the Genius Loci. It was not quite a public event, though the Commend atore Boni is so well known to the higher journalism, and even to fiction (as the reader of Anatole France's *La Pierre Blanche* will not have forgotten), that nothing which he archseologically does is without public interest, and this excursion in the domain of antiquity was expected to result in identifying the site of the Temple of Jupiter Stator. It was conjectured that the temple vowed to this specific Jupiter for his public spirit in stopping the flight of a highly demoralized Roman army would be found where we actually found it. Archaaology seems to proceed by hypothesis, like other sciences, and to enjoy a forecast of events before they are actually accomplished. I do not say that I was very vividly aware of the event in question; I could not go now and show where the temple stood, but when I read of it in a cablegram to the American newspapers I almost felt that I had dug it up with my own hands.

Of many other facts I was at the time vividly aware: of the charm of finding the archaeologist in an upper room of the mediaeval church which is turning itself into his study, of listening to his prefatory talk, so informal and so easy that one did not realize how learned it was, and then of following him down to the scene of his researches and hearing him speak wisely, poetically, humorously, even, of what he believed he had reason to expect to find. We stood with him by the Arch of Titus and saw how the sculptures had been broken from it in the fragments found at its base, and how the carved marbles had been burned for lime in the kiln built a few feet off, so that those who wanted the lime need not have the trouble of carrying the sculptures away before burning them. A handful of iridescent glass from a house-drain near by, where it had been thrown by the servants after breaking it, testified of the continuity of human nature in the domestics of all ages. A somewhat bewildering suggestion of the depth at which the different periods of Rome underlie one another spoke from the mouth of the imperial well or cistern which had been sunk on the top of a republican well or cistern at another corner of the arch. In a place not far off, looking like a potter's clay pit, were graves so old that they seem to have antedated the skill of man to spell any record of himself; and in the small building which seems the provisional repository of the archaeologist's finds we saw skeletons of the immemorial dead in the coffins of split trees still shutting them imperfectly in. Mostly the bones and bark were of the same indifferent interest, but the eternal pathos of human grief appealed from what mortal part remained of a little child, with beads on her tattered tunic and an ivory bracelet on her withered arm. History in the presence of such world-old atomies seemed an infant babbling of yesterday, in what it could say of the Rome of the Popes, the Rome of the Emperors, the Rome of the Republicans, the Rome of the Kings, the Rome of the Shepherds and Cowherds, through which a shaft sunk in the Forum would successively pierce in reaching those aboriginals whose sepulchres alone witnessed that they had ever lived.

It is the voluble sorrow common to all the emotional visitors in Rome that the past of the different generations has not been treated by the present with due tenderness, and the Colosseum is a case notoriously in point. But, if it was an Italian archaeologist who destroyed the wilding growths in the Colosseum and scraped it to a bareness which nature is again trying to clothe with grass and weeds, it ought to be remembered that it is another Italian archaeologist who has set laurels all up and down the slopes of the Forum, and has invited roses and honeysuckles to bloom wherever they shall not interfere with science, but may best help repair the wounds he must needs deal the soil in researches which seem no mere dissections, but feats of a conservative, almost a constructive surgery. It is said that the German archaeologists objected to those laurels where the birds sing so sweetly; perhaps they thought them not strictly scientific; but when the German Kaiser, who always knows so much better than all the other Germans put together, visited the Forum, he liked them, and he parted from the Genius Loci with the imperial charge, "Laurels, laurels, evermore laurels." After that the emotional tourist must be hard indeed to please who would begrudge his laurels to Commendatore Boni, or would not wish him a perpetual crown of them.

IV. THE ANGLO-AMERICAN NEIGHBORHOOD OF THE SPANISH STEPS

It is not every undeserving American who can have the erudition and divination of the Genius Loci in answer to his unuttered prayer during a visit to even a small part of the Roman Forum. But failing the company of the Commendatore Boni, which is without price, there are to be had for a very little money the guidance and philosophy, and, for all I know, the friendship of several peripatetic historians who lead people about the ruins in Rome, and instruct them in the fable, and doubtless in the moral, of the things they see. If I had profited by their learning, so much greater, or at least securer, than any the average American has about him, I should now be tiring the reader with knowledge which I am so willingly leaving him to imagine in me. If he is like the average American, he has really once had some nodding acquaintance with the facts, but history is apt to forsake you on the scene of it, and to come lagging back when it is too late. In this psychological experience you feel the need of help which the peripatetic historian supplies to the groups of perhaps rather oblivious than ignorant tourists of all nations in all languages, but preferably English. We Anglo-Saxons seem to be the most oblivious or most ignorant; but I would not slight our occasionally available culture any more than I would imply that those peripatetic historians are at all like the cicerones whom they have so largely replaced. I believe they are instructed and scholarly men; I offer them my respect; and I wish now that I had been one of their daily disciples, for it is full sixty years since I read Goldsmith's *History of Rome.* As I saw them, somewhat beyond earshot, they and their disciples formed a spectacle which was always interesting, and, so far as the human desire for information is affecting, was also affecting. The listeners to the lecturers would carry back to their respective villages and towns, or the yet simpler circles of our ordinary city lift, vastly more association with the storied scene than I had brought to it or should bring away. In fact, there is nothing more impressive in the floating foreign society of Rome than its zeal for self-improvement. No one classes himself with his fellow-tourists, though if he happens to be a traveller he is really one of them; and it is with difficulty I keep myself from the appearance of patronizing them in these praises, which are for the most part reverently meant. Their zeal never seemed to be without knowledge, whatever their age or sex; the intensity of their application reached to all the historical and actual interests, to the religious as well as the social, the political as well as the financial; but, fitly in Rome, it seemed specially turned to the study of antiquity, in the remoter or the nearer past. There was given last winter a series of lectures at the American School of Archaeology by the head of it, which were followed with eager attention by hearers who packed the room. But these lectures, which were so admirably first in. the means of intelligent study, seemed only one of the means by which my fellow-tourists were climbing the different branches of knowledge. All round my apathy I felt, where I did not see, the energy of the others; with my mind's ear I heard a rustle as of the turning leaves of Baedekers, of Murrays, of Hares, and of the many general histories and monographs of which these intelligent authorities advised the supplementary reading.

If I am not so mistaken as I might very well be, however, the local language is less studied than it was in former times, when far fewer Italians spoke English. My own Italian was of that date; but, though I began by using it, I found myself so often helped for a forgotten meaning that I became subtly demoralized and fell luxuriously into the habit of speaking English like a native of Rome. Yet tacitly, secretly perhaps, there may have been many people who were taking up Italian as zealously as many more were taking up antiquity.

One day in the Piazza di Spagna, in a modest little violet of a tea-room, which was venturing to open in the face of the old-established and densely thronged parterre opposite, I noted from my Roman version of a buttered muffin a tall, young Scandinavian girl, clad in complete corduroy, gray in color to the very cap surmounting her bandeaux of dark-red hair. She looked like some of those athletic-minded young women of Ibsen's plays, and the pile of books on the table beside her tea suggested a student character. When she had finished her tea she put these books back into a leather bag, which they filled to a rigid repletion, and, after a few laconic phrases with the tea-girl, she went out like going off the stage. Her powerful demeanor somehow implied severe studies; but the tea-girl—a massive, confident, confiding Roman—said, No, she was studying Italian, and all those books related to the language, for which she had a passion. She was a Swede; and here the student being exhausted as a topic, and my own nationality being ascertained, What steps, the tea-girl asked, should one take if one wished to go to New York in order to secure a place as cashier in a restaurant

My facts were not equal to the demand upon them, nor are they equal to anything like exact knowledge of the intellectual pursuits of the many studious foreign youth of all ages and sexes whom one meets in Rome. As I say, our acquaintance with Italian is far less useful, however ornamental, than it used to be. The Romans are so quick that they understand you when they speak no English, and take your meaning before you can formulate it in their own tongue. A classically languaged friend of mine, who was hard bested in bargaining for rooms, tried his potential landlord in Latin, and was promptly answered in Latin. It was a charming proof that in the home of the Church her mother-speech had never ceased to be spoken by some of her children, but I never heard of any Americans, except my friend, recurring to their college courses in order to meet the

W. D. Howells

modern Latins in their ancient parlance. In spite of this instance, and that of the Swedish votary of Italian, I decided that the studies of most strangers were archaeological rather than philological, historical rather than literary, topographical rather than critical. I do not say that I had due confirmation of my theory from the talk of the fellow-sojourners whom one is always meeting at teas and lunches and dinners in Rome. Generally the talk did not get beyond an exchange of enthusiasms for the place, and of experiences of the morning, in the respective researches of the talkers.

Such of us as were staying the winter, of course held aloof from the hurried passers-through, or looked with kindly tolerance on their struggles to get more out of Rome in a given moment than she perhaps yielded with perfect acquiescence. We fancied that she kept something back; she is very subtle, and has her reserves even with people who pass a whole winter within her gates. The fact is, there are a great many of her, though we knew her afar as one mighty personality. There is the antique Rome, the mediaeval Rome, the modern Rome; but that is only the beginning. There is the Rome of the State and the Rome of the Church, which divide between them the Rome of politics and the Rome of fashion; but here is a field so vast that Ave may not enter it without danger of being promptly lost in it. There is the Rome of the visiting nationalities, severally and collectively; there is especially the Anglo-American Rome, which if not so populous as the German, for instance, is more important to the Anglo-Saxons. It sees a great deal of itself socially, but not to the exclusion of the sympathetic Southern temperaments which seem to have a strange but not unnatural affinity with it. So far as we might guess, it was a little more Clerical than Liberal in its local politics; if you were very Liberal, it was well to be careful, for Conversion lurked under many exteriors which gave no outward sign of it; if the White of the monarchy and the Black of the papacy divide the best Roman families, of course foreigners are more intensely one or the other than the natives. But Anglo-Saxon life was easy for one not self-obliged to be of either opinion or party; and it was pleasant in most of its conditions. In Rome our internationalities seemed to have certain quarters largely to themselves. In spite of our abhorrence of the destruction and construction which have made modern Rome so wholesome and delightful, most of us had our habitations in the new quarters; but certain pleasanter of the older streets, like the Via Sistina, Via del Babuino, Via Capo le Case, Via Gregoriana, were our sojourn or our resort. Especially in the two first our language filled the outer air to the exclusion of other conversation, and within doors the shopmen spoke it at least as well as the English think the Americans speak it. It was pleasant to meet the honest English faces, to recognize the English fashions, to note the English walk; and if these were oftener present than their American counterparts, it was not from our habitual minority, but from our occasional sparsity through the panic that had frightened us into a homekeeping foreign to our natures.

In like manner our hyphenated nationalities have the Piazza di Spagna for their own. There are the two English book-stores and the circulating libraries, in each of which the books are so torn and dirty that you think they cannot be quite so bad in the other till you try it; there seems nothing for it, then, but to wash and iron the different Tauchnitz authors, and afterward darn and mend them. The books on sale are, of course, not so bad; they are even quite clean; and except for giving out on the points of interest where you could most wish them to abound, there is nothing in them to complain of. There is less than nothing to complain of in the tea-room which enjoys our international favor except that at the most psychological moment of the afternoon you cannot get a table, in spite of the teas going on in the fashionable hotels and the friendly houses everywhere. The toast is exceptional; the muffins so far from home are at least reminiscent of their native island; the tea and butter are alike blameless. The company, to the eye of the friend of man, is still more acceptable, for, if the Americans have dwindled, the English have increased; and there is nothing more endearing than the sight of a roomful of English people at their afternoon tea in a strange land. No type seems to predominate; there are bohemians as obvious as clerics; there are old ladies and young, alike freshly fair; there are the white beards of age and the clean-shaven cheeks of youth among the men; some are fashionable and some outrageously not; peculiarities of all kinds abound without conflicting. Some talk, frankly audible, and others are frankly silent, but a deep, wide purr, tacit or explicit, close upon a muted hymn of thanksgiving, in that assemblage of mutually repellent personalities, for the nonce united, would best denote the universal content.

Hard by this tea-room there is a public elevator by which the reader will no doubt rather ascend with me than, climb the Spanish Steps without me; after the first time, I never climbed them. The elevator costs but ten centimes, and I will pay for both; there is sometimes drama thrown in that is worth twice the money; for there is war, more or less roaring, set between the old man who works the elevator and the young man who sells the tickets to it. The law is that the elevator will hold only eight persons, but one memorable afternoon the ticket-seller insisted upon giving a ticket to a tall, young English girl who formed an unlawful ninth. The elevator-man, a precisian of the old school, expelled her; the ticket-seller came forward and reinstated her; again the elder stood upon the letter of the law; again the younger demanded its violation. The Tuscan tongue in their Roman mouths flew into unintelligibility, while the poor girl was put into the elevator and out of it; and the respective parties to the quarrel were enjoying it so much that it might never have ended if she had not taken the affair into her own hands. She finally followed the ticket-seller back to his desk, to which he retired after each act of the melodrama, and threw her ticket violently down. "Here is your ticket!" she said in English so severe that he could not help understanding and cowering before it. "Give me back my money!" He was too much stupefied by her decision of character to speak; and he returned her centimes in silence while we got into our cage and mounted to the top, and the elevator-man furiously repeated to himself his side of the recent argument all the way up. This did not prevent his touching his hat to each of us in parting, and assuring us that he revered us; a thing that only old-fashioned Romans seem to do nowadays, in the supposed decay of manners which the comfortable classes everywhere like to note in the uncomfortable. Then some ladies of our number went off on a platform across the house-tops to which the elevator had brought us, as if they expected to go down the chimneys to their apartments; and the rest of us expanded into the Piazza Trinita de' Monti; and I stopped to lounge against the uppermost balustrade of the Spanish Steps.

It is notable, but not surprising, how soon one forms the habit of this, for, seen from above, the Spanish Steps are only less enchanting than the Spanish Steps seen from below, whence they are absolutely the most charming sight in the world. The reader, if he has nothing better than a post-card (which I could have bought him on the spot for fifty a franc), knows how the successive stairways part and flow downward to right and left, like the parted waters of a cascade, and lose themselves at the bottom in banks of flowers. No lovelier architectural effect was ever realized from a happy fancy; but, of course, the pictorial effect is richer from below, especially from the Via dei Condotti, where it opens into the Piazza di Spagna. I suppose there must be hours of the day, and certainly there are hours of the night, when in this prospect the Steps have not the sunset on them. But most of the time they have the sunset on them, warm, tender; a sunset that begins with the banks of daffodils and lilies and anemones and carnations and roses and almond blossoms, keeping the downpour of the marble cascades from flooding the piazza, and mounts, mellowing and yellowing, up their gray stone, until it reaches the Church of Trinita de' Monti at the top.

There it lingers, I should say, till dawn, bathing the golden-brown facade in an effulgence that lifelong absence cannot eclipse when once it has blessed your sight. It is beauty that rather makes the heart ache, and the charm of the Steps from above is something that you can bear better if you are very, very worthy, or have the conceit of feeling yourself so. It is a charm that imparts itself more in detail and is less exclusively the effect of perpetual sunset. From the parapet against which you lean you have a perfecter conception of the architectural form than you get from below, and you are never tired of seeing the successive falls of the Steps dividing themselves and then coming together on the broad landings and again parting and coming together.

If there were once many models, male, female, and infant, brigands, peasants, sages, and martyrs, lounging on the Spanish Steps, as it seems to me there used to be, and as every one has heard say, waiting there for the artists to come and carry them off to their studios and transfer them to their canvases, they are now no longer there in noticeable number. I saw some small boys in steeple-crowned soft hats and short jackets, with their little legs wound round with the favorite bandaging of brigands; and some mothers suitable for Madonnas, perhaps, with babes at the breast; there was a patriarchal old man or two, ready no doubt to pose for the prophets, or, at a pinch, for yet more celestial persons; but for the rest the Steps were rather given up to flower-girls, fruit-peddlers, and beggars pure and simple, on levels distinctly below those infested by the post-card peddlers. The whole neighborhood abounds in opportunities for charity, and at the corner of the Via Sistina there is a one-legged beggar who professes to black shoes in the intervals of alms-taking, and who early made me his prey. If sometimes I fancied escaping by him to my lounge against the parapet of the steps, he joyously overtook me with a swiftness of which few two-legged men are capable; he wore a soldier's cap, and I hoped, for the credit of our species, that he had lost his leg in battle, but I do not know.

On a Sunday evening I once hung there a long time, watching with one eye the people who were coining back from their promenade on the Pincian Hill, and with the other the groups descending and ascending the Steps. On the first landing below me there was a boy who gratified me, I dare say unconsciously, by trying to stand on his hands; and a little dramatic spectacle added itself to this feat of the circus. Two pretty girls, smartly dressed in hats and gowns exactly alike, and doubtless sisters, if not twins, passed down to the same level. One was with a handsome young officer, and walked staidly beside him, as if content with her quality of captive or captor. The other was with a civilian, of whom she was apparently not sure. Suddenly she ran away from him to the verge of the next fall of steps, possibly to show him how charmingly she was dressed, possibly to tempt him by her grace in flight to follow her madly. But he followed sanely and slowly, and she waited for him to come up, in a capricious quiet, as if she had not done anything or meant anything. That was all; but I am not hard to suit; and it was richly enough for me.

Her little comedy came to its denouement just under the shoulder of the rose-roofed terrace jutting from a lowish, plainish house on the left, beyond certain palms and eucalyptus-trees. It is one of the most sacred shrines in Rome, for it was in this house that the "young English poet whose name was writ in water" died to deathless fame three or fourscore years ago. It is the Keats house, which when he lived in it was the house of Severn the painter, his host and friend. I had visited it for the kind sake of the one and the dear sake of the others when I first visited Rome in 1864; and it was one of the earliest stations of my second pilgrimage. It is now in form for any and all visitors, but the day I went it had not yet been put in its present simple and tasteful keeping. A somewhat shrill and scraping-voiced matron inquired my pleasure when she followed me into the ground-floor entrance from somewhere without, and then, understanding, called hor young daughter, who led me up to the room where Keats mused his last verse and breathed his last sigh. It is a very little room, looking down over the Spanish Steps, with their dike of bloom, across the piazza to the narrow stretch of the Via del Babuino. I must have stood in it with Severn and heard him talk of Keats and his ultimate days and hours; for I remember some such talk, but not the details of it. He was a very gentle old man and fondly proud of his goodness to the poor dying poet, as he well might be, and I was glad to be one of the many Americans who, he said, came to grieve with him for the dead poet.

Now, on my later visit, it was a cold, rainy day, and it was chill within the house and without, and I imputed my weather to the time of Keats's sojourn, and thought of him sitting by his table there in that bare, narrow, stony room and coughing at the dismal outlook. Afterward I saw the whole place put in order and warmed by a generous stove, for people who came to see the Keats and Shelley collections of books and pictures; but still the sense of that day remains. The young girl sympathized with my sympathy, and wished to find a rose for me in the trellis through which the rain dripped. She could not, and I suggested that there would be roses in the spring. "No," she persisted, "sometimes it makes them in the winter," but I had to come away through the reeking streets without one.

When it rains, it rains easily in Rome. But the weather was divine the evening I looked one of my latest looks down on the Spanish Steps. The sun had sunk rather wanly beyond the city, but a cheerful light of electrics shone up at me from the Via dei Condotti. I stood and thought of as much as I could summon from the past, and I was strongest, I do not know why, with the persecutions of the early Christians. Presently a smell of dinner came from the hotels around and the houses below, and I was reminded to go home to my own *table d'hote*. My one-legged beggar seemed to have gone to his, and I escaped him; but I was intercepted by the sight of an old woman asleep over her store of matches. She was not wakened by the fall of my ten-centime piece in her tray, but the boy drowsing beside her roused himself, and roused her to the dreamy expression of a gratitude quite out of scale with my alms.

W. D. Howells

V. AN EFFORT TO BE HONEST WITH ANTIQUITY

My visit to the Roman Forum when the Genius Loci verified to my ignorance and the intelligence of my companions the well-conjectured site of the Temple of Jupiter Stator was not the first nor yet the second visit I had paid the place. There had been intermediate mornings when I met two friends there, indefinitely more instructed, with whom I sauntered from point to point, preying upon their knowledge for my emotion concerning each. Information is an excellent thing —in others; and but for these friends I should not now be able to say that this mouldering heap of brickwork, rather than that, was Julius Caesar's house; or just where it was that Antony made his oration over the waxen effigy which served him for Caesar's body. They helped me realize how the business life and largely the social life of Rome centred in the Forum, but spared me so much detail that my fancy could play about among its vanished edifices without inconvenience from the clutter of shops and courts and monuments which were ultimately to hem it in and finally to stifle it. They knew their Forum so well that they could not only gratify any curiosity I had, but could supply me with curiosity when I had none. For the moment I was aware that this spot or that, though it looked so improbable, was the scene of deeds which will reverberate forever; they taught me to be tolerant of what I had too lightly supposed fables as serious traditions closely verging on facts. I learned to believe again that the wolf suckled Romulus and Remus, because she had her den no great way off on the Palatine, and that Romulus himself had really lived, since he had died and was buried in the Forum, where they showed me his tomb, or as much of it as I could imagine in the sullen little cellar so called. They also showed me the rostrum where the Roman orators addressed the mass-meetings of the republican times, and they showed me the lake, or the puddle left of it, into which Curtius (or one of three heroes of the name) leaped at an earlier day as a specific for the pestilence which the medical science of the period had failed to control. In our stroll about the place we were joined by one of the several cats living in the Forum, which offered us collectively its acquaintance, as if wishing to make us feel at home. It joined us and it quitted us from time to time, as the whim took it, but it did not abandon us wholly till we showed a disposition to believe in that lake of Curtius, so called after those three public-spirited heroes, the first being a foreigner. Then the cat, which had more than once stretched itself as if bored, turned from us in contempt and went and lay down in a sunny corner near the tomb of Romulus, and fell asleep.

It is quite possible that my reader does not know, as lately I did not, that the Roman Forum is but one of several forums connected with it by ways long centuries since buried fathoms deep and built upon many stories high. But I am now able to assure him that in the whole region between the Roman Forum and the Forum of Trajan, which were formerly opened into each other by the removal of a hill as tall as the top of Trajan's Column, you pass over other forums hidden beneath your feet or wheels. You cannot be stayed there, however, by the wonders which archaeology will yet reveal in them (for archaeology has its relentless eye upon every inch of the ground above them), but you will certainly pause at the Forum of Trajan, where archaeology, as it is in Commendatore Boni, has had its way already. In fact, until his work in the Roman Forum is finished, the Forum of Trajan must remain his greatest achievement, and the sculptured column of the great emperor must serve equally as the archaeologist's monument. I do not remember why in the old time I should have kept coming to look at that column and study the sculptured history of Trajan's campaigns, toiling around it to its top. I think one could then get close to its base, as now one cannot, what with the deepening of the Forum to its antique level and the enclosure of the whole space with an iron rail. The area below is free only to a large company of those cats which seem to have their dwelling among all the ruins and restorations of ancient Rome. People come to feed the Trajan cats with the fish sold near by for the purpose, and one morning, in pausing to view his column from the respectful distance I had to keep, I counted no less than thirteen of his cats in his forum. They were of every age and color, but much more respectable in appearance than the cats of the Pantheon, which have no such sunny expanse as that forum for their quarters, but only a very damp corner beside the temple, and seem to have suffered in their looks and health from the situation. It was afterward with dismay that I realized the fatal number of the Trajan cats coming to their breakfast that morning so unconscious of evil omen in the figure; but as there are probably no statistics of mortality among the cats of Rome, I shall never know whether any of the thirteen has rendered up one of their hundred and seventeen lives.

However, if I allowed myself to go on about the cats of Rome, either ancient or modern, there would be no end. For instance, in a statuary's shop in the Via Sistina there is a large yellow cat, which I one day saw dressing the hair of the statuary's boy. It performed this office with a very motherly anxiety, seated on the top of a high rotary table where ordinarily the statuary worked at his carving, and pausing from time to time, as it licked the boy's thick, black locks, to get the effect of its labors. On other days or at other hours it slept under the table-top, unvexed by the hammering that went on over its head. Even in Rome, where cats are so abundant, it was a notable cat.

If you visit the Roman Forum in the morning you are only too apt to be hurried home by remembrance of the lunch-hour.

That, at any rate, was my case, but I was not so hungry that I would not pause on my way hotelward at what used to be the Temple of Vesta in my earlier time, but which, is now superseded by the more authentic temple in the Forum. I had long revered the first in its former quality, and I now paid it the tribute of unwilling renunciation. It is so nearly a perfect relic of ancient Rome and so much more impressive, in its all but unbroken peristyle, than the later but recumbent claimant to its identity that I am sure the owners of the little bronze or alabaster copies of it scattered over the world must share my pious reluctance. The custodian is still very proud of it, and would have lectured me upon it much longer than I let him; as it was, he kept me while he could cast a blazing copy of the *Popolo Romano* into the cavernous crypt under it, apparently to show me how deep it was. He may have had other reasons; but in any case I urge the traveller to allow him to do it, for it costs no additional fee, and it seems to do him so much good. If it is not very near lunch-time, let the traveller look well about him in the dusty little piazza there, for the Temple of Fortune, with its bruised but beautiful facade, is hard by, as much in the form that Servius Tullius gave it as could well be expected after all this time.

Perhaps the Circus of Marcellus is on the traveller's way home to lunch; but he will always be passing the segment of its arcaded wall, filled in with mediaeval masonry; and he need not stop, especially if he has his cab by the hour, for there is nothing more to be seen of the circus. A glimpse, through overhanging foliage, of the steps to the Campidoglio, with Castor and Pollux beside their horses at top, may be a fortunate accident of his course. If this happens it will help to rehabilitate for him the Rome of the paganism to which these divinities remained true through all temptations to Judaize during the unnumbered centuries of their sojourn, forgotten, in the Ghetto. It is hardly possible that his glimpse will include even the top of Marcus Aurelius's head where he

W. D. Howells

sits his bronze charger—an extremely fat one—so majestically in the piazza beyond those brothers, as if conscious of being the most noble equestrian statue which has ridden down to us from antiquity.

A more purposed sight of all this will, of course, supply any defects of chance, though I myself always liked chance encounters with the monuments of the past. I had constantly cherished a remembrance of the nobly beautiful facade which is all that is left of the Temple of Neptune, and I meant deliberately to revisit it if I could find out where it was. A kind fortuity befriended me when one day, driving through the little piazza where it lurks behind the Piazza Colonna, I looked up, and there, in awe-striking procession, stood the mighty antique columns sustaining the entablature of mediaeval stucco with their fluted marble. I could not say why their poor, defaced, immortal grandeur should have always so affected me, for I do not know that my veneration was due it more than many other fragments of the past; but no arch or pillar of them all seems so impressive, so pathetic. To make the reader the greatest possible confidence, I will own that I passed five times through the Piazza Colonna to my tailor's in the next piazza (at Rome your tailor wishes you to try on till you have almost worn your new clothes out in the ordeal) before I realized that the Column of Marcus Aurelius was not the more famous Column of Trajan. There is, in fact, a strong family likeness between these columns, both being bandaged round from bottom to top with the tale of the imperial achievements and having a general effect in common; but there is no brother or cousin to the dignity of that melancholy yet vigorous ruin of the Temple of Neptune, or anything that resembles it in the whole of ancient Rome. It survives having been a custom-house and being a stock-exchange without apparent ignominy, while one feels an incongruity, to say the least, in the Column of Marcus Aurelius looking down on the sign of the Mutual Life

Insurance Company of New York. Whether this is worse than for the Palazzo di Venezia to confront the American Express Company where it is housed on the other side of the piazza I cannot say. What I can say is that I believe the Temple of Neptune would have been superior to either fate; though I may be mistaken.

Ruin, nearly everywhere in Rome, has to be very patient of the environment; and even the monuments of the past which are in comparatively good repair have not always the keeping that the past would probably have chosen for them. One that suffers as little as any, if not the very least, is the Pantheon, on whose glorious porch you are apt to come suddenly, either from a narrow street beside it or across its piazza, beyond the fountain fringed with post-card boys and their bargains. In spite of them, the sight of the temple does mightily lift the heart; and though you may have had, as I had, forty-odd years to believe in it, you must waver in doubt of its reality whenever you see it. It seems too great to be true, standing there in its immortal sublimity, the temple of all the gods by pagan creation, and all the saints by Christian consecration, and challenging your veneration equally as classic or catholic. It is worthy the honor ascribed to it in the very latest edition of Murray's *Handbook* as "the best-preserved monument of ancient Rome"; worthy the praise of the fastidious and difficult Hare as "the most perfect pagan building in the city"; worthy whatever higher laud my unconsulted Baedeker bestows upon it. But I speak of the outside; and let not the traveller grieve if he comes upon it at the noon hour, as I did last, and finds its vast bronze doors closing against him until three o'clock; there are many sadder things in life than not seeing the interior of the Pantheon. The gods are all gone, and the saints are gone or going, for the State has taken the Pantheon from the Church and is making it a national mausoleum. Victor Emmanuel the Great and Umberto the Kind already lie there; but otherwise the wide Cyclopean eye of the opening in the roof of the rotunda looks down upon a vacancy which even your own name, as written in the visitors' book, in the keeping of a solemn beadle, does not suffice to fill, and which the lingering side altars scarcely relieve.

I proved the fact by successive visits; but, after all my content with the outside of the Pantheon, I came to think that what you want in Rome is not the best-preserved monument, not the most perfect pagan building, but the most ruinous ruin you can get. I am not sure that you get this in the mouldering memorials of the past on the Palatine Hill, but you get something more nearly like it than anything I can think of at the moment. In that imperial and patrician and plutocratic residential quarter you see, if you are of the moderately moneyed middle class, what the pride of life must always come to when it has its way; and your consolation is full if you pause to reflect how some day Fifth Avenue and the two millionaire blocks eastward will be as the Palatine now is.

Riches and power are of the same make in every time, though they may wear different faces from age to age; and it will be well for the very wealthy members of our smart set to keep this fact in mind when they visit that huge sepulchre of human vainglory.

But I will not pretend that I did so myself that matchless April morning when I climbed over the ruins of the Palatine and found the sun rather sickeningly hot there. That is to say, it was so in the open spaces which were respectively called the house of this emperor and that, the temple of this deity or that, whose divine honors half the Caesars shared; in the Stadium, beside the Lupercal, and the like. The Lupercal was really imaginable as the home of the patroness wolf of Rome, being a wild knot of hill fitly overgrown with brambles and bushes, and looking very probably the spot where Caesar would thrice have refused the crown that Antony offered him. But for the rest, one ruin might very well pass for another; a temple with a broken statue and the stumps of a few columns could very easily deceive any one but an archaeologist. Fortunately we had the charming companionship of one of the most amiable of archaeologists, who was none the less learned for being a woman; and she made even me dimly aware of identities which would else have been lost upon me. To be sure, I think that without help I should have known the Stadium when I came to it, because it seemed studied from that in Cambridge, Massachusetts, and, though it was indefinitely more dilapidated, was so obviously meant for the same sorts of games and races. I do not know but it was larger than the Cambridge Stadium, though I will not speak so confidently of its size as of that deathly cold in the vaults and subterranean passages by which we found our way to the burning upper air out of the foundations and basements of palaces and temples and libraries and theatres that had ceased to be.

One of the most comfortable of these galleries was that in which Caligula was justly done to death, or, if not Caligula, it was some other tyrant who deserved as little to live. But for our guide I should not have remembered his slaughter there, and how much satisfaction it had given me when I first read of it in Goldsmith's *History of Rome;* and really you must not acquaint yourself too early with such facts, for you forget them just when you could turn them to account. History is apt to forsake you in the scene of it and come lagging hack afterward; and you cannot hope always to have an archaeologist at your elbow to remind you of things you have forgotten or possibly have not known. Suetonius, Plutarch, De Quincey, Gibbon, these are no bad preparations for a visit to the Palatine, but it is better to have read them yesterday than the day before if you wish to draw suddenly

W. D. Howells

upon them for associations with any specific spot. If I were to go again to the Palatine, I would take care to fortify myself with such structural facts from Hare's *Walks in Rome,* or from Murray, or even from Baedeker, as that it was the home of Augustus and Tiberius, Domitian and Nero and Caligula and Septimius Severus and Germanicus, and a very few of their next friends, and that it radically differed from the Forum in being exclusively private and personal to the residents, while that was inclusively public and common to the whole world. I strongly urge the reader to fortify himself on this point, for otherwise he will miss such significance as the place may possibly have for him. Let him not trust to his impressions from his general reading; there is nothing so treacherous; he may have general reading enough to sink a ship, but unless he has a cargo taken newly on board he will find himself tossing without ballast on those billowy slopes of the Palatine, where he will vainly try for definite anchorage.

The billowy effect of the Palatine, inconvenient to the explorer, is its greatest charm from afar, in whatever morning or evening light, or sun or rain, you get its soft, brownish, greenish, velvety masses. Distance on it is best, and distance in time as well as space. If you can believe the stucco reconstruction opposite the Forum gate, ruin has been even kinder to the Palatine than to the Forum, with which it was equally ugly when in repair, if taken in the altogether, however beautiful in detail. As you see it in that reproduction, it is a horror, and a very vulgar horror, such a horror as only unlimited wealth and uncontrolled power can produce. If you will think of individualism gone mad, and each successive personality crushing out and oversloughing some other, without that regard for proportion and propriety which only the sense of a superior collective right can inspire, you will imagine the Palatine. Mount Morris, at One Hundred and Twenty-fifth Street, if unscrupulously built upon by the multimillionaires thronging to New York and seeking to house themselves each more splendidly and spaciously than the other, would offer a suggestion in miniature of what the Palatine seems to have been like in its glory. But the ruined Mount Morris, even allowing for the natural growth of the landscape in two thousand years, could show no such prospect twenty centuries hence as we got that morning from a bit of wilding garden near the Convent of San Bonaventura, on the brow of the Palatine. Some snowy tops pillowed themselves on the utmost horizon, and across the Campagna the broken aqueducts stalked and fell down and stumbled to their legs again. The Baths of Caracalla bulked up in rugged, monstrous fragments, and then in the foreground, filling the whole eye, the Colosseum rose and stood, and all Rome sank round it. The Forum lay deep under us, vainly struggling with the broken syllables of its demolition to impart a sense of its past, and at our feet in that bit of garden where the roses were blooming and the plum-trees were blowing and the birds were singing, there stretched itself in the grass a fallen pillar wreathed with the folds of a marble serpent, the emblem of the oldest worship under the sun, as I was proud to remember without present help. It was the same immemorial, universal faith which the Mound Builders of our own West symbolized in the huge earthen serpents they shaped uncounted ages before the red savages came to wonder at them, and doubtless it had been welcomed by Rome in her large, loose, cynical toleration, together with cults which, like that of Isis and Osiris, were fads of yesterday beside it. Somehow it gave the humanest touch in the complex impression of the overhistoried scene. It made one feel very old, yet very young—old with the age and young with the youth of the world—and very much at home.

W. D. Howells

VI. PERSONAL RELATIONS WITH THE PAST

I was myself part of the antiquity with which I have been trying to be honest; and, though my date was no earlier than the seventh decade of the nineteenth century, still so many and such cataclysmal changes had passed over Rome since my time that I was, as far as concerned my own consciousness, practically of the period of the Pantheon, say. The Pantheon, in fact, was among my first associations with Rome. I lodged very near it, in the next piazza, so that, if we were not contemporaries, we were companions, and I could not go out of my hotel to look up a more permanent sojourn without passing by it. Perhaps I wished to pass by it, and might really have found my way to the Corso without the Pantheon's help.

I have no longer a definite idea why I should have made my sojourn in the very simple and modest little street called Via del Gambero, which runs along behind the Corso apparently till it gets tired and then stops. But very possibly it was because the Via del Gambero was so simple and modest that I chose it as the measure of my means; or possibly I may have heard of the apartment I took in it from wayfarers passing through Venice, where I then lived, and able to commend it from their own experience of it; people in that kind day used to do such things. However it was, I took the apartment, and found it, though small, apt for me, as Ariosto said of his house, and I dwelt in it with my family a month or more in great comfort and content. In fact, it seemed to us the pleasantest apartment in Rome, where the apartments of passing strangers were not so proud under Pius IX. as they are under Victor Emmanuel III. I do not know why it should have been called the Street of the Lobster, but it may have been in an obscure play of the fancy with the notion of a backward gait in it that I came to believe that, in the many improvements which had befallen Rome, Via del Gambero had disappeared. Destroyed, some traveller from antique lands had told me, I dare say; obliterated, wiped out by the march of municipal progress. At any rate, I had so long resigned the hope of revisiting the quiet scene that when I revisited Rome last winter, after the flight of ages, and one day found myself in a shop on the Corso, it was from something like a hardy irony that I asked the shopman if a street called Via del Gambero still existed in that neighborhood. I said that I had once lodged in it forty-odd years before; but I believed it had been demolished. Not at all, the shopman said; it was just behind his place; and what was the number of the house? I told him, and he laughed for joy in being able to do me a pleasure; me, a stranger from the strange land of sky-scratchers *(grattacieli),* as the Italians not inadequately translate sky-scrapers. If I would favor him through his back shop he would show me how close I was upon it; and from his threshold he pointed to the corner twenty yards off, which, when I had turned it, left me almost at my own door.

In that transmuted Rome Via del Gambero, at least, was wholly unchanged, and there was not a wrinkle in the front of the house where we had sojourned so comfortably, so contentedly, in our incredible youth. I had not quite the courage to ring and ask if we were at home; but, standing across the way and looking up at the window, it seemed to me that I might have seen my own young face peering out in a somewhat suspicious question of the old eyes staring up so fixedly at it. Who was I, and what was I doing there? Was I waiting, hanging idly about, to see the Armenian archbishop coming to carry my other self in his red coach to the Sistine Chapel, where we were to hear Pius IX. say mass? There was no harm in my hanging about, but the street was narrow and there was a chance of my being ground up by some passing cart against the wall there behind me if I was not careful. I could not tell my proud young double that we were one, and that I was going in the archbishop's red coach as well; he would never have believed it of my gray hairs and sunken figure. I could not even ask him what had become of the grocer near by, whom I used to get some homely supplies of, perhaps eggs or oranges, or the like, when I came out in the December mornings, and who, when I said that it was very cold, would own that it was *un poco rigidetto,* or a little bit stiffish. The ice on the pavement, not clean-swept as now, but slopped and frozen, had been witness of that; the ice was gone and the grocer with it; and where really was I? At the window up there, or leaning against the apse of the church opposite? What church was it, anyway? I never knew; I never asked. Why should I insist upon a common identity with a man of twenty-seven to whom my threescore and ten could only bring perplexity, to say the least, and very likely vexation? I went away from Via del Gambero, where the piety of the reader will seek either of myselves in vain. In my earlier date one used to see the red legs of the French soldiers about the Roman streets, and the fierce faces of the French officers, fierce as if they felt themselves wrongfully there and were braving it out against their consciences. Very likely they had no conscience about it; they had come there over the dead body of the Roman Republic at the will of their rascal president, and they were staying there by the will of their rascal emperor, to keep on his throne the pope from whom the Italians had hoped for unity and liberty. No one is very much to blame for anything, I suppose, and very likely Pius IX. had not voluntarily disappointed his countrymen, who may have expected too much. But then the French had been there fifteen years, and were to be there another fifteen years yet. Now they are gone, with the archbishop's red coach, and the complaisant grocer, and the young man of twenty-seven in Via del Gambero, and the rest of the things that the sun looked on and will look on the like of again, no doubt, in our monotonous round of him.

To-day, instead of the red legs of the French soldiers, you see the blue legs of the Italian soldiers, and instead of the fierce faces of their officers, the serious, intelligent, mostly spectacled faces of the Italian officers, in sweeping cloaks of tender blue verging on lavender. They are soldierly men none the less for their gentler aspect, and perhaps something the more; and a better thing yet is that there are comparatively few of them. There are few of the privates also, far fewer than the priests and the students of the ecclesiastical schools, who dress like priests and go dashing through the streets in files and troops.

I have an impression that one sees about the proportion of Italian soldiers in Rome that one sees of American soldiers in Washington, or, at least, not many more. The barracks are apparently outside the walls; there you meet cavalry going and coming, and detachments of *bersaglieri;* or riflemen, pushing on at their quick trot, or plainer infantry trudging wearily. Certainly, in a capital where the Church holds itself prisoner, there is no show of force on the part of its captors; and this is pleasant to the friend of man and the lover of Italy for other reasons. In the absence of the military you can imagine that not only does the state not wish to boast its political supremacy in the ancient capital of the Church, but it does not desire to show the potentiality of holding its own against the republic which is instinct there. The monarchy is the consensus of all the differing wills in Italy, which naturally would not for the most part have chosen a monarchy. But never was a monarchy so mild-mannered or seated so firmly, for the present at least, in the affection and reason of its people.

This is not the place (as writers say who have not prepared themselves with the requisite ideas at a given point) to speak of the situation in Rome; and I meant only to note that there are more ecclesiastics than conscripts to be seen there. Of all the varying costumes of the varying schools, none is so pleasing, so vivid, as that of the German students as they rush swiftly by in their flying robes of scarlet. The red matches the ruddy health in their cheeks, and there is a sort of gladness in their fling that wins the liking as well as the looking; so that almost one would not mind being a German student of theology one's self. There are other-costumes running in color from violet, and blue with orange sashes, to unrelieved black and black trimmed with red; but I cannot remember which nationality wears which.

I am not sure but one sees as many priests in Rome now as in the times when they ruled it; and I am no such Protestant that I will pretend I do not like a monsignore when I meet him, either in the street or at afternoon tea, as one sometimes may. I have no grudge against priests of any rank; but I did not seek to see them at the functions, as I used in the old days to do. Shall I say that I now rather tolerated than welcomed myself there through the hospitality which so freely opens the churches of the Church to all comers of whatever creed? What right had I, a heretic and recusant, to come staring and standing round where the faithful were kneeling and praying? If we could conceive of our fast-locked conventicles being thrown as freely open, could we conceive of Catholics wandering up and down their naves and aisles while the hymning or preaching went on? After being so high-minded in the matter, shall I confess that I was a good deal kept out of the churches by the cold in them? It was a sort of stored cold, much greater than that outside, though there was something warming to the fancy, at least, in the smoke and smell of the incense.

Even with the Church of the Capuchins, which we lived opposite, I was dilatory, though in my mediaeval days it had been one of the first places to which I hurried. In those days everybody said you must be sure and go to the Capuchins', because Guide's "St. Michael and the Enemy" was there, and still more because the wonderful bone mosaics in the cemetery under the church were not on any account to be missed. I suspect that in both these matters I had then a very crude taste, but it was not from my greater refinement that I now let the Capuchin church go on long un-revisited. It was, for one thing, too instantly and constantly accessible across the street there; and it is well known human nature is such that it will not seek the line of the least resistance as long as it can help. Besides, I could hardly believe that it was really the Capuchin church which I had once so hastened to see, and I neglected it almost two months, contenting myself with the display of those hand-bills on the convent walls, spreading largely and glaringly incongruous over it. When I did go I found the Guido ridiculous, of course, in the painter's imagination of the archangel as a sort of dancing figure in a *tableau vivant,* and yet of a sublime authority in the execution. To be more honest, I had little feeling about it and less knowledge.

It was not so cold in the church as I had expected; and in the succession of side chapels, beginning with the St. Michael's and opening into one another, we found a kind of domesticity close upon cosiness, which we were enjoying for its own sake, when we were aware of a pale, gentle young girl who seemed to be alone there. She asked, in our unmistakable native accents, if we were going to see the Capuchin mosaics in their place below; and one of us said, promptly, No, indeed; but relented at the shadow of disappointment that came over the girl's face, and asked, Was she going? The girl said, Oh, she guessed she could see them some other time; and then she who had spoken ordered him who had not spoken to go with her. I do not know what question of propriety engaged them with reference to her going alone with the handsome young monk waiting to accompany her; but he was certainly too handsome for a monk of any age. We followed him, however, and I had my usual nausea on viewing the decoration of the ceilings and walls of the place below; it always makes me sick to go into that place; between realizing that I am of the same make as the brothers composing those mosaics, and trying to imagine what the intricate patterns will do at the Resurrection Day, I cannot command myself. Neither am I supported by the sight of some skeletons, the raw material of that grewsome artistry, deposited whole in their coffins in the niches next the ground, though their skulls smile so reassuringly from their cowls; their cheeriness cannot make me like them. But my companion seemed to be merely interested; and I fancied her deciding that it all quite came up to her expectations, while I translated for her from the monk that the dead used to be left in the hallowed earth from Jerusalem covering the ground before they were taken up and decoratively employed, but that since the Italian occupation of Rome the art had fallen into abeyance. She said nothing, but when we came out she stood a moment on the pavement beside our cab and confessed herself a New England girl, from an inland town, who was travelling with relatives. She had been sick, and she had come alone, as soon as she could get out, to see the wonders of the Capuchin church, because she had heard so much of them. We said we hoped she had been pleased, and she said, "Oh yes, indeed," and then she said, "Well, good-bye," and gently tilted away, leaving us glad that there could still be in an old, spoiled world such sweetness and innocence and easily gratified love of the beautiful.

Taking Rome so easily, so provisionally, while waiting the eventualities of the colds which mild climates are sure to give their frequenters from the winterlands, I became aware of a latent anxiety respecting St. Peter's. I did not feel that the church would really get away without our meeting, but I felt that it was somehow culpably hazardous in me to be taking chances with it. As a family, we might never collectively visit it, and, in fact, we never did; but one day I drove boldly (if secretly) off alone and renewed my acquaintance with this contemporary of mine; for, if you have been in Rome a generation and a half ago, you find that you are coeval not only with the regal, the republican, and the imperial Rome, but with each Rome of the successive popes, down, at least, to that of Pius IX. St. Peter's will not be, by any means, your oldest friend, but it will be an acquaintance of such long standing that you may not wish to use it with all the frankness which its faults invite. If you say, when you drive into its piazza between the sublime colonnades which stretch forth their mighty embrace as if to take the whole world to the church's heart, that here is the best of St. Peter's, you will not be wrong. If you say that here is grandeur, and that there where the temple fronts you grandiosity begins, you will be rhetorical, but, again, you will not be wrong. The day of my furtive visit was sober and already waning, with a breeze in which the fountains streamed flaglike, and with a gentle sky on which the population of statues above the colonnades defined themselves in leisure attitudes, so recognizable all that I am sure if they had come down and taken me by the hand we could have called one another by name without a moment's hesitation. Every detail of a prospect which is without its peer on earth, but may very possibly be matched in Paradise, had been so deeply stamped in my remembrance that I smiled for pleasure in finding myself in an environment far more familiar than any other I could think of at the time. It was measurably the same within the church, but it was not quite the same in the reserves I was obliged to make, the reefs I was obliged to take in my rapture. The fact is, that unless you delight in a hugeness whose bareness no ornamentation can, or does at least, conceal, you do not find the interior of St. Peter's adequate to the exterior. In the mere article of hugeness, even, it fails through the interposition of the baldachin midway of the vast nave, and each detail seems to fail of the office of beauty more lamentably than another.

I had known, I had never forgotten, that St. Peter's was very, very baroque, but I had not known, I had not remembered how baroque it was. It is not so badly baroque as the Church of the Jesuits either in Rome or in Venice, or as the Cathedral at Wuerzburg; but still it is badly baroque, though, again, not so baroque in the architecture as in the sculpture. In the statues of most of the saints and popes it could not be more baroque; they swagger in their niches or over their tombs in an excess of decadent taste for which the most bigoted agnostic, however Protestant he may be, must generously grieve. It is not conceivably the taste of the church or the faith; it is the taste of the wicked world, now withered and wasted to powerlessness, which overruled both for evil in art from its evil life. The saints and the popes are, assthetically, lamentable enough; but the allegories in bronze or marble, which are mostly the sixteenth-century notions of the Virtues, are inexpressible—some of these creatures ought really to be put out of the place; but I suppose their friends would say they ought to be left as typical of the period. In the case of that merciless miscreant, Queen Christina of Sweden, who has her monument in St. Peter's, there would be people to say she must have her monument in some place; but, all the same, remembering Monaldeschi—how he was stabbed to death by her command, the kinder assassins staying their hands from time to time, while his confessor went vainly to implore her pardon—it is shocking to find her tomb in the prime church in Christendom. At first it offends one to see certain pontiffs with mustaches and imperials and goatees; but, if one reflects that so they wore them in life, one perceives right in it; only when one comes to earlier or later popes, bearded in medieval majority or shaven in the decent modern fashion, one can endure those others only as part of the prevailing baroque of the church. Canova was not so Greek or even so classic as one used to think him, but one hardly has a moment of repose in St. Peter's till one comes to a monument by him and rests in its quiet. It is tame, it is even weak, if you like; but compared with the frantic agglomeration of gilt clouds and sunbursts, and marble and bronze figures in the high-altar, it is heavenly serene and lovely.

There were not many people in St. Peter's that afternoon, so that I could give undisturbed attention to the workman repairing the pavement at one point and grinding the marble smooth with a slow, secular movement, as if he were part of its age-Ions: waste and repair. Another day, the last day I came, there were companies of the personally conducted, following their leaders about and listening to the lectures in several languages, which no more stirred the immense tranquillity than they themselves qualified the spacious vacancy of the temple: you were vaguely sensible of the one and of the other like things heard and seen in a drowse. It was a pleasant vagueness in which all angularities of feeling were lost, and you were disposed to a tolerance of the things that had hurt or offended you before. As a contemporary of the edifice, throughout its growth, you could account for them more and more as of their periods. Perhaps through your genial reconciliation there came, however dimly, a suggestion of something unnatural and alien in your presence there as a mere sightseer, or, at best, a connoisseur much or little instructed. If you had been there, say, as a worshipper, would you have been afflicted by the incongruities of the sculptures or by the whole baroque keeping? Possibly this consideration made you go away much modester than you came. "After all," you may have said, "it is not a gallery; it is not a museum. It is a house of prayer," and you emerged, let us hope, humbled, and in so far fitted for renewed joy in the beauty, the glory of the sublime colonnades.

VII. CHANCES IN CHURCHES

If any one were to ask me which was the most beautiful
church in Rome I should temporize, and perhaps I should
end by saying that there was none. Ecclesiastical Rome
seems to have inherited the instinct of imperial Rome for
ugliness; only, where imperial Rome used the instinct
collectively, ecclesiastical Rome has used it distributively in
the innumerable churches, each less lovely than the other.
This position will do to hedge from; it is a bold outpost from
which I may be driven in, especially by travellers who have
seen the churches I did not see. I took my chances, they
theirs; for nobody can singly see all the churches in Rome;
that would need a syndicate.

If imperial Rome was beautiful in detail because it had the
Greeks to imagine the things it so hideously grouped,
ecclesiastical Rome may be unbeautiful in detail because it
had not the Goths to realize the beauty of its religious
aspiration—that is, if it was the Goths who invented Gothic
architecture; I do not suppose it was. Anyway, there is said
to be but one Gothic church in Rome, and this I did not visit,
perhaps because I felt that I must inure myself to the
prevalent baroque, or perhaps from mere perversity. I can
merely say in self-defence that, on the outside, Santa Maria
sopra Minerva no more promised an inner beauty than Il
Gesu, which is the most baroque church in Rome, without
the power of coming together for a unity of effect which
baroque churches sometimes have. It is a tumult of virtuosity
in painting, in scuplture, in architecture. Statues sprawl into
frescoed figures at points in the roof, and frescoed figures
emerge in marble at others. Marvels of riches are lavished
upon chapels and altars, which again are so burdened with
bronze gilded or silver plated, and precious stones wrought
and unwrought, that the soul, or if not the soul the taste,

shrinks dismayed from them. Execution in default of inspiration has had its way to the last excess; there is nothing that it has not done to show what it can do; and all that it has done is a triumph of misguided skill and power. But it would be a mistake for the spectator to imagine that anything has been done from the spirit in which he receives it; everything is the expression of devoted faith in the forms that the art of the time offered.

In the monstrous marble tableau, say, of "Religion Triumphing Over Heresy," he may be very sure that the artist was not winking an ironical eye where he made Faith spurning Schism with her foot look very much like a lady of imperfect breeding who has lost her temper; he was most devoutly in earnest, or at least those were so, both cleric and laic, for whom he wrought his prodigy. We others, pagans or Protestants, had better understand that the children of the Church, and especially the poor children, were serious through all the shows that seem to us preposterous; they had not renounced something for nothing; if they bowed that very fallible thing, Reason, to Dogma, they got faith for their reward and could gladly accept whatever symbol of it was offered them.

No matter how baroque any church was, it could express something of this sincerity, and in their way the worshippers seemed always simply at home in it. In San Lorenzo in Lucina, where I went to see the truly sublime "Crucifixion" by Guido (there is also a bar of St. Lawrence's gridiron to be seen, but I did not know it at the time) I liked the unconsciousness of the girl kneeling before the high altar and provisionally gossiping with the young sacristan before she began her devotions. She gave her mind to them when he asked me if I wished to see the Guido, for I could see her lips moving while she shared my veneration of that most affecting masterpiece; the more genuinely affecting because

W. D. Howells

it expresses the rapture and not the anguish of the Passion. I have no doubt she was grateful when the sacristan proposed my having the electric light turned on it, and when, though that I knew it would cost me something more, I assented.

They have the electric light now in all the holy places, and notably in the dungeon where St. Peter was imprisoned, and where the custodian was so proud of it, as the lastest improvement, and as far more satisfactory than candles. The shrine of the miraculous Bambino in the Church of Ara Coeli is also lighted by electricity, which spares no detail of the child's apparel and appearance. To other eyes than those of faith it has the effect of a life-size but not life-like doll, piously bedizened and jewelled over, but rather ill-humored looking, or, if not that, proud looking or severe looking. To the eyes in which its sickbed visits have dried the tears it must wear an aspect of heavenly pity and beauty; and I am very willing to believe that these are the eyes which see it aright. As it was, and taking it literally, it seemed far less mechanical and unfeeling than the monk who pulled it out and pushed it back on its wheeled platform. But he must get tired of showing it to the unbelievers who come out of curiosity, and very likely I should, if I were in his place, as nonchalantly wipe across the glass front of the shrine the card with the Bambino's legend printed in various languages on it, which you may then buy with the blessing from the glass for whatever you choose to give.

Where art and antiquity are so abundant as in Rome, the Bambino incident is probably what the reader, when he has visited the Church of Ara Coeli will chiefly remember, and I will not pretend to be any better than the reader, though I will say that I have a persistent sense of something important about the roof; and there are the Pinturrichio frescos, which an old Sienese like me must have the taste for. The not easily praiseful Hare says it is "one of the most interesting of

Christian churches," and without allowing that there are any other sorts of churches I may allow that this is one of the least unlovely in Rome. Trinita de' Monti seemed to be another, but only, I dare say, subjectively, because of the exquisite pleasure we had one afternoon in March when we went into it for the nuns' singing of the Benediction. That, we had been told, was something which no one coming to Rome should miss; and we were so anxious not to miss it that on our way to the Pincian Hill we stopped at the foot of the church-steps, and reassured ourselves of the hour through the kindness of an English-speaking nurse-maid at the bottom and of a gentle nun at the top, who both told us the hour would be exactly five.

When we came back at that time and bought our way into the church by rightful payment to the two blind beggars who guarded its doors, we found it packed with people who bad been more literally punctual. They were of all nations, but a large part were Anglo-Americans, and a young girl of this race rose and gave her seat, with a sweet insistence that would not be denied, to that one of us who deserved it most. He who was left leaning against the soft side of a pillar hesitated whether to make some young priests spreading over undue space on one of the benches push up, and he enjoyed a rich moment of self-satisfaction in his forbearance. He was there, to be sure, an alien and a heretic, out of mere curiosity, and they were there probably so rapt in their devout attention that they did not notice their errant step-brother, and so did not think to offer him the hospitality of their mother church's house. But he would not make any such allowance; he condemned them with the unsparing severity of the strap-hanger in a trolley-car, who blushes with shame for the serried rows of men sitting behind their newspapers. When he was at his wit's end to find excuse for them a priest on another bench made room, and he sank down glad to forgive and forget; but now he would not have yielded his place to any other Protesant in Christendom.

In the collective curiosity he lost the sense of self-reproach for his own, and eagerly bent his gaze on the group of officiating priests at the high altar beyond the grille of the choir. The altar was all a blaze of electric lights, and there was a novel effect in their composition in the crosses resting diagonally on either side of it. Next the grille showed the feathers and fashions of the mothers and sisters of the young girls from the school of the adjoining Convent of the Sacred Heart, and midway between these visitors, like a flock of white birds stooping on some heavenly plain, the white veils of the girls stretched in lovely levels to left and right. Nothing could have attuned the spirit for the surprise awaiting it like this angelic sight; and when the voices of the nuns fell suddenly from the organ gallery, behind all the people, like the singing of the morning stars molten in one adoring music and falling from the zenith down, whatever moments of innocent joy life might have had it could have had none surpassing that.

But when we came out the self-mockery with which life is apt to recover itself from any exaltation began. In returning from the Pincio the only cab we had been able to get was the last left of the very worst cabs in Rome, and we had bidden the driver wait for us at the church-steps, not without some hope that he would play us false. But there he was, true to his word, with such disciplined fidelity as that of the Roman sentinels who used to die at their posts; and we mounted to ours with the muted prayer that we, at least, might reach home alive. This did not seem probable when the driver whipped up his horse. It appeared to have aged and sickened while we were in the church, though we had thought it looked as bad as could be before, and it lurched alarmingly from side to side, recovering itself with a plunge of its heavy head away from the side in which its body was sinking. The driver swayed on his box, having fallen equally decrepit in spite of the restoratives he seemed to have applied for his years and infirmities. His clothes had put on some such effect of extreme decay as those of Rip Van Winkle in the third act; there was danger that he would fall on top of his falling horse, and that their raiment would mingle in one scandalous ruin. Via Sistina had never been so full of people before; never before had it been so long to that point where we were to turn out of it into the friendly obscurity of the little cross street which would bring us to our hotel. We could not consent to arrive in that form; we made the driver stop, and we got out and began overpaying him to release us. But the more generously we overpaid him the more nobly he insisted upon serving us to our door. At last, by such a lavish expenditure as ought richly to provide for the few remaining years of himself and his horse, we prevailed with him to let us go, and reached our hotel glad, almost proud, to arrive on foot.

Hare tells me, now it is too late, that I may reach the Church of Santa Maggiore by keeping straight on through the long, long straightness of the Via Sistina. I reached that church by quite another way after many postponements; for I thought I remembered all about it from my visit in 1864. But really nothing had remained to me save a sense of the exceptional dignity of the church, and the sole fact that the roof of its most noble nave is thickly plated with the first gold mined in South America, which Ferdinand and Isabella gave that least estimable of the popes, Alexander VI. Now I know that it is far richer than any gold could make it in the treasures of history and legend, which fairly encrust it in every part. Doubtless some portion of this wealth my fellow-sightseers were striving to store up out of the guide-books which they bore in their hands and from which they strained their eyes to the memorable points as they slowly paced through the temple. Some were reading one to another in bated voices, and I thought them ridiculous; but perhaps they were wise, and rather he was ridiculous who marched by them and contented himself with a general sense of the grandeur, the splendor. More than any other church except that of San Paolo fuori le Mura, Santa Maria Maggiore imparts this sense, for, as I have already pretended, St. Peter's fails of it. Without as well as within the church is spacious and impressive from its spaciousness; but it seems more densely fringed than most others with peddlers of post-cards and mosaic pins. On going in you can plunge through their ranks, but in coming out you do not so easily escape. One boy pursued me quite to my cab, in spite of my denials of hand and tongue. There he stayed the driver while he made a last, a humorous appeal. "Skiddoo?" he asked in my native speech. "Yes," I sullenly replied, "skiddoo!" But it is now one of the regrets which I shall always feel for my wasted opportunities in Rome that I did not buy all his post-cards. Patient gayety like his merited as much.

As it was, I drove callously away from Santa Maria Maggiore to San Pietro in Vincoli, where I expected to renew my veneration for Michelangelo's Moses. That famous figure is no longer so much in the minds of men as it used to be, I think; and, if one were to be quite honest with one's self as to the why and wherefore of one's earlier veneration, one might not get a very distinct or convincing reply. Do sculptors and painters suffer periods of slight as authors do? Are Raphael and Michelangelo only provisionally eclipsed by Botticelli and by Donatello and Mino da Fiesole, or are they remanded to a lasting limbo? I find I have said in my notes that the Moses is improbable and unimpressive, and I pretended a more genuine joy in the heads of the two Pollajuolo brothers which startle you from their tomb as you enter the church. Is the true, then, better than the ideal, or is it only my grovelling spirit which prefers it? What I scarcely venture to say is that those two men evidently lived and still live, and that Michelangelo's prophet never lived; I scarcely venture, because I remember with tenderness how certain clear and sweet spirits used to bow their reason before the Moses as before a dogma of art which must be implicitly accepted. Do they still do so, those clear and sweet spirits

The archaeologist who was driving my cab that morning had pointed out to me on the way to this church the tower on which Nero stood fiddling while Rome was burning. It is a strong, square, mediaeval structure which will serve the purpose of legend yet many centuries, if progress does not pull it down; but the fiddle no longer exists, apparently, and Nero himself is dead. When I came out and mounted into my cab, my driver showed me with his whip, beyond a garden wall, a second tower, very beautiful against the blue sky, above the slim cypresses, which he said was the scene of the wicked revels of Lucrezia Borgia. I do not know why it has been chosen for this distinction above other towers; but it was a great satisfaction to have it identified. Very possibly I had seen both of these memorable towers in my former Roman sojourn, but I did not remember them, whereas I renewed my old impressions of San Paolo fuori le Mura in almost every detail.

That is the most majestic church in Rome, I think, and I suppose it is, for a cold splendor, unequalled anywhere. Somehow, from its form and from the great propriety of its decoration, it far surpasses St. Peter's. The antic touch of the baroque is scarcely present in it, for, being newly rebuilt after the fire which destroyed the fourth-century basilica in 1823, its faults are not those of sixteenth-century excess. It would be a very bold or a very young connoisseur who should venture to appraise its merits beyond this negative valuation; and timid age can affirm no more than that it came away with its sensibilities unwounded. Tradition and history combine with the stately architecture, which reverently

W. D. Howells

includes every possible relic of the original fabric, to render the immense temple venerable; and as it is still in process of construction, with a colonnaded porch in scale and keeping with the body of the basilica, it offers to the eye of wonder the actual spectacle of that unstinted outlay of riches which has filled Rome with its multitudes of pious monuments— monuments mainly ugly, but potent with the imagination even in their ugliness through the piety of their origin. Where did all that riches come from

Out of what unfathomable opulence, out of what pitiable penury, out of what fear, out of what love? One fancies the dying hands of wealth that released their gift to the sacred use, the knotted hands of work that spared it from their need. The giving continues in this latest Christian age as in the earliest, and Rome is increasingly Rome in a world which its thinkers think no longer believes.

From San Paolo we were going to another shrine, more hallowed to our literary sense, and we drove through the sweet morning sunshine and bird-singing, past pale-pink clouds of almond bloom on the garden slopes, with snowy heights far beyond, to the simple graveyard where Keats and Shelley lie. Our way to the Protestant cemetery held by some shabby apartment-houses of that very modern Rome which was largely so jerry-built, and which I would not leave out of the landscape if I could, for I think their shabbiness rather heightens your sense of the peaceful loveliness to which you come under the cypresses, among the damp aisles, so thickly studded with the stones recording the death in exile of the English strangers lying there far from home. In a faulty perspective of memory, I had always seen the graves of the two poets side by side; but the heart of Shelley rests in a prouder part of the cemetery, where the paths between the finer tombs are carefully kept; and the dust of Keats lies in an old, plain, almost neglected corner, well off beyond a dividing trench. It seems an ungracious chance which has so parted the two poets so inextricably united in their fame; it is as if here, too, the world would have its way; but, of course, it is only at the worst an ungracious chance. Keats, at least, has the companionship of the painter Severn, the friend on whose "fond breast his parting soul relied," and who has here followed him into the dust.

A few withered daisies had been scattered in the thin grass over the poet, and one hardly dared lift one's eyes from them to the heartbreaking epitaph which one could not spell for tears.

W. D. Howells

VIII. A FEW VILLAS

It was but a few minutes' walk from the hotel to the Porta
Pinciana, and, if you took this short walk, you found yourself
almost before you knew it in the Villa Borghese. You might
then, on your first Sunday in Rome, have fancied yourself in
Central Park, for all difference in the easily satisfied Sunday-
afternoon crowd. But with me a difference began in the
grove of stone-pines, and their desultory stretch toward the
Casino, where in the simple young times which are now the
old we had hurried, with our Kugler in our hands and other
reading in our heads, to see Titian's Sacred and Profane Love
(it has got another name now) and Canova's Pauline
Bonaparte, who was also the Princess Borghese, and all the
rest of the precious gallery. However, if I had any purpose of
visiting the Casino now, I put it aside, and contented myself
with the gentle sun, the gentle shade, and the sweet air,
which might have had less dust in it, breathing over grass as
green in late January as in early June. I did not care so much
for a mounted corporal who was jumping his horse over a
two-foot barrier in the circular path rounding between the
Villa Borghese and the Pincian Hill, though his admirers
hung in rows on the rail beside it so thickly that I could
hardly have got a place to see him if I had tried. But there
was room enough to the fathers and mothers who had
brought their children, and young lovers who had brought
each other for the afternoon's outing, just as the people in
Central Park do, and, no doubt, just as any Sunday crowd
must do in the planet Mars, if the inhabitants are human.
There was a *vacherie* nearby where not many persons were
drinking milk or even coffee; it is never the notion of the
Italians that amusement can be had only through the
purchase of refreshments.

I did not get as far as the Casino till the last Sunday of our

Roman stay, though we came again and again to the park (as we should call it, rather than villa), sometimes to walk, sometimes to drive, and always to rejoice in its loveliness. It was not now a very guarded, if once a very studied, loveliness; not quite neglect, but a forgottenness to which it took kindly, had fallen upon it; the drives seemed largely left to take care of themselves, the walks were such as the frequenters chose to make over the grass or through the woods; the buildings—the aviary, the conservatory, the dairy, the stables—which formed part of the old pleasance, stood about, as if in an absent-minded indifference to their various roles. The weather had grown a little more wintry, or, at least, autumnal, as the season advanced toward spring, and one day at the end of February, when we were passing a woody hollow, the fallen leaves stirred crisply with a sound like that of late October at home. We had been at some pains and expense to put home four thousand miles away, but this sound was the sweetest and dearest we had heard in Rome, and it strangely attuned our spirits to the enjoyment of the fake antiquities, the broken arches, pediments, columns, statues, which, in a region glutted with ruin, the landscape architect of the Villa Borghese had fancied putting about in pleasing stages of artificial dilapidation. But there was nothing faked in the dishevelled grass of the little stadium, with its gra-dines around the sides, and the game of tennis which some young girls were playing in it. Neither was there anything ungenuine in the rapture of the boy whom we saw racing through the dead leaves of that woody hollow in chase of the wild fancies that fly before boyhood; and I hope that the charm of the plinths and statues in the careless grounds behind the soft, old, yellow Casino was a real charm. At any rate, these things all consoled, and the turf under the pines, now thickly starred with daisies, gave every assurance of being original.

When we came last the daisies were mingled with clustering

W. D. Howells

anemones, which seem a greatly overrated sort of flower, crude and harsh in color, like cheap calico. If it were not for their pretty name I do not see how people could like them; yet the children that day were pouncing upon them and pulling them by handfuls; for the Villa Borghese is now state property and is free to the children of the people in a measure quite beyond Central Park. They can apparently pull anything they want, except mushrooms; there are signs advising people that the state draws the line at mushrooms.

It was once more a Sunday, and it was a free day in the Casino. The trodden earth sent up its homely, kindly smell from many feet on their way to the galleries, which we found full of people looking greater intelligence than the frequenters of such places commonly betray. They might have been such more cultivated sight-seers as could not afford to come on the paydays, and, if they had not crowded the room so, one might have been glad as well as proud to be of their number. They did not really keep one from older friends, from the statues and the pictures which were as familiarly there in 1908 as in 1864. In a world of vicissitudes such things do not change; the Sacred and Profane Love of Titian, though it had changed its name, had not changed its nature, and was as divinely serene, as richly beautiful as before. The Veroneses still glowed from the walls, dimming with their Venetian effulgence all the other pictures but the Botticellis and the Francias, and comforting one with the hope that, if one had always felt their beauty so much, one might, without suspecting it, have always had some little sense of art. But it was probably only a literary sense of art, such as moves the observer when he finds himself again in the presence of Canova's Pauline Borghese. That is there, on the terms which were those no less of her character than of her time, in the lasting enjoyment of a publicity which her husband denied it in his lifetime; but it had no more to say now than it had so many, many years ago. As, a piece of personal history it is amusing enough, and as a sermon in stone it preaches whatever moral you choose to read into it. But as the masterpiece of the sculptor it testifies to an ideal of his art for which the world has reason to be grateful. Criticism does not now put Canova on the height where we once looked up to him; but criticism is a fickle thing, especially in its final judgments; and one cannot remember the behavior of the Virtues in some of the baroque churches without paying homage to the portrait of a lady who, whatever she was, was not a Virtue, but who yet helped the sculptor to realize in her statue a Venus of exceptional propriety. Tame, yes, we may now safely declare Canova to have been, but sane we must allow; and we must never forget that he has been the inspiration in modern sculpture of the eternal Greek truth of repose from which the art had so wildly wandered, He, more than any other, stayed it in the mad career on which Michelangelo, however remotely, had started it; and we owe it to him that the best marbles now no longer strut or swagger or bully.

It was by one of those accidents which are the best fortunes of travel that I visited the Villa Papa Giulio, when I thought I was merely going to the Piazza del Popolo, to which one cannot go too often. A chance look at my guide-book beguiled me with the notion that the villa was just outside the gate; but it was a deceit which I should be glad to have practised on me every February 17th of my life. If the villa was farther off than I thought, the way to it lay for a while through a tramwayed suburban street delightfully encumbered with wide-horned oxen drawing heavy wagon-loads of grain, donkeys pulling carts laden with vegetables, and children and hens and dogs playing their several parts in a perspective through which one would like to continue indefinitely. But after awhile a dim, cool, curving lane leaves this street and irresistibly invites your cab to follow it; and sooner than you could ask you get to the villa gate. There a gatekeeper tacitly wonders at your arriving before he is well awake, and will keep you a good five minutes while he parleys with another custodian before he can bring himself to sell you a ticket and let you into the beautiful, old, orange-gray cloistered court, where there is a young architect with the T-square of his calling sketching some point of it, and a gardener gently hacking off from the parent stems such palm-leaves as have survived their usefulness. Beyond is the famous fountained court, and a classic temple to the right, and other structures responsive to the impulses of the good Pope Julius III., who was never tired of adding to this pleasure palace of his. It was his favorite resort, with all his court, from the Vatican, and his favorite amusement in it was the somewhat academic diversion of proverbs, which Ranke says sometimes "mingled blushes with the smiles of his guests."

Lest the reader should think I have gone direct to Ranke for this knowledge, I will own that I got it at second-hand out of Hare's *Walks in Rome,* where he tells us also that the pope used to come to his villa every day by water, and that "the richly decorated barge, filled with venerable ecclesiastics, gliding through the osier-fringed banks of the Tiber, . . . would make a fine subject for a picture." No doubt, and if I owned such a picture I would lose no time in public-spiritedly bestowing it on the first needy gallery. Our author is, as usual, terribly severe on the Italian government for some wrong done the villa, I could not well make out what. But it seems to involve the present disposition of the Etruscan antiquities in the upper rooms of the casino, where these, the most precious witnesses of that rather inarticulate civilization, must in any arrangement exhaust the most instructed interest. Just when the amateur archaeologist, however, is sinking under his learning, the custodian opens a window and lets him look out on a beautiful hill beyond certain gardens, where a bird is singing angelically. I suppose it is the same bird which sings all through these papers, and I am sorry I do not know its name. But we will call it a blackcap: blackcap has a sweet, saucy sound like its own note, and is the pretty translation of *caponero,* a name which the bird might gladly know itself by.

Villa Papa Giulio is but a little place compared with something on the scale of the Villa Pamfili Doria though from its casino it has a charm far beyond that. What it may once have been as to grounds and gardens there is little to show now, and the Pamfili Doria itself had not much to show in gardens, though it had grounds, and to spare. It is, in fact, a large park, though whether larger than the Villa Borghese I cannot say. But it has not been taken by the state, and it is so far off on its hills that it is safe from the overrunning of city feet. It is safe even from city wheels, unless they are those of livery carriages, for numbered cabs are not suffered in its proud precincts. You partake of this pride when you come in your rubber-tired *remise,* and have the consolation of being part of the beautiful exclusiveness. It costs you fifteen francs, but one must suffer for being patrician, even for a single afternoon. Outside we had the satisfaction of seeing innumerable numbered cabs drawn up, and within the villa gates of meeting or passing the plebeians who had come in them, and were now walking while we were smoothly rolling in our victoria. The day was everything we could ask, very warm and bright below the Janiculum, on which we had mounted, and here on the summit delicious with cool currents of air. There had been beggars, on the way up, at every point where our horses must be walked, and we had paid our way handsomely, so that when we went back they bowed without asking again; this is a convention at Rome which no self-respecting beggar will violate; they all touch their hats in recognition of it.

The beautiful prospect from a certain curve of the drive after

W. D. Howells

yon have passed the formal sunken garden, at which you pause, is the greatest beauty of the Villa Pamfili Doria. You stop to look at it by the impulse of your coachman, and then you keep on driving round, in the long ellipse which the road describes, through grassy and woody slopes and levels, watered by a pleasant stream, and through long aisles of pine and ilex. We thought twice round was enough, and told the driver so, to his evident surprise and to our own regret, so far as the long aisle of ilex was concerned, for I do not suppose there is a more perfect thing of its kind in the world. The shade under the thick sun-proof roofing of horizontal boughs was practically as old as night, and on our second passage of its dim length it had some Capuchin monks walking down it, who formed the fittest possible human interest in the perspective. Off on the grass at one side some Ursuline nuns were sitting with their pupils, laughing and talking, and one nun was playing ball with the smaller girls, and mingling with their shouts her own gay, innocent cries of joy as she romped among them. Nothing could have been prettier, sweeter, or better suited to the place; all was very simple, and apparently the whole place was hospitably free to the poor women who ranged over it, digging chiccory for salad out of the meadows. The daisies were thick as white clover, and the harsh purple of the anemones showed everywhere.

The casino is plainer than the casino of the Villa Borghese, and is not public like that; its sculptures have been taken to the Doria palace in the city; and there is no longer any excuse for curiosity even to try penetrating it. It stands on the left of the road by which you leave the villa, and to the right on the grassy incline in full view of the casino was something that puzzled us at first. It did not seem probable that the gigantic capital letters grown in box should be spelling the English name Mary, but it proved that they were, and later it proved that this was the name of the noble English lady whom the late Prince Pamfill Doria had

married. Whether they marked her grave or merely comme-
morated her, it was easy to impute a pathos to the fancy of
having them there, which it might not have been so easy to
verify. You cannot attempt to pass over any ground in Rome
without danger of sinking into historical depths from which
it will be hard to extricate yourself, and it is best to heed
one's steps and keep them to the day's activities. But one
could not well visit the Villa Pamfili Doria without at least
wishing to remember that in 1849 Garibaldi held it for weeks
against the whole French army, in his defence of republican
Rome. A votive temple within the villa grounds commemo-
rates the invaders who fell in this struggle; on a neighboring
height the Italian leader triumphs in the monument his
adoring country has raised to him.

If we are to believe the censorious Hare, the love of the
hero's countrymen went rather far when the Roman
municipality, to please him, tried to change the course of the
Tiber in conformity with a scheme of his, and so spoiled the
beauty of the Farnesina garden Avithout effecting a too-
difficult piece of engineering. The less passionate Murray
says merely that "a large slice of this garden was cut off to
widen the river for the Tiber embankment," and let us hope
that it was no worse. I suppose we must have seen the villa
in its glory when we went, in 1864, to see the Raphael
frescos in the casino there, but in the touching melancholy of
the wasted and neglected grounds we easily accepted the
present as an image of the past. For all we remembered, the
weed-grown, green-mossed gravel-paths of the sort of
bewildered garden that remained, with its quenched fountain,
its vases of dead or dying plants, and its dishevelled
shrubbery, were what had always been; and it was of such a
charm that we were gratefully content with it. The truth is,
one cannot do much with beauty in perfect repair; the
splendor that belongs to somebody else, unless it belongs
also to everybody else, wounds one's vulgar pride and

inspires envious doubts of the owner's rightful possession. But when the blight of ruin has fallen upon it, when dilapidation and disintegration have begun their work of atonement and exculpation, then our hearts melt in compassion of the waning magnificence and in a soft pity for the expropriated possessor, to whom we attribute every fine and endearing quality. It is this which makes us such friends of the past and such critics of the present, and enables us to enjoy the adversity of others without a pang of the jealousy which their prosperity excites.

There was much to please a somewhat peculiar taste in our visit to the Farnesina. The gateman, being an Italian official, had not been at the gate when we arrived, but came running and smiling from his gossip with the door-keeper of the casino, and this was a good deal in itself; but the door-keeper, amiably obese, was better still in her acceptance of the joke with which the hand-mirror for the easier study of the roof frescos was accepted. "It is more convenient," she suggested, and at the counter-suggestion, "Yes, especially for people with short necks," she shook with gelatinous laughter, and burst into the generous cry, "Oh, how delightful!" Perhaps this was because she, too, had experienced the advantage of perusing the frescos in the hand-mirror's reversal. At any rate, she would not be satisfied till she had returned a Roland for that easy Oliver. Her chance came in showing a Rubens in one of the rooms, with the master's usual assortment of billowy beauties, when she could say— and she ought to have known—that they had eaten too much macaroni. It was not much of a joke; but one hears so few jokes in Rome.

Do I linger in this study of simple character because I feel myself unequal to the ecstasies which the frescos of Raphael and his school in that pleasure dome demanded of me? Something like that, I suppose, but I do not pride myself on my inability. It seemed to me that the coloring of the frescos had lost whatever tenderness it once had; and that what was never meant to be matter of conscious perception, but only of the vague sense which it is the office of decoration to impart, had grown less pleasing with the passage of time. There in the first hall was the story of Cupid and Psyche in the literal illustration of Apuleius, and there in another hall was Galatea on her shell with her Nymphs and Tritons and Amorini; and there were Perseus and Medusa and Icarus and Phaeton and the rest of them. But, if I gave way to all the frankness of my nature, I should own the subjects fallen sillv through the old age of an outworn life and redeemed only by the wonderful skill with which they are rendered. At the same time, I will say in self-defence that, if I had a very long summer in which to keep coming and dwelling long hours in the company of these frescos, I think I might live back into the spirit which invented the fables, and enjoy even more the amusing taste that was never tired of their repetition. Masterly conception and incomparable execution are there in histories which are the dreams of worlds almost as extinct as the dead planets whose last rays still reach us and in whose death-glimmer we can fancy, if we will, a unity of life with our own not impossible nor improbable. But more than some such appeal the Raphaels and the Giulio Romanos of the Farnesina hardly make to the eye untrained in the art which created them, or unversed in the technique by which they will live till the last line moulders and the last tint fades.

We came out and stood a long time looking up in the pale afternoon light at the beautiful face of the tenderly aging but not yet decrepit casino. It was utterly charming, and it prompted many vagaries which I might easily have mistaken for ideas. This is perhaps the best of such experiences, and, after you have been with famous works of art and have got them well over and done with, it is natural and it is not unjust that you should wish to make them some return, if not in kind, then in quantity. You will try to believe that you have thought about them, and you should not too strictly inquire as to the fact. It is some such forbearance that accounts for a good deal of the appreciation and even the criticism of works of art.

IX. DRAMATIC INCIDENTS

If the joke of the door-keeper at the Farnesina was not so delicate in any sense as some other jokes, it had, at least, the merit of being voluntary. In fact, it is the only voluntary joke which I remember hearing in the Tuscan tongue from the Roman mouth during a stay of three months in the Eternal City. This was very disappointing, for I had always thought of the Italians as gay and as liking to laugh and to make laugh. In Venice, where I used to live, the gondoliers were full of jokes, good, bad, and indifferent, and an infection of humor seemed to spread from them to all the lower classes, who were as ready to joke as the lower classes of Irish, and who otherwise often reminded one of them. The joking hahit extended as far down as Florence, even as Siena, and at Naples I had found cabmen who tempered their predacity with *bonhomie.* But the Romans were preferably serious, at least with the average American, though, if I had tried them in their English instead of my Italian, it might have been different. At times I thought, they felt the weight of being Romans, as it had descended to them from antiquity, and that the strain of supporting it had sobered them. In any case, though there was shouting by night, and some singing of not at all the Neapolitan quality and still less the Neapolitan quantity, there was no laughing, or, as far as I could see, smiling by day.

Yet one day there was a tragedy in front of the hotel next ours which would have made a dog laugh, as the saying is, unless it was a Roman dog. It was a quarrel, more or less murderous, between a fat, elderly man and an agile stripling of not half his age or girth, of whom the tumult about them permitted only fleeting glimpses. By these the elder seemed to be laboriously laying about him with a five-foot club and the younger to be making wild dashes at him and then

W. D. Howells

escaping to the skirts of the cabmen, mounted and dismounted, who surrounded them. Now and then a cabman drove out of the mellay very excitedly, and then turned and drove excitedly back into the thick of it. All the while the dismounted cabmen pressed about the combatants with their hands on one another's backs and their heads peering carefully over one another's shoulders. On the very outermost rim of these, more careful than any, was one of those strange images whom you see about Italian towns in couples, with red-braided swallowtail coats and cocked hats, those carabinieres—namely, who are soldiers in war and policemen in times of peace. Any spectator from a foreign land would have thought it the business of such an officer of the law to press in and stop the fighting; but he did not so interpret his duty. He gingerly touched the shoulders next him with the tips of his fingers, and now and then lifted himself on the tips of his toes to look if the fight had stopped of itself or not.

At last the fat, elderly man, whom his friends—and all the throng except that one wicked youth seemed his friends—were caressing in untimely embraces and coaxing in tones of tender entreaty, burst from them, and, aiming at the head of his enemy, flung his club, to the imminent peril of all the bystanders, and missed him. Then he frankly put himself in the hands of his friends, who lifted him into a cab, where one of them mounted with him and stayed him on the seat, while the cabman drove rapidly away. The wicked youth had vanished in unknown space; but the carabiniere, attended by a group of admirers, marched boldly up the middle of the street, and the crowd, with whatever reluctance, persuaded itself to disperse, though the cabmen, to the number of ten or twenty, continued to drive around in concentric circles and irregular ellipses. In five minutes not an eye-witness of the fray remained, such being the fear of the law, not so much in those who break it as in those who see it broken, and who dread incurring the vengeance of the culprit, if he is acquitted, or of his family if he is convicted on their testimony. The quarrel had gone on a full quarter of an hour, but the concierge of the hotel in front of which it had raged professed to have known nothing of it, having, he said, been in-doors all the time. A cabman whom we eliminated from the hysterical company of his fellows and persuaded to drive us away to see a church attempted to ignore the whole affair when asked about it. With difficulty he could be made to recollect it, and then he dismissed it as a trifle. "Oh," he said, "chiacchiere di donnicciuole," which is something like "Clatter of little old women," a thing not worth noticing. He had, if we could believe him, not cared to know how it began or ended, and he would not talk about it.

Later, still interested by the action of the carabiniere in guarding the public security in his own person, I asked an Italian gentleman, who owned to have seen the affair, why the officer did not break through the crowd and arrest the fighters. "They had knives," he explained, and it seemed a good reason for the carabiniere's forbearance, as far as it went; but I thought of the short work the brute locust of an Irish policeman at home would have made of the knives. My friend said he had himself gone to one of the municipal police who was looking on at a pleasant remove and said, "Those fellows have knives; they will kill each other," and the municipal policeman had answered, with the calm of an antique Roman sentinel on duty in time of earthquake, "Let them kill."

I could not approve of so much impartiality, but afterward it seemed to me I had little to be proud of in the shorter and easier method of our own police, as contrasted with the caution of that Roman carabiniere who left the combatants to the mild might of their friends' moral suasion. It was better that the youth should escape, if he did, without a vexatious criminal trial; he may have been no more to blame than the other, who, I learned, had been carried off, in the honorable manner I saw, to a doctor and had his stab looked to. It was not dangerous, and the whole affair ended so. Besides, as I learned, still longer afterward, when it was quite safe for a cabman from the same stand to speak, the combatants were not Romans, but peasants from the Campagna, who had come in with their market-carts and had become heated with the bad spirits which the peasants have the habit of drinking five or six glasses of when they visit Rome. "What we call benzine," my cabman explained. "We Romans," he added from a moral height, "drink only a glass or two of wine, and we never carry knives."

He may have been right concerning the peacefulness of the Romans and their sobriety, and I am bound to say that I never saw any other violent scene during my stay. Sometimes I heard loud quarrelling among our cabmen, and sometimes I was the subject of it, when one driver snatched me, an impartial prey, from another. But the bad feeling, if there was really any, quickly passed, and some other day I fell to the cabman who had been wronged of me. I had not always the fine sense of being booty which I had one day on coming out of a church and blundering toward the wrong cab. Then the driver whom I had left waiting at the door seized me from the very cab of an unjust rival with the indignant cry, "E roba mia!" (He's my stuff!). It was not quite the phrase I would have chosen, but I had no quarrel, generally speaking, with the cabmen of Rome. To be sure, they have not a rubber tire among them, and their dress leaves much to be desired in professional uniformity. Not one of them looks like a cabman, but many of them in pict-uresqueness of hats and coats look like brigands. I think they would each prefer to have a fur-lined overcoat, which the Roman of any class likes to wear well into the spring; but they mostly content themselves with an Astrakhan collar, more or less mangy. For the rest, some of them will point out the objects of interest as you pass, and they are proud to do so; they are not extortionate, and, if you overpay them ever so little (which is quite worth while), they will not stand upon a matter of lawful fare. A two-cent tip contents them, one of four cents makes them your friends for life; as for a five-cent tip, I do not know what it does, but I advise the reader when he goes to Rome to try it and see.

One fine thing is that the cabmen are in great super-abundance in Rome, and the number of barrel-ribbed, ewe-necked, and broken-kneed horses is in no greater proportion than in Paris. Still, the average is large, though, if you will go to the stand, you may select any horse you please without offence. It was a cheerful sight, verging upon gayety, to see every morning the crowd of cabs at our stand and to hear the drivers' talk, sometimes rising into protest and mutual upbraiding. But one Thursday morning, the brightest of the spring, a Sunday silence had fallen on the place, and a Sabbath solitude deepened to the eye the mystery that had first addressed itself to the ear. Then, suddenly, we knew that we were in the presence of that Italian conception of a general strike which interprets itself as a *sciopero*. It is saying very little of that two days' strike to say that it was far the most impressive experience of our Roman winter; in some sort it was the most impressive experience of my life, for I beheld in it a reduced and imperfect image of what labor could do if it universally chose to do nothing. The dream of William Morris was that a world which we know is pretty much wrong could be put right by this simple process. The trouble has always been to get all sorts of labor to join in the universal strike, but in the Italian *sciopero* of four years ago the miracle was wrought from one end of the peninsula to the other.

In the Roman strike of last April a partial miracle of the

same nature was illustratively wrought, with the same alarming effect on the imagination.

As with the national strike, the inspiration of the Roman strike came from the government's violent dealing with a popular manifestation which only threatened to be mischievous. A stone-mason was killed by falling from a scaffolding, and his funeral was attended by so many hundreds, amounting to thousands, of workmen that the police conceived, not quite unjustifiably, that it was to be made the occasion of a demonstration, especially as the proposed route of the procession lay through the Piazza di Venezia, under the windows of the Austrian Embassy, Austria being always a red rag to the Italian bull and peculiarly irritating through the reservation of the Palazzo Venezia to the ancient enemy at the cession of Venice to Italy. The mourners were therefore forbidden to pass that way, and the police forces were drawn up in the Piazza Gesu, before the Jesuit church, with a strong detachment of troops to support them. Their wisdom in all this was very questionable after what followed, for the mourners insisted on their rights and would go no way but through the Piazza di Venezia. When the dispute was at its height two wagons laden with bricks appeared on the scene. The mourners swarmed upon them, broke the bricks into bats, and hurled them at the police. They had apparently the simple-hearted expectation that the police would stand this indefinitely, but the brickbats hurt, and in their paroxysms of pain the sufferers began firing their revolvers at the mourners. Four persons were killed, with the usual proportion of innocent spectators. At night the labor unions met, and the *sciopero* was proclaimed as an expression of the popular indignation; but the police had been left with the victory. Whether it was not in some sort a defeat I do not know, but a retired English officer, whom I had no reason to think a radical, said to me that he thought it a great mistake to have let the police oppose the people with firearms. Soldiers should alone be used for such work; they alone knew when to fire and when to stop, and they never acted without orders. In fact, the troops supporting the police took no part in the fray, as the workmen's press recognized with patriotic rejoicing.

The next morning a signal silence prevailed throughout the city, where not a wheel stirred or the sound of a hoof broke the hush of the streets. We had noted already that there were seven Sundays every week in Rome, as was fit in the capital of the Christian religion, but this Thursday was of an intenser Sabbath stillness than any first day of the week that we had yet known. There was the clack of passing feet in the street under our windows, but we looked out upon a yawning void where the busy cabs had clustered, and the cabmen had socially chaffed and quarrelled, and entreated the stranger in the cabman's superstition that a stranger never knows when he wants a cab. Now he could have walked all over Rome without being once invited to drive. Except for here and there a private carriage, or the coupe evidently of a doctor, the streets were empty, and the tourists had to join the citizens in their pedestrian exercise.

The shopkeepers had been notified to close their places of business on the tacit condition of having their windows broken for non-compliance, but in the early forenoon they were still slowly and partially putting up their shutters. You could get in through the darkened doors up till noon; after that it was more and more difficult. But it would be hard to say how far and how deep the *sciopero* went. In our hotel we knew of it only the second day through the failure of the morning rolls, for there had been no baking overnight. Most of the in-door service was of Swiss or other foreign extraction, and the mechanism of our comfort, our luxury, was operated as usual. Our floor *facchino,* or porter, went to the meeting of the unions in the evening, being an Italian.

Otherwise the strike fell especially on the helpless and guiltless foreigner, who might be, and very often was, in sympathy with the strikers. He had to walk to the ruins, the galleries, the gardens, the churches, if he wanted anything of them; he could not get a carriage even from a stable.

Between the hotels and the station the omnibus traffic was suspended. The railroads being national, push-carts manned by the government employes carried the baggage to and fro, but if one wanted to arrive or depart one had to do it on foot. Tragical scenes presented themselves in relation to this fact. In the afternoon, as I walked up the street toward the great railroad station, I saw coming down the middle of it a strange procession of ladies and gentlemen of every age, gray-haired elders and children of tender years, mixed with porters and push-carts, footing it into the region of the fashionable hotels. They were all laden according to their strength, and people who had never done a stroke of work in their lives were actually carrying their own hand-bags, rugs, and umbrella-cases. It was terrible.

It was terrible for what it was, and terrible for what it suggested, if ever that poor dull beast of labor took the bit permanently into its teeth, or, worse yet, hung back in the breeching and inexorably balked. What would then become of us others, us ladies and gentlemen who had never done a stroke of work and never wished to do one? Should we be forced to the hard necessity of beginning? Could we remain in the comfortable belief that we gave work, or must we be made to own distastefully that it had always been given to us? Should we be able to flatter ourselves with the notion that we had once had dependents because we had money, or should we realize that we had always been dependents because of our having money?

These were the hateful doubts which the Roman strike

suggested to the witness, or, at least, one of the witnesses, who has here the pleasure of unburdening himself upon the reader. Yet there was something amusing in the situation; there was a joke—that rarest of all things in Rome—latent in it, which one suspected only from the amiable, the all-but-smiling behavior of the strikers. There was not the slightest disorder during the two days that the strike lasted. When it was called off at a meeting of the unions on Saturday night, one of the seven Sundays of the Roman week dawned upon an activity at the neighboring cab-stand no peacefuller and not much gayer than the silence and solitude of the mornings previous. As for the general effect in the city, you would hardly have known that particular Sunday from those which had gone by the names of Friday and Saturday. Throughout Italy there is now a Sunday-closing law whose effect in a land once of joyous Sabbaths strikes some such chill to the heart as pierces it in Boston on that day, or in the farther eastern or western avenues of New York, when the Family Entrances are religiously locked.

The Italian state has, in fact, so far taken the matter in charge as to have established a secular holiday, coming once a week, which has almost disestablished the holidays of the Church, formerly of much more frequent occurrence. This secular holiday, which every workman has a right to, he may neither give nor sell to his master. He may not even loaf it away in the place where he works, lest he should be clandestinely employed. He must go out of the shop or house or factory or foundry, and spend his ten hours where he cannot be suspected of employing them in productive industry for hire. This law has been enacted in accordance with the will of the unions and no doubt in correction of great abuses. Neither masters nor men now recognize the old-fashioned *festa* as they once did. Whether the men like the new holiday so well, I did not get any of them explicitly to say. Of course, they cannot all take it at once; they must take it turn about, and they may not find their enforced leisure so lively as the old voluntary saints' days, when their comrades were resting, too. As for the masters, one of the employers of labor, whom I found filling his man's place, would merely say: "It is the new law. No doubt we shall adjust ourselves to it." He did not complain.

X. SEEING ROME AS ROMANS SEE US

Shortly after our settlement in the Eternal City, which has so much more time to be seen than the sojourner has to see it, I pleased myself with the notion of surprising it by visiting in a studied succession the many different piazzas. This, I thought, would acquaint me with the different churches, and on the way to them I should make friends with the various quarters. Everything, old or new, would have the charm of the unexpected; no lurking ruin would escape me; no monument, whether column or obelisk, statue, "storied urn or animated bust" or mere tablet, would be safe from my indirect research. Before I knew it, I should know Rome by heart, and this would be something to boast of long after I had forgotten it.

I could not say what suggested so admirable a notion, but it may have been coining by chance one day on the statue of Giordano Bruno, and realizing that it stood in the Campo di Fieri, on the spot where he was burned three hundred years ago for abetting Copernicus in his sacrilegious system of astronomy, and for divers other heresies, as well as the violation of his monastic vows. I saw it with the thrill which the solemn figure, heavily draped, deeply hooded, must impart as mere mystery, and I made haste to come again in the knowledge of what it was that had moved me so. Naturally I was not moved in the same measure a second time. It was not that the environment was, to my mind, unworthy the martyr, though I found the market at the foot of the statue given over, not to flowers, as the name of the place might imply, but to such homely fruits of the earth as potatoes, carrots, cabbages, and, above all, onions. There was a placidity in the simple scene that pleased me: I liked the quiet gossiping of the old market-women over their baskets of vegetables; the confidential fashion in which a gentle crone came to my elbow and begged of me in undertone, as if she meant the matter to go no further, was even nattering. But the solemnity of the face that looked down on the scene was spoiled by the ribbon drawn across it to fasten a wreath on the head, in the effort of some mistaken zealot of free thought to enhance its majesty by decoration. It was the moment when the society calling itself by Giordano Bruno's name was making an effort for the suppression of ecclesiastical instruction in the public schools; and on the anniversary of his martyrdom his effigy had suffered this unmeant hurt. In all the churches there had been printed appeals to parents against the agnostic attack on the altar and the home, and there had been some of the open tumults which seem in Rome to express every social emotion. But the clericals had triumphed, and an observer more anxious than I to give a mystical meaning to accident might have interpreted the disfiguring ribbon over Bruno's bronze lips as a new silencing of the heretic.

I certainly did not construe it so, and, if my notion of serially visiting the piazzas of Rome was not prompted by my chance glimpse of the Campo di Fiori, it was certainly not relinquished because of any mischance in my meditated vision of it. I had merely reflected that I could not hope to carry out my scheme without greater expense both in time and money than I could well afford, for, though cabs in Rome are swift and cheap, yet the piazzas are many and widely distributed; and I finally decided to indulge myself in a novelty of adventure verging close upon originality. It had always seemed to me that the happy strangers mounted on the tiers of seats that rise from front to back on the motor-chariots for seeing New York and looking down, even from the lowest place, on the life of our streets had a peculiar, almost a bird's-eye view of it which I might well find the means of a fresh impression. But I never had the courage, for reasons which I have not the courage to give, though the reader can perhaps imagine them. In Rome I did not feel that the like reasons held; of all the unknown, I was one of the most unknown; by me nobody would be put to the shame of recognizing an acquaintance on the benches of the like chariot, or forced to the cruelty of cutting him in my person. When once I had fully realized this, it was only a question of the time when I should yield to the temptation which renewed itself as often as I saw the stately automobile passing through the storied streets, with its English legend of "Touring Rome" inscribed on the back of the rear seat. There remained the question whether I should go alone or whether I should ask the countenance of friends in so bold an enterprise. When I suggested it to some persons of the more courageous sex, they did not wait to be asked to go with me; they instantly entreated to be allowed to go; they said they had always wished to see Rome in that way; and we only waited to be chosen by the raw and blustery afternoon which made us its own for the occasion.

It was the eve of the last sad day of such shrunken and faded carnival as is still left to Rome, and there were signs of it in the straggling groups of children in holiday costume, and in here and there a pair of young girls in a cab, safely masked against identification and venting, in the sense of wild escape, the joyous spirits kept in restraint all the rest of the year. Already in the Corso, where our touring-car waited for us at the first corner, a great cafe was turning itself inside out with a spread of chairs and tables over the sidewalk, which we found thronged on our return with spectators far out-numbering the merrymakers of the carnival. Our car was not nearly so packed, and when we mounted to the benches we found that the last and highest of them was left to the sole occupancy of a young man, well enough dressed (his yellow gloves may have been more than well enough) and well-mannered enough, who continued enigmatical to the last. There was a German couple and there were some

French-speaking people; the rest of us were bound in the tie of our common English. The agent of the enterprise accompanied us, an international of undetermined race, and beside the chauffeur sat the middle-aged, anxious-looking Italian who presently arose when we made our first stop in the Piazza Colonna and harangued us in three languages—successively, of course—concerning the Column of Marcus Aurelius. He did not use the megaphone of his American confrere; and from the shudder which the first sound of his voice must have sent through a less fastidious substance than mine I perceived that an address by megaphone I could not have borne, to that extreme of excess even my modernism could not go. As it was, there was an instant when I could have wished to be on foot, or even in a cab, with a red Baedeker in my hand; and yet, as the orator went on, I had to own that he was giving me a better account of the column than I could have got for myself out of the guide-book. He spoke first in French, with an Italian accent and occasionally an Italian idiom; then he spoke in English, and then in a German which suffered from his knowledge of English.

He sat down, looking rather spent with his effort, and on the way to our next stop, at the Temple of Neptune, the agent examined us upon our necessities in the article of language. He himself spoke such good English that we could not do otherwise than declare that we could get on perfectly with an address in French. The German pair, perhaps from patriotic grudge, denied a working knowledge of the unfriendly tongue. The solitary on the back seat, being asked in his turn, graciously answered, "Toutes les langues me sont egales," and thereafter we suffered with the orator only through French and German.

The reply which decided the matter launched us upon yet wider conjecture regarding the unknown: was he a retired courier, a concierge out of place, a professor of languages on his holiday, or merely an amateur of philological studies? His declared proficiency was manifested in unexpected measure as we drove away from the Temple of Neptune on through the narrow street leading to it. Every motor has its peculiar note, and our car had something like the scream of a wild animal in pain, such as might have justly alarmed a stouter spirit than that of the poor little cab-horse which we encountered at the corner of this street. It reared, it plunged; when our chauffeur held us in it still backed and filled so dangerously that the mother and children overflowing the cab followed the example of the driver in spilling to the ground. Then our good international, the agent, jumped down and, mounting to the coachman's seat, took the reins and urged the horse forward, while its driver pulled it by the bridle. All was of no effect till the solitary of the back seat rose in his place and shouted to the frightened creature in choice American: "What d' you mean, there? Come on! Come on, you fool!" Then, as if it had been an "impenitent mule" in some far-distant Far-Western incarnation, this Eoman cab-horse recognized the voice of authority; it nerved itself against the imaginary danger, and came steadily forward; our agent regained his place, and we moved shriekingly on to the next object of interest. It was not quite the note blown from level tubes of brass in the progress of a conqueror, but we did not lack the cheers of a disinterested populace, which at several points impartially applauded our orator's French and German versions of his not always tacit Italian.

Our height above the cheers helped preserve us from the sense of anything ironical in them, and there was an advantage in the outlook from our elevation which the wayfarer in cab or on foot can only imagine. No such wayfarer can realize the vast scope and compass of our excursion, which was but one of two excursions made on alternate afternoons by the Touring-Rome wagons. It included, perhaps not quite in the following order, after the Temple of Neptune, such objects of prime importance as the Palazzo Madama, where Catharine de' Medici once dwelt and where the Italian Senate now holds its sessions; the Fountain of Trevi, the Pantheon, the Piazza Navona, the new Palace of Justice and the Cavour monument beyond the Tiber, the Castle of Sant' Angelo, the Vatican and St. Peter's, the Janiculum and the Garibaldi monument on it, and the stupendous prospect of the city from that supreme top, the bridge that Horatius held in Macaulay's ballad, the island in the Tiber formed after the expulsion of the Tarquins by the river sand and drift catching on the seed-corn thrown into the stream from the fields consecrated to Mars, the Temple of Fortune, the once-supposed House of Eienzi, and the former Temple of Vesta; the Palatine Hill and the Aventine Hill, the Circus Maximus, the Colosseum, the Campidoglio, the Theatre of Marcellus, the worst slum in Rome, where the worst boy in Rome, flown with Carnival, will try to board your passing car; back to Piazza Colonna through Piazza Monte Citerio, where the Italian House of Deputies meets in the plain old palace of the same name.

The mere mention of these storied places will kindle in the reader's fancy a fire which he will feel all the need of if ever he verifies my account of them in touring Rome on so cold an afternoon as that of our excursion. The wind rose with our ascent of every elevation, if it did not fall with our return to a lower level; on the Janiculum it blew a blizzard in which the incongruous ilexes and laurels bowed and writhed, and some groups of almond trees in their pale bloom on a distant upland mocked us with a derisive image of spring. At the foot of the steps to the Campidoglio, where some of our party dismounted to go up and view the statue of Marcus Aurelius, it was so cold that nothing but the sense of a strong common interest prevented those who remained from persuading the chauffeur to go on without the sight-seers.

But we forbore, both because we knew we were then very near the end of our tour, and because we felt it would have been cruel to abandon the lady who had got out of the car only by turning herself sidewise and could not have made her way home on foot without sufferings which would justly have brought us to shame. Certain idle particulars will always cling to the memory which lets so many ennobling facts slip from it; and I find myself helpless against the recollection of this poor lady's wearing a thick motoring-veil which no curiosity could pierce, but which, when she lifted it, revealed a complexion of heated copper and a gray mustache such as nature vouchsafes to few women.

The crowd, which thickened most in the Piazza di Venezia, had grown more and more carnivalesque in attire and behavior. We had been obliged to avoid the more densely peopled streets because, as our international explained, if the car had slowed at any point the revellers would have joined our excursion of their own initiative and accompanied us to the end in overwhelming numbers. They wellnigh blocked the entrance of the Corso when we got back to it, and the cafe where we had agreed to have tea was so packed that our gay escapade began to look rather gloomy in the retrospect. But suddenly a table was vacated; a waiter was caught, in the vain attempt to ignore us, and given such a comprehensive order that we could see respect kindling in his eyes, and before we could reasonably have hoped it he spread before us tea and bread and butter and tarts and little cakes, while scores of hungry spectators stood round and flatteringly envied us. In this happy climax our adventure showed as a royal progress throughout. We counted up the wonders of our three hours' course in an absolutely novel light; and we said that touring Rome was a thing not only not to be despised, but to be forever proud of.

For myself, I decided that if I were some poor hurried

fellow-countryman of mine, doing Europe in a month and obliged to scamp Rome with a couple of days, I would not fail to spend two of them in what I must always think of as a triumphal chariot. I resolved to take the second excursion, not the next day perhaps, but certainly the day after the next, and complete the most compendious impression of ancient, mediaeval, and modern Rome that one can have; but the firmest resolution sometimes has not force to hold one to it. The second excursion remains for a second sojourn, when perhaps I may be able to solve the question whether I was moved by a fine instinct of proportion or by mere innate meanness in giving our orator at parting just two francs in recognition of his eloquence. No one else, indeed, gave him anything, and he seemed rather surprised by my tempered munificence. It might have been mystically adjusted to the number of languages he used in addressing us; if he had held to three languages I might have made it three francs; but now I shall never be certain till I take the second excursion with a company which imperatively requires English as well as French and German, and with no solitary in yellow gloves to whom all languages are alike.

To this end I ought to have thrown a copper coin into the Fountain of Trevi as we passed it. You may return to Rome without doing this, but it is well known that if you do it you are sure to come back. The Fountain of Trevi is alone worth coming back for, and I could not see that it poured scanter streams than it formerly poured over brimming brinks or from the clefts of the artificial rocks that spread in fine disorder about the feet of its sea-gods and sea-horses; but they who mourn the old papal rule accuse the present Italian government of stinting the supply of water. To me there seemed no stint of water in any of the fountains of Rome. In some a mere wasteful spilth seems the sole design of the artist, as in the Fontana Paolina on the Janiculum, where the cold wash of its deluge seemed to add a piercing chill to our windy afternoon. The other fountains have each a quaint grace or absolute charm or pleasing absurdity, whether the waters shower over groups of more or less irrelevant statuary in their basins or spout into the air in columns unfurling flags of spray and keeping the pavement about them green with tender mould. The most sympathetic is the Fountain of the Triton, who blows the water through his wreathed horn and on the coldest day seems not to mind its refluent splash on his mossy back; in fact, he seems rather to like it.

He is one of many tritons, rivers, sea-gods, and aqueous allegories similarly employed in Rome and similarly indifferent to what flesh and blood might find the hardship of their calling. I had rashly said to myself that their respective fountains needed the sun on them to be just what one could wish, but the first gray days taught me better. Then the thinly clouded sky dropped a softened light over their glitter and sparkle and gave them a spirituality as much removed from the suggestion of physical cold as any diaphanous apparition would suggest. Then they seemed rapt into a finer beauty than that of earth, though I will not pretend that they were alike beautiful. No fountain can be quite ugly, but some fountains can be quite stupid, like, for instance, those which give its pretty name to the Street of the Four Fountains and which consist of two extremely plain Virtues and two very dull old Rivers, diagonally dozing at each other over their urns in niches of the four converging edifices. They are not quite so idiotic under their disproportionate foliage as the conventional Egyptian lions of the Fountain of Moses, with manes like the wigs of so many lord chancellors, and with thin streams of water drooling from the tubes between their lips. But these are the exceptional fountains; there are few sculptured or architectural designs which the showering or spouting water does not retrieve from error; and in Rome the water (deliciously potable) is so abundant that it has force to do almost anything for beauty, even where, as in the Fontana

Paolina, it is merely a torrent tumbling over a facade. It is lavished everywhere; in the Piazza Navona alone there are three fountains, but then the Piazza Navona is very long, and three fountains are few enough for it, even though one is that famous Fountain of Bernini, in which he has made one of the usual rivers—the Nile, I believe—holding his hand before his eyes in mock terror of the ungainly facade of a rival architect's church opposite, lest it shall fall and crush him. That, however, is the least merit of the fountain; and without any fountain the Piazza Navona would be charming; it is such a vast lake of sunshine and is so wide as well as long, and is so mellowed with such rich browns and golden grays in the noble edifices.

I do not know, now, what all the edifices are, but there are churches, more than one, and palaces, and the reader can find their names in any of the guidebooks. If I were buying piazzas in Rome I should begin with the Navona, but there are enough to suit all purses and tastes. The fountains would be thrown in, I suppose, along with the churches and palaces; but I really never inquired, and, in fact, not having carried out my plan of visiting them all, I am in no position to advise intending purchasers. What I can say is that if you are in a hurry to inspect, that kind of property, and in immediate need of a piazza, you cannot do better than take the wagon for touring Rome. In two days you can visit every piazza worth having, including the Piazza di Spagna, where there is a fountain in the form of a marble galley in which you can embark for any fairyland you like, through the Via del Babuino and the Piazza del Popolo. Come to think of it, I am not so sure but I would as soon have the Piazza del Popolo as the Piazza Navona. If the fountains are not so fine, they are still very fine, and the Pincian Hill overtops one side of the place, with foliaged drives and gardened walks descending into it.

Everything of importance that did not happen elsewhere in Rome seems to have happened in the Piazza del Popolo, and I may name as a few of its attractions for investors the facts that it was here Sulla's funeral pyre was kindled; that Nero was buried on the left side of it, and out of his tomb grew a huge walnut-tree, the haunt of demoniacal crows till the Madonna appeared to Paschal II. and bade him cut it down; that the arch-heretic Luther sojourned in the Augustinian convent here while in Rome; that the dignitaries of Church and State received Christina of Sweden here when, after her conversion, she visited the city; that Lucrezia Borgia celebrated her betrothal in one of the churches; that it used to be a favorite place for executing brigands, whose wives then became artists' models, and whose sons, if they were like Cardinal Antonelli, became princes of the Church. So I learn from Hare in his *Walks in Rome,* and, if he enables me to boast the rivalry of the Piazza Navona in no such array of merits, still I will not deny my love for it. Certainly it was not a favorite place for executing brigands, but the miracle which saved St. Agnes from, cruel shame was wrought in the vaulted chambers under the church of her name there, and that is something beyond all the wonders of the Piazza del Popolo for its pathos and for its poetry. But, if the Piazza Navona had no other claim on me, I should find a peculiar pleasure in the old custom of stopping the escapes from its fountains and flooding with water the place I saw flooded with sun, for the patricians to wade and drive about in during the very hot weather and eat ices and drink coffee, while the plebeians looked sumptuously down on them from the galleries built around the lake.

W. D. Howells

XI. IN AND ABOUT THE VATICAN

It would be a very bold or very incompetent observer of the Roman situation who should venture upon a decided opinion of the relations of the monarchy and the papacy. You hear it said with intimations of special authority in the matter, that both king and pope are well content with the situation, and it is clearly explained how and why they are so; but I did not understand how or why at the moment of the explanation, or else I have now forgotten whatever was clear in it. I believe, however, it was to the effect that the pope willingly remained self-prisoned in the Vatican because, if he came out, he might not only invalidate a future claim upon the sovereign dignity which the Italian occupation had invaded, but he might incur risks from the more unfriendly extremists which would at least be very offensive. On his part, it was said that the king used the embarrassment occasioned by the pope's attitude as his own defence against the anti-Clericals, who otherwise would have urged him to far more hostile measures with the Church. The king and the pope were therefore not very real enemies, it was said by those who tried to believe themselves better informed than others.

To the passing or tarrying stranger the situation does not offer many dramatic aspects. When you are going to St. Peter's, if you will look up at the plain wall of the Vatican palace you will see two windows with their shutters open, and these are the windows of the rooms where Pius X. lives, a voluntary captive; the closed blinds are those of the rooms where Leo XIII. died, a voluntary captive. Whatever we think of the wisdom or the reason of the papal protest against the occupation of the States of the Church by the Italian people, these windows have their pathos. The pope immures himself in the Vatican and takes his walks in the Vatican gardens, whose beauty I could have envied him, if he had not been a prisoner, when I caught a glimpse of them one morning, with the high walls of their privet and laurel alleys blackening in the sun.

But otherwise the severest Protestant could not cherish so unkind a feeling toward the gentle priest whom all men speak well of for his piety and humility. It is a touching fact of his private life that his three maiden sisters, who wish to be as near him as they can, have their simple lodging over a shop for the sale of holy images in a street opening into the Piazza of St. Peter's. We all know that they are of a Venetian family neither rich nor great; their pride and joy is solely in him, as it well might be, and it is said that when they come to hear him in some high function at the Sistine Chapel their rapture of affection and devotion is as evident as it is sweet and touching.

Their relation to him is the supremely poetic fact of a situation which even one who knows of it merely by hearsay cannot refuse to feel. The tragical effect of the situation is in the straining and sundering of family ties among those who take one side or the other in the difference of the monarchy and papacy. I do not know how equally Roman society, in the large or the small sense, is divided into the Black of the Papists and the White of the Monarchists (for the mediaeval names of Neri and Bianchi are revived in the modern differences), but one cannot help hearing of instances in which their political and religious opinions part fathers and sons and mothers and daughters. These are promptly noted to the least-inquiring foreigner, and his imagination is kindled by the attribution of like variances to the members of the reigning family, who are reported respectively blacker and whiter if they are not as positively black or white as the nobles. Some of these are said to meet one another only in secret across the gulf that divides them openly; but how far the cleavage may descend among other classes I cannot venture to conjecture; I can only testify to some expressions of priest-hatred which might have shocked a hardier heretical substance than mine.

One Sunday we went to the wonderful old Church of San Clemente, which is built three deep into the earth or high into the air, one story above or below the other, in the three successive periods of imperial, mediaeval, and modern Rome. It was the day when the church is illuminated, and the visitors come with their Baedekers and Hares and Murrays to identify its antiquities of architecture and fresco; it was full of people, and, if I fancied an unusual proportion of English-speaking converts among them, that might well have been, since the adjoining convent belongs to the Irish Dominicans. But I carried with me through all the historic and artistic interest of the place the sensation left by two inscriptions daubed in black on the white convent wall next the church. One of these read: "VV. la Repubblica" (Long live the Republic), and the other: "M. ai Preti" (Death to the Priests). No attempt had been made to efface them, and as they expressed an equal hatred for the monarchy and the papacy, neither laity nor clergy may have felt obliged to interfere. Perhaps, however, it was rightly inferred that the ferocity of one inscription might be best left to counteract the influence of the other. I know that with regard to the priests you experience some such effect from the atrocious attacks in the chief satirical paper of Rome, The name of this paper was given me, with a deprecation not unmixed with recognition of its cleverness, by an Italian friend whom I was making my creditor for some knowledge of Roman journalism; and the sole copy of it which I bought was handed to me with a sort of smiling abhorrence by the kindly old kiosk woman whom I liked best to buy my daily papers of. When I came to look it through, I made more and more haste, for its satire of the priests was of an indecency so rank that it seemed to offend the nose as well as the eye. To turn from the paper was easy, but from the fact of its popularity a painful impression remained. It was not a question of whether the priests were so bad as all that, but whether its many readers believed them so, or believed them bad short of it, in the kind of wickedness they were accused of.

There can be no doubt of the constant rancor between the Clericals and the Radicals in their different phases throughout Italy. There can be almost no doubt that the Radicals will have their way increasingly, and that if, for instance, the catechism is kept in the public schools this year, it will be cast out some other year not far hence. Much, of course, depends upon whether the status can maintain itself. It is, like the status everywhere and always, very anomalous; but it is difficult to imagine either the monarchy or the papacy yielding at any point. Apparently the State is the more self-assertive of the two, but this is through the patriotism which is the political life of the people. It must always be remembered that when the Italians entered Rome and made it the capital of their kingdom they did not drive out the French troops, which had already been withdrawn; they drove out the papal troops, the picturesque and inefficient foreign volunteers who remained behind. Every memorial of that event, therefore, is a blow at the Church, so far as the Church is identified with the lost temporal power. One of the chief avenues is named Twenty-second September Street because the national troops entered Rome on that date; the tablets on the Porta Pia where they entered, the monument on the Pincio to the Cairoli brothers, who died for Italy; the statues of Garibaldi, of Cavour, of Victor Emmanuel everywhere painfully remind the papacy of its lost sovereignty. But the national feeling has gone in its expression beyond and behind the patriotic occupation of Rome; and no one who suffered conspicuously, at any time in the past, for freedom of thought through the piety of the fallen power is suffered to be forgotten. On its side the

W. D. Howells

Church enters its perpetual protest in the self-imprisonment of the pope; and here and there, according to its opportunity, it makes record of what it has suffered from the State. For instance, at St. John Lateran, which theoretically forms part of the Leonine City of the Popes and is therefore extraterritorial to Italy, a stretch of wall is suffered to remain scarred by the cannon-shot which the monarchy fired when it took Rome from the papacy.

Doubtless there are other monuments of the kind, but their enumeration would not throw greater light on a situation which endures with no apparent promise of change. The patience of the Church is infinite; it lives and it outlives. Remembering that Arianism was older than Protestantism when Catholicism finally survived it, we must not be surprised if the Roman Church shall hold out against the Italian State not merely decades, but centuries. In the meanwhile to its children from other lands it means Rome above all the other Romes; and on us, its step-children of different faiths or unfaiths, its prison-house—if we choose so to think of the Vatican—has a supreme claim, if we love the sculpture of pagan Rome or the painting of Christian Rome.

We swarm to its galleries in every variety of nationality, with guide-books in every tongue, and we are very queer, for the most part, to any one of our number who can sufficiently exteriorate himself to get the rest of us in perspective. It is probably well that most of us do not stagger under any great knowledge of the crushing history of the place, which has been the scene of the most terrible experiences of the race, the most touching, the most august. Provisionally ignorant, at least, we begin to appear at the earliest practicable hour before the outermost stairway of the Vatican, and, while the Swiss Guards still have on their long, blue cloaks to keep their black and yellow legs warm, mount to the Sistine Chapel. Here we help instruct one another, as we stand about or sit about in twos and threes or larger groups, reading aloud from our polyglot Baedekers while we join in identifying the different facts. Here, stupendously familiar, whether we have seen it before or not, is Michelangelo's giant fresco of the Judgment, as prodigious as we imagined or remembered it; here are his mighty Prophets and his mighty Sibyls; and here below them, in incomparably greater charm, are the frescos of Botticelli, with the grace of his Primavera playing through them all like a strain of music and taking the soul with joy.

It is the same crowd in the Raphael Stanze, but rather silenter, for by now we have taught ourselves enough from our Baedekers at least to read them under our breaths, and we talk low before the frescos and the canvases. Some of us are even mute in the presence of the School of Athens, whatever reserves we may utter concerning the Transfiguration. If we are honest, we more or less own what our impressions really are from those other famous works, concerning which our impressions are otherwise altogether and inexpressibly unimportant; it is a question of ethics and not aesthetics, as most of our simple-hearted company suppose it to be; and, if we are dishonest, we pretend to have felt and thought things at first-hand from them which we have learned at second-hand from our reading. I will confess, for my small part, that I had more pleasure in the coloring and feeling of some of the older canvases and in here and there a Titian than in all the Raphaels in the Stanze of his name.

I was not knowing his works for the first time; no one perhaps does that, such is the multiplicity of the copies of them; and I vividly remembered them from my acquaintance with the originals four decades before, as I had remembered the Michelangelos; but in their presence and in the presence of so many other masterpieces in the different rooms, with

W. D. Howells

their horrible miracles and atrocious martyrdoms, I realized as for the first time what a bloody religion ours was. It was such relief, such rest, to go from those broilings and beheadings and crucifixions and flayings and stabbings into the long, tranquil aisles of the museum where the marble men and women, created for earthly immortality by Greek art, welcomed me to their serenity and sanity. The earlier gods might have been the devils which the early Christians fancied them, but they did not look it; they did not look as if it was they that had loosed the terrors upon mankind out of which the true faith has but barely struggled at last, now when its relaxing grasp seems slipping from the human mind. I remembered those peaceful pagans so perfectly that I could have gone confidently to this or that and hailed him friend; and though I might not have liked to claim the acquaintance of all of them in the flesh, in the marble I fled to it as refuge from the cruel visions of Christian art. If this is perhaps saying too much, I wish also to hedge from the wholesale censure of my fellow-sight-seers which I may have seemed to imply. They did not prevail so clutteringly in the sculpture galleries as in the Sistine Chapel and the Stanze. One could have the statues as much to one's self as one liked; there were courts with murmuring fountains in them; and there was a view of Rome from a certain window, where no fellow-tourist intruded between one and the innumerable roofs and domes and towers, and the heights beyond whose snows there was nothing but blue sky. It was a beautiful morning, with a sun mild as English summer, which did not prevent the afternoon from turning cold with wind and raining and hailing and snowing. This in turn did not keep off a fine red sunset, with an evening star of glittering silver that brightened as the sunset faded. At Rome the weather can be of as many minds in March as in April at New York.

But through all one's remembrance of the Roman winter a

sentiment of spring plays enchantingly, like that grace of Botticelli's Primavera in his Sistine frescos. It is not a sentiment of summer, though it is sometimes a summer warmth which you feel, and except in the steam-heated hotels it does not penetrate to the interiors. In the galleries and the churches you must blow your nails if you wish to thaw your fingers, but, if you go out-of-doors, there is a radiant imitation of May awaiting you. She takes you by your thick glove and leads you in your fur-lined overcoat through sullen streets that open upon sunny squares, with fountains streaming into the crystal air, and makes you own that this is the Italian winter as advertised—that is, if you are a wanderer and a stranger; if you are an Italian and at home you keep in the out-door warmth, but shun the sun, and in-doors you wrap up more thickly than ever, or you go to bed if you have a more luxurious prejudice against shivering. If you are a beggar, as you very well may be in Rome, you impart your personal heat to a specific curbstone or the spot which you select as being most in the path of charity, and cling to it from dawn till dark. Or you acquire somehow the rights of a chair just within the padded curtain of a church, and do not leave it till the hour for closing. The Roman beggars are of all claims upon pity, but preferably I should say they were blind, and some of these are quite young girls, and mostly rather cheerful. But the very gayest beggar I remember was a legless man at the gate of the Vatican Museum; the saddest was a sullen dwarf on the way to this cripple, whose gloom a donative even of twenty-five centessimi did not suffice to abate.

W. D. Howells

XII. SUPERFICIAL OBSERVATIONS AND CONJECTURES

It had seemed to me that in the afternoons of the old papal times, so dear to foreigners who never knew them, I used to see a series of patrician ladies driving round and round on the Pincio, reclining in their landaus and shielding their complexions from the November suns of the year 1864 with the fringed parasols of the period. In the doubt which attends all recollections of the past, after age renders us uncertain of the present, I hastened on my second Sunday at Rome in February, 1908, to enjoy this vision, if possible. I found the Pincio unexpectedly near; I found the sunshine; I found the familiar winter warmth which in Southern climates is so unlike the summer warmth in ours; but the drive which I had remembered as a long ellipse had narrowed to a little circle, where one could not have driven round faster than a slow trot without danger of vertigo. I did not find that series of apparent principessas or imaginable marchesas leaning at their lovely lengths in their landaus. I found in over-whelming majority the numbered victorias, which pass for cabs in Rome, full of decent tourists, together with a great variety of people on foot, but not much fashion and no swells that my snobbish soul could be sure of. There was, indeed, one fine moment when, at a retired point of the drive, I saw two private carriages drawn up side by side in their encounter, with two stout old ladies, whom I decided to be dowager countesses at the least, partially projected from their opposing windows and lost in a delightful exchange, as I hoped, of scandal. But the only other impressive personality was that of an elderly, obviously American gentleman, in the solitary silk hat and long frock-coat of the scene. There were other Americans, but none so formal; the English were in all degrees of informality down to tan shoes and at least one travelling-cap. The women's dress, whether they were on foot or in cabs, was not striking, though more than half of them were foreigners and could easily have afforded to outdress the Italians, especially the work people, though these were there in their best.

There was a band-stand in the space first reached by the promenaders, and there ought clearly to have been a band, but I was convinced that there was to be none by a brief colloquy between one of the cab-drivers (doubtless goaded to it by his fair freight) and the gentlest of Roman policemen, whose response was given in accents of hopeful compassion:

CABMAN: *"Musica, no?"* (No music?)

POLICEMAN: *"Forse l' avremo oramai"* (Perhaps we shall have it presently.)

We did not have it at all that Sunday, possibly because it was the day after the assassination of the King of Portugal, and the flags were at half-mast everywhere. So we went, such of us as liked, to the parapet overlooking the Piazza del Popolo, and commanding one of those prospects of Rome which are equally incomparable from every elevation. I, for my part, made the dizzying circuit of the brief drive on foot in the dark shadows of the roofing ilexes (if they are ilexes), and then strolled back and forth on the paths set thick with plinths bearing the heads of the innumerable national great— the poets, historians, artists, scientists, politicians, heroes— from the ancient Roman to the modern Italian times. I particularly looked up the poets of the last hundred years, because I had written about them in one of my many forgotten books, till I fancied a growing consciousness in them at this encounter with an admirer; they, at least, seemed to remember my book. Then I went off to the cafe overlooking them in their different alleys, and had tea next a man who was taking lemon instead of milk in his. Here I was

W. D. Howells

beset with an impassioned longing to know whether he was a Russian or American, since the English always take milk in their tea, but I could not ask, and when I had suffered my question as long as I could in his presence I escaped from it, if you can call it escaping, to the more poignant question of what it would be like to come, Sunday after Sunday, to the Pincio, in the life-long voluntary exile of some Americans I knew, who meant to spend the rest of their years under the spell of Rome. I thought, upon the whole, that it would be a dull, sad fate, for somehow we seem born in a certain country in order to die in it, and I went home, to come again other Sundays to the Pincio, but not all the Sundays I promised myself.

On one of these Sundays I found Roman boys playing an inscrutable game among the busts of their storied compatriots, a sort of "I spy" or "Hide and go whoop," counting who should be "It" in an Italian version of "Oneary, ory, ickory, an," and then scattering in every direction behind the plinths and bushes. They were not more molestive than boys always are in a world which ought to be left entirely to old people, and I could not see that they did any harm. But somebody must have done harm, for not only was a bust here and there scribbled over in pencil, but the bust of Machiavelli had its nose freshly broken off in a jagged fracture that was very hurting to look at. This may have been done by some mistaken moralist, who saw in the old republican adviser of princes that enemy of mankind which he was once reputed to be. At any rate, I will not attribute the mutilation to the boys of Rome, whom I saw at other times foregoing so many opportunities of mischief in the Villa Bor-ghese. One of them even refused money from me there when I misunderstood his application for matches and offered him some coppers. He put my tip aside with a dignified wave of his hand and a proud backward step; and, indeed, I ought to have seen from the flat, broad cap he wore that he was a school-boy of civil condition. The Romans are not nearly so dramatic as the Neapolitans or Venetians or even as the Tuscans; but once in the same pleasance I saw a controversy between school-boys which was carried on with an animation full of beauty and finish. They argued back and forth, not violently, but vividly, and one whom I admired most enforced his reasons with charming gesticulations, whirling from his opponents with quick turns of his body and many a renunciatory retirement, and then facing about and advancing again upon the unconvinced. I decided that his admirable drama had been studied from the histrionics of his mother in domestic scenes; and, if I had been one of those other boys, I should have come over to his side instantly.

The Roman manners vary from Roman to Roman, just as our own manners, if we had any, would vary from New-Yorker to New-Yorker. Zola thinks the whole population is more or less spoiled with the conceit of Rome's ancient greatness, and shows it. One could hardly blame them if this were so; but I did not see any strong proof of it, though I could have imagined it on occasion. I should say rather that they had a republican simplicity of manner, and I liked this better in the shop people and work people than the civility overflowing into servility which one finds among the like folk, for instance, in England. I heard complaints from foreigners that the old-time deference of the lower classes was gone, but I did not miss it. Once in a cafe, indeed, the waiter spoke to me in *Voi* (you) instead of *Lei* (lordship), but the Neapolitans often do this, and I took it for a friendly effort to put me at my ease in a strange tongue with a more accustomed form. We were trying to come together on the kind of tea I wanted, but we failed, if I wanted it strong, for I got it very weak and tepid. I thought another day that it would be stronger if I could get it brought hotter, but it was not, and so I went no more to a place where I was liable to be called You instead of Lordship and still get weak tea. I think this was a mistake of mine and a loss, for at that cafe I saw some old-fashioned Italian types drinking their black coffee at afternoon tea-time out of tumblers, and others calling for pen and ink and writing letters, and ladies sweetly asking for newspapers and reading them there; and I ought to have continued coming to study them.

As to my conjectures of republican quality in the Romans, I had explicit confirmation from a very intelligent Italian who said of the anomalous social and political situation in Rome: "We Italians are naturally republicans, and, if it were a question of any other reigning family, we should have the republic. But we feel that we owe everything, the very existence of the nation, to the house of Savoy, and we are loyal to it in our gratitude. Especially we are true to the present king." It is known, of course, that Menotti Garibaldi continues the republican that his father always was, but I heard of his saying that, if a republic were established, Victor Emmanuel III. would be overwhelmingly chosen the first president. It is the Socialists who hold off unrelentingly from the monarchy, and not the republicans, as they can be differenced from them. One of the well-known Roman anomalies is that some members of the oldest families are or have been Socialists; and such a noble was reproached because he would not go to thank the king in recognition of some signal proof of his public spirit and unselfish patriotism. He owned the generosity of the king's behavior and his claim upon popular acknowledgment, but he said that he had taught the young men of his party the duty of ignoring the monarchy, and he could not go counter to the doctrine he had preached.

If I venture to speak now of a very extraordinary trait of the municipal situation at Rome, it must be without the least pretence to authority or to more than such superficial knowledge as the most incurious visitor to Rome can hardly help having. In the capital of Christendom, where the head of the Church dwells in a tradition of supremacy hardly less Italian than Christian, the syndic, or mayor, is a Jew, and not merely a Jew, but an alien Jew, English by birth and education, a Londoner and an Oxford man. More yet, he is a Freemason, which in Italy means things anathema to the Church, and he is a very prominent Freemason. With reference to the State, his official existence, though not inimical, is through the fusion of the political parties which elected him hardly less anomalous. This combination overthrew the late Clerical city government, and it included Liberals, Republicans, Socialists, and all the other anti-Clericals. Whatever liberalism or republicanism means, socialism cannot mean less than the economic solution of regality and aristocracy in Europe, and in Italy as elsewhere. It does not mean the old-fashioned revolution; it means simply the effacement of all social differences by equal industrial obligations. So far as the Socialists can characterize it, therefore, the actual municipal government of Rome is as antimonarchical as it is antipapal. But the syndic of Rome is a man of education, of culture, of intelligence, and he is evidently a man of consummate tact. He has known how to reconcile the warring elements, which made peace in his election, to one another and to their outside antagonists, to the Church and to the State, as well as to himself, in the course he holds over a very rugged way. His opportunities of downfall are pretty constant, it will be seen, when it is explained that if a measure with which he is identified fails in the city council it becomes his duty to resign, like the prime-minister of England in the like case with Parliament, But Mr. Nathan, who is as alien in his name as in his race and religion, and is known orally to the Romans as Signor Nahtahn, has not yet been obliged to resign. He has felt his way through every difficulty, and has not yet been identified with any fatally compromising measure. In such an extremely embarrassing predicament as that created by the conflict between the labor unions and the police early in April, and eventuating in the two days' strike, he knew how to do the wise thing and the right thing. As to the incident, he held his hand and he held his tongue, but he went to visit the wounded workmen in the hospital, and he condoled with their families. He was somewhat blamed for that, but his action kept for him the confidence of that large body of his supporters who earn their living with their hands.

It is said that the common Romans do not willingly earn their living with their hands; that they like better being idle and, so far as they can, ornamental. In this they would not differ from the uncommon Romans, the moneyed, the leisured, the pedigreed classes, who reproach them for their indolence; but I do not know whether they are so indolent as all that or not. I heard it said that they no longer want work, and that when they get it they do not do it well—a supposed effect of the socialism which is supposed to have spoiled their manners. I heard it said more intelligently, as I thought, that they are not easily disciplined, and that they cannot be successfully associated in the industries requiring workmen to toil in large bodies together; they will not stand that. Also I heard it said, as I thought again rather intelligently, that where work is given them to do after a certain model, they will conform perfectly for the first three or four times; then their fatal creativeness comes into play, and they begin to better their instruction by trying to improve upon the patterns—that is, they are artists, not artisans. They must please their fancy in their work or they cannot do it well. From my own experience I cannot say whether this is generally or only sometimes true, but I can affirm that where they delayed or erred in their work they took their failure very amiably. I never saw sweeter patience than that of the Roman matron who had undertaken a small job of getting spots out of a garment, and who quite surpassed me in self-control when she announced, day after appointed day, that the work was not done yet or not done perfectly; she was politeness itself.

On the other hand, some young ladies at a fashionable concert which the queen-mother honored with her presence did not seem very polite. They kept on their immense hats, as women still do in all public places on the European continent, and they seized as many chairs as they could for friends who did not come, and at supreme moments they stood up on their chairs and spoiled such poor chance of seeing the queen-mother as the stranger might have had. While the good King Umberto lived the stranger would have had many other chances, for it is said that the queen showed herself with him to the people at the windows of their palace every afternoon; but in her widowhood she lives retired, though now and then her carriage may be seen passing through the streets, with four special policemen on bicycles following it. These waited about the doorway of the concert-hall that afternoon and formed a very simple, if effective, guard. In fact, it might be said that in its relations with the popular life the reigning family could hardly be simpler. The present king and queen are not so much seen in public as King Umberto and Queen Margherita were, but it is known from many words and deeds that King Victor Emmanuel wishes to be the friend, if not the acquaintance, of his people. When it was proposed to push the present tunnel, with its walks and drives and trolley-lines, under the Quirinal Palace and gardens, so as to connect the two principal business quarters of the city, the king was notified that the noise and jar of the traffic in it might interfere with his comfort. He asked if the tunnel would be for the general advantage, and, when this could not be denied, he gave his consent in words to some such effect as "That settles it." When the German Emperor last visited Rome he is said to have had some state question as to whether he should drive on a certain occasion to the Palatine with the king's horses or the pope's. He who told the story did not remember how the question was solved by the emperor, but he said, "Our king walked."

All this does not mean republican simplicity in the king; a citizen king is doubtless a contradiction in terms anywhere out of France, and even there Louis Philippe found the part difficult. But there is no doubt that the King of Italy means to be the best sort of constituional king, and, as he is in every way an uncommon man, he will probably succeed. One may fancy in him, if one likes, something of that almost touching anxiety of thoughtful Italians to be and to do all that they can for Italy, in a patriotism that seems as enlightened as it is devoted. If I had any criticism to make of such Italians it would be that they expected, or that they asked, too much of themselves. To be sure, they have a right to expect much, for they have done wonders with a country which, without great natural resources except of heart and brain, entered bankrupt into its national existence, and has now grown financially to the dimensions of its vast treasury building, with a paper currency at par and of equal validity with French and English money. If the industrial conditions in Italy were so bad as we compassionate outsiders have been taught to suppose, this financial change is one of the most important events accomplished in Europe since the great era of the racial unifications began. No one will pretend that there have not been great errors of administration in Italy, but apparently the Italians have known how to learn wisdom from their folly. There has been a great deal of industrial adversity; the cost of living has advanced; the taxes are very heavy, and the burdens are unequally adjusted; many speculators have been ruined, and much honestly invested money has been lost. But wages have increased with the prices and rents and taxes, and in a country where every ounce of coal that drives a wheel of production or transportation has to be brought a thousand miles manufactures and railroads have been multiplied.

The state has now taken over the roads and has added their cost to that of its expensive army and navy, but no reasonable witness can doubt that the Italians will be equal to this as well as their other national undertakings. These in Rome are peculiarly difficult and onerous, because they must be commensurate with the scale of antiquity. In a city surviving amid the colossal ruins of the past it would be grotesque to build anything of the modest modern dimensions such as would satisfy the eye in other capitals. The Palace of Finance, at a time when Italian paper was at a discount almost equal to that of American paper during the Civil War, had to be prophetic of the present solvency in size. The yet-unfinished Palace of Justice (one dare not recognize its beauty above one's breath) must be planned so huge that the highest story had to be left off if the foundations were to support the superstructure; the memorial of Victor Emmanuel II. must be of a vastness in keeping with the monuments of imperial Rome, some of which it will partly obscure. Yet as the nation has grown in strength under burdens and duties, it will doubtless prove adequate to the colossal architectural enterprises of its capital. Private speculation in Rome brought disaster twenty-five years ago, but now the city has overflowed with new life the edifices that long stood like empty sepulchres, and public enterprises cannot finally fail; otherwise we should not be digging the Panama Canal or be trying to keep the New York streets in repair. We may confide in the ability of the Italians to carry out their undertakings and to pay the cost out of their own pockets. It is easy to criticise them, but we cannot criticise them more severely than they criticise themselves; and perhaps, as our censure cannot profit them, we might with advantage to ourselves, now and then, convert it into recognition of the great things they have accomplished.

W. D. Howells

XIII. CASUAL IMPRESSIONS

The day that we arrived in Rome the unclouded sun was
yellow on the white dust of the streets, which is never laid by
a municipal watering-cart, though sometimes it is sprinkled
into mire from the garden-hose of the abutting hotels; and in
my rashness I said that for Rome you want sun and you want
youth. Yet there followed many gray days when my age
found Rome very well indeed, and I would not have the
septuagenarian keep away because he is no longer in the
sunny sixties. He may see through his glasses some things
hidden even from the eyes of the early forties. If he drives
out beyond the Porta Pia, say, some bright afternoon, and
notes how the avenue between the beautiful old villas is also
bordered by many vacant lots advertised for sale as well as
built up with pleasant new houses, he will be able to carry
away with him the significant fact that a convenient and
public-spirited trolley-line has the same suburban effect in
Rome, Italy, as in Rome, New York. If he meets some
squadrons of cavalry or some regiments of foot, in that
military necessity of constant movement which the civilian
can never understand, he may make the useful reflection that
it is much better to have the troops out of the city than in it,
and he can praise the wisdom of the Italian government
accordingly. On the neighboring mountains the presence or
absence of snow forms the difference between summer and
winter in Rome, and will suggest the question whether, after
all, our one continental weather is better than the many local
weathers of Europe; and perhaps he will acquire national
modesty in owning that there is something more picturesque
in the indications of those azure or silvery tops than in his
morning paper's announcement that there is or is not a lower
pressure in the region of the lakes.

At any rate, I would not have him note the intimations of

such a drive at less worth than those of any more conventional fact of his Roman sojourn. If one is quite honest, or merely as honest as one may be with safety, one will often own to one's self that something merely incidental to one's purpose, in visiting this memorable place or that, was of greater charm and greater value than the fulfilment of a direct purpose. One happy morning I went, being in the vicinity, to renew the acquaintance with the Tarpeian Rock, which I had hastened to make on my first visit to Rome. I had then found it so far from such a frightfully precipitous height as I had led myself to expect that I came away and rather mocked it in print. But now, possibly because the years had moderated all my expectations in life, I thought the Tarpeian Rock very respectably steep and quite impressively lofty; either the houses at its foot had sunk with their chimneys and balconies, or the rock had risen, so that one could no longer be hurled from it with impunity. We looked at it from an arbor of the lovely little garden which we were let into beyond the top of the rock, and which was the pleasance of some sort of hospital. I think there were probably flowers there, since it was a garden, but what was best was the almond-tree covering the whole space with a roof of bloom, and in this roof a score of birds that sang divinely.

I am aware of bringing a great many birds into these papers; but really Rome would not be Rome without them; and I could not exaggerate their number or the sweetness of their song. They particularly abounded in the cloistered and gardened close of the Cistercian Convent, which three hundred years ago ensconsed itself within the ruinous Baths of Diocletian. I have no fable at hand to explain what seems the special preference of the birds for this garden; it is possibly an idiosyncrasy, something like that of the cats which make Trajan's Forum their favorite resort. All that I can positively say is that if I were a bird I would ask nothing better than to frequent the cypresses of that garden and tune my numbers for the entertainment of the audience of extraordinary monsters in the aisles below, which bea'in plinths of clipped privet and end marble heads of horses, bulls, elephants, rhinoceroses, and their like. I do not pretend to be exact in their nomination; they may be other animals; but I am sure of their attention to the birds. I am not quite so sure of the attention of the antique shapes in the rooms of the Ludovisi collection looking into the close. I fancy them preoccupied with the in-doors cold, so great in all Italian galleries, and scarcely tempered for them by the remote and solitary brazier over which the custodians take turns in stifling themselves. They cannot come down into the sun and song of the garden, to which the American tourist may return from visiting them, to thaw out his love of the beautiful.

They are not so many or so famous as their marble brothers and sisters in the Vatican Museum, but the tourist should not miss seeing them. Neither should he miss any accessible detail of the environing ruins of the Diocletian Baths. Let him not think because they are so handy, and so next door, as it were, to the railway station where he arrives, and to Cook's office where he goes for his letters next morning, that they are of less merit than other monuments of imperial Rome. They are not only colossally vast, but they are singularly noble, as well as so admirably convenient. Because they are so convenient, the modern Romans have turned their cavernous immensity to account in the trades and industries, and have built them up in carpenters' and blacksmiths' and plumbers' shops, where there is a cheerful hammering and banging much better than the sullen silence of more remote and difficult ruins. In color they are a very agreeable reddish brown, though not so soft to the eye as the velvety masses of the Palatine, which at any distance great enough to obscure their excavation have a beauty like that of primitive nature. I do not know but you see these best from the glazed terrace of that restaurant on the Aventine which is the resort of the well-advised Romans and visitors, and from which you look across to the mount of fallen and buried grandeur over a champaign of gardens and orchards. All round is a landscape which I was not able to think of as less than tremendous, with the whole of Rome in it, and the snow-topped hills about it—a scene to which you may well give more than a moment from the varied company at the other tables, where English, German, French, and Americans, as well as Italians, are returning to the simple life in their enjoyment of the local dishes, washed down with golden draughts of local wine, served ciderwise in generous jugs.

If your mind is, as ours was in that place, to drive farther and see the chapter-house of the Knights of Malta, clinging to the height over the Tiber, and looking up and down its yellow torrent and the black boats along the shore, with universal Rome melting into the distance, you must not fail to stop at the old, old Church of St. Sabina. You will naturally want to see this, not only because there in the cloister (as the ladies can ascertain at the window let into the wall for their dangerous eyes to peer through from the outside) is the successor of the orange-tree transplanted from the Holy Land by St. Dominic six or seven hundred years ago; not only because one of the doors of the church, covered with Bible stories, is thought the oldest wood-carving in the world, but also because there will be sitting in his white robes on a bench beside the nave an aged Dominican monk reading some holy book, with his spectacles fallen forward on his nose and his cowl fallen back on his neck, and his wide tonsure gleaming glacially in the pale light, whom nothing in the church or its visitors can distract from his devotions.

It is very, very cold in there, but he probably would not, if he could, follow you into the warm outer world and on into the garden of the Knights, who came here after they had misruled Malta for centuries and finally rendered a facile submission to General Bonaparte of the French Republican army in 1798. Their fixing here cannot be called anything so vigorous as their last stand; but, without specific reference to the easy-chairs in their chapter-house, it may be fitly called their last seat; and, if it is true that none of plebeian blood may enjoy the order's privileges, the place will afford another of those satisfactions which the best of all possible worlds is always offering its admirers. Even if one were disposed to moralize the comfortable end of the poor Knights harshly, one must admit that their view of Rome is one of the unrivalled views, and that the glimpse of St. Peter's through the key-hole of their garden-gate is little short of tin-rivalled. I could not manage the glimpse myself, but I can testify to the unique character of the avenue of clipped box and laurel which the key-hole also commands. Lovers of the super-natural, of which I am the first, will like to be reminded, or perhaps instructed, that the Church of the Priory stands on the spot where Remus had a seance with the spiritual authorities and was advised against building Rome where he proposed, being shown only six vultures as against twelve that Romulus saw in favor of his chosen site. The fact gave the Aventine Hill the fame of bad luck, but any one may safely visit it now, after the long time that has passed.

I do not, however, advise visiting it above any other place in Rome. What I always say is, take your chances with any or every time or place; you cannot fail of some impression which you will always like recurring to as characteristically delightful. For instance, I once walked home from the Piazza di Spagna with some carnival masks frolicking about me through the sun-shotten golden dust of the delicious evening air, and I had a pleasure from the experience which I shall never forget. It was as rich as that I got from the rosy twilight in Avhich I wandered homeward another time from the Piazza di Venezia and found myself passing the Fountain of Trevi, and lingered long there and would not throw my penny into its waters because I knew I could not help coming back to Rome anyhow. Yet another time I was driving through a certain piazza where the peasants stand night long waiting to be hired by the proprietors who come to find them there, and suddenly the piety of the Middle Ages stood before me in the figure of the Brotherhood of the Misericordia, draped to the foot and hooded in their gray, unbleached linen. The brothers were ranged in a file at the doors of the church ready to visit the house of sickness or of mourning, barefooted, with their eyes showing spectrally through their masks and their hands coming soft and white out of their sleeves and betraying the lily class that neither toils nor spins and yet is bound, as in the past, to the poorest and humblest through the only Church that knows how to unite them in the offering and acceptance of reciprocal religious duties.

In Rome, as elsewhere in Catholic countries, it seemed to me that the worshippers were mostly of the poorer classes and were mostly old women, but in the Church of the Jesuits I saw worshippers almost as well dressed as the average of our Christian Scientists, and in that church, whose name I forget, but which is in the wide street or narrow piazza below the windows of the palace where the last Stuarts lived and died, my ineradicable love of gentility was flattered and my faith in the final sanctification of good society restored by the sight of gentlemen coming to and going from prayer with their silk hats in their hands.

The performance of ritual implies a certain measure of mechanism, and the wonder is that in the Catholic churches it is not more mechanical than it actually is. I was no great frequenter of functions, and I cannot claim that my superior spirituality was ever deeply wounded; sometimes it was even supported and consoled. I noted, without offence, in the

Church of San Giuseppe how the young monk, who preached an eloquent sermon on the saint's life and character, exhausted himself before he exhausted his topic, and sat down between the successive heads of his discourse and took a good rest. It was the saint's day, which seemed more generally observed than any other saint's day in Rome, and his baroque church in Via Capo le Case was thronged with people, mostly poor and largely peasants, who were apparently not so fatigued by the preacher's shrill, hard delivery as he was himself. There were many children, whom their elders held up to see, and there was one young girl in a hat as wide as a barrel-head standing up where others sat, and blotting out the prospect of half the church with her flaring brim and flaunting feathers. The worshippers came and went, and while the monk preached and reposed a man crept dizzyingly round the cornice with a taper at the end of a long pole lighting the chandeliers, while two other men on the floor kindled the candles before the altars. As soon as their work was completed, the monk, as if he had been preaching against time, sat definitely down and left us to the rapture of the perfected splendor. The high-altar was canopied and curtained in crimson, fringed with gold, and against this the candle-flames floated like yellow flowers. Suddenly, amid the hush and expectance, a tenor voice pealed from the organ-loft, and a train of priests issued from the sacristy and elbowed and shouldered their way through the crowd to the high-altar, where their intoning, like so many

"Silver snarling trumpets 'gan to glide,"

and those flower-like flames and that tenor voice seemed to sing together, and all sense of mortal agency in the effect was lost.

How much our pale Northern faith has suffered from the

elimination of the drama which is so large an element in the worship of the South could not he conjectured without offence to both. Drama I have said, but, if I had said opera, it would have been equally with the will merely to recognize the fact and not to censure it. Many have imagined a concert of praise in heaven, and portrayed it as a spectacle of which the elder Christian worship seems emulous. Go, therefore, to Rome, dear fellow-Protestant, with any measure of ignorance short of mine, but leave as much of your prejudice behind you as you can. You are not more likely to become a convert because of your tolerance; in fact, you may be the safer for it; and it will prepare you for a gentler pleasure than you would otherwise enjoy in the rites and ceremonies which seem exotic in our wintrier world, but which are here native to the climate, or, at least, could not have had their origin under any but oriental or meridional skies. The kindlier mood will help you to a truer appreciation of that peculiar keeping of the churches which the stranger is apt to encounter in his approach. Be tender of the hapless mendicants at the door; they are not there for their pleasure, those blind and halt and old. Be modestly receptive of the good office of the whole tribe of cicerones, of custodians, of sacristans; they can save you time, which, though it is not quite the same as money, even in Rome is worth saving, and are the repository of many rejected fables waiting to be recognized as facts again. I, for instance, committed the potential error of wholly rejecting with scorn the services of an authorized guide to the Church of St. John Lateran because he said the tariff was three francs. But after wandering, the helpless prey of my own Baedeker, up and down the huge temple, I was glad to find him waiting my emergence where I had left him, in the church porch, one of the most pathetic figures that ever wrung the remorseful heart.

His poor black clothes showed the lustre of inveterate wear;

his waistcoat would have been the better for a whole bottle of benzine; his shoes, if they did not share the polish of those threadbare textures, reciprocated the effect of his broken-spirited cuffs and collar, and the forlorn gentility of his hat. His beard had not been shaved for three days; I do not know why, but doubtless for as good a reason as that his shirt had not been washed for seven. It was with something like a cry for pardon of my previous brutality that I now closed with his unabated demand of a three-franc fee, and we went with him wherever he would, from one holy edifice to another of those that constitute the church; but I will not ask the reader to follow us in the cab which he mounted into with us, but which would not conveniently hold four. Let him look it all up in the admirably compendious pages of Hare and Murray, and believe, if he can, that I missed nothing of that history and mystery. If I speak merely of the marvellous baptistery, it is doubtless not because the other parts were not equally worthy of my wonder, but because I would not have even an enemy miss the music of the singing doors, mighty valves of bronze which, when they turn upon their hinges, emit a murmur of grief or a moan of remorse for whatever heathen uses they once served the wicked Caracalla at his baths. Not to have heard their rich harmony would he like not having heard the echo in the baptistery of Pisa, a life-long loss.

Heaven knows how punctiliously our guide would have acquainted us with every particular of the Lateran group, which for a thousand years before the Vatican was the home of the popes. We begged off from this and that, but even indolence like mine would not spare itself the sight of the Scala Santa. That was another of the things which I distinctly remembered from the year 1864, and I did not find the spectacle of the modern penitents covering the holy steps different in 1908. Now, as then, there was something incongruous in their fashions and aspirations, but one could not doubt that it was a genuine piety that nerved them to climb up and down the hard ascent on their knees, or, at the worst, that it was good exercise. Still, I would rather leave my reader the sense of that most noble fagade of the church, with its lofty balustraded entablature, where the gigantic Christ and ten of his saints look out forever to the Alban hills.

XIV. TIVOLI AND FRASCATI

One of the most agreeable illusions of travel is a sort of expectation that if you will give objects of interest time enough they will present themselves to you, and, if they will not actually come to you in your hotel, will happen in your way when you go out. This was my notion of the right way of seeing Rome, but, as the days of my winter passed, so many memorable monuments failed not merely to seek me out, but stiffly held aloof from me in my walks abroad, that I began to feel anxious lest I should miss them altogether. I had, for instance, always had the friendliest curiosity concerning Tivoli and Frascati as the two most amiable Roman neighborhoods, and hoped to see both of them in some informal and casual sort; but they persisted so long in keeping off on their respective hills that I saw something positive on niy part must be done. Clearly I must make the advances; and so when, one morning of mid-March, a friend sent to ask if we would not motor out to Tivoli with him and his family, I closed eagerly with the chance of a compromise which would save feeling all round. My friend has never yet known how he was bringing Tivoli and me together after a mutual diffidence, but, as he was a poet, I am sure he will be glad to know now.

Our road across the Campagna lay the greater part of the distance beside the tram-line, but at other points parted with it and stretched rough, if lately mended, and smooth, if long neglected, between the wide, lonely pastures and narrow drill-sown fields of wheat. The Campagna is said to be ploughed only once in five years by the peasants for the proprietors, who have philosophized its fertility as something that can be better restored by the activities of nature in that time than by phosphates in less. As they are mostly Roman patricians, they have always felt able to wait; but now it is said that northern Italian capital and enterprise are coming in, and the Campagna will soon be cropped every season, though as yet its chief yield seemed to be the two-year-old colts we saw browsing about. For some distance we had the company of the different aqueducts, but their broken stretches presently ceased altogether, and then for other human association we had, besides the fencings of the meadows, only the huts and shelters scattered among the grassy humps and hollows. There were more humps than I had remembered of the Campagna, and probably they were the rounded and turfed-over chunks of antiquity which otherwhere showed their naked masonry unsoftened and unfriended by the passing centuries. At times a dusty hamlet, that seemed to crop up from the roadside ditches, followed us a little way with children that shouted for joy in our motor and dogs that barked for pleasure in their joy. Women with the square linen head-dress of the Roman peasants stood and stared, and sallow men, each with his jacket hanging from one of his shoulders, seemed stalking backward from us as we whirled by. Here and there we scared a horse or a mule, but we did not so much as run over a hen; and both man and beast are becoming here, as elsewhere, reconciled to the automobile. Now and then a carter would set his team slantwise in our course and stay us out of good-humored deviltry, and when he let us pass would fling some chaff to the fresh-faced English youngster who was our chauffeur.

"I suppose you don't always understand what those fellows say," I suggested from my seat beside him.

"No, sir," he confessed. "But I give it to 'em back in English," he added, joyously.

He rather liked these encounters, apparently, but not the beds of sharp, broken stone with which the road was repaired. It was his belief that there was not a steam-roller in all Italy, and he seemed to reserve an opinion of the government's motives in the matter with respect to motors, as if he thought them bad.

The scenery of the Campagna was not varied. Once we came to a battlemented tomb, of mighty girth and height, as perdurable in its masonry as the naked, stony hills that in the distance propped the mountains fainting along the horizon under their burden of snow. But as we drew nearer Tivoli the hills drew nearer us, and now they were no longer naked, but densely covered with the gray, interminable stretch of the olive forests. The olive is the tree which, of all others, is the friend of civilized man; it is older and kinder even than the apple, which is its next rival in beneficence; but these two kinds are so like each other, in the mass, that this boundless forest of olives around Tivoli offered an image of all the aggregated apple-orchards in the world. Where the trees came closest to the road they seemed to watch our passing, each with its trunk aslant and its branches akimbo, in a humorous make-believe of being in some joke with us, like so many gnarled and twisted apple-trees, used to children's play-fellowship. You felt a racial intimacy with the whimsical and antic shapes which your brief personal consciousness denied in vain; and you rose among the slopes around Tivoli with a sense of home-coming from the desert of the Campagna. But in the distance to which the olive forests stretched they lost this effect of tricksy familiarity. They looked like a gray sea against the horizon; more fantastically yet, they seemed a vast hoar silence, full of mystery and loneliness.

If Tivoli does not flourish so frankly on its oil as Frascati on its wine, it is perhaps because it has of late years tacitly prospered as much on the electricity which its wonderful and beautiful waterfalls enable it to furnish as abundantly to Rome as our own Niagara to Buffalo. The scrupulous Hare, whose *Walks in Rome* include Tivoli, does not, indeed, advise you to visit the electrical works, but he says that if you have not strength enough for all the interests and attractions of Tivoli it will be wise to give yourself entirely to the cascades and to the Villa d'Este, and this was what we instinctively did, but in the reverse order. Chance rewarded us before we left the villa with a sight of the electric plant, which just below the villa walls smokes industriously away with a round, redbrick chimney almost as lofty and as ugly as some chimney in America. On our way to and fro we necessarily passed through the town, which, with its widish but not straightish chief street, I found as clean as Rome itself, and looking, after the long tumult of its history, beginning well back in fable, as peaceable as Montclair, New Jersey. It had its charm, and, if I could have spent two weeks there instead of two hours, I might impart its effect in much more circumstance than I can now promise the reader. Most of my little time I gladly gave to the villa, which, with the manifold classic associations of the region, attracts the stranger and helps the cataracts sum up all that most people can keep of Tivoli.

The Villa d'Este is not yet a ruin, but it is ruinous enough to win the fancy without cumbering it with the mere rubbish of decay. Some neglected pleasances are so far gone that you cannot wish to live in them, but the forgottenness of the Villa d'Este hospitably allured me to instant and permanent occupation, so that when I heard it could now be bought, casino and all, for thirty thousand dollars, nothing but the want of the money kept me from making the purchase. I indeed recognized certain difficulties in living there the year round; but who lives anywhere the year round if he can help it? The casino, standing among the simpler town buildings on the plateau above the gardens, would be a little inclement, for all its frescoing and stuccoing by the sixteenth-century arts, and in its noble halls, amid the painted and modelled

W. D. Howells

figures, the new American proprietor would shiver with the former host and guests after the first autumn chill began; but while it was yet summer it Avould be as delicious there as in the aisles and avenues of the garden which its balustrated terrace looked into. From that level you descend by marble steps which must have some trouble in knowing themselves from the cascades pouring down the broken steeps beside them, and companionably sharing their seclusion among the cypresses and ilexes. You are never out of the sight and sound of the plunging water, which is still trained in falls and fountains, or left to a pathetic dribble through the tattered stucco of the neglected grots. It is now a good three centuries and a half since the Cardinal Ippolito d'.Este had these gardens laid out and his pleasure-house built overlooking them; and his gardener did not plan so substantially as his architect. In fact, you might suppose that the landscapist wrought with an eye to the loveliness of the ruin it all would soon fall into, and, where he used stone, used it fragilely, so that it would ultimately suggest old frayed and broken lace. Clearly he meant some of the cataracts to face one another, and to have a centre from which they could all be seen—say the still, dull-green basin which occupies a large space in the grounds between them. But he must have meant this for a surprise to the spectator, who easily misses it under the trees overleaning the moss-grown walks which hardly kept themselves from running wild. There is a sense of crumbling decorations of statues, broken in their rococo caverns; of cypresses carelessly grouped and fallen out of their proper straightness and slimness; of unkempt bushes crowding the space beneath; of fragmentary gods or giants half hid in the tangling grasses. It all has the air of something impatiently done for eager luxury, and its greatest charm is such as might have been expected to be won from eventual waste and wreck. If there was design in the treatment of the propitious ground, self-shaped to an irregular amphitheatre, it is now obscured, and the cultiavted tourist of our day may reasonably please himself with the belief that he is having a better time there than the academic Roman of the sixteenth century.

Academic it all is, however hastily and nonchalantly, and I feel that I have so signally failed to make the charm of the villa felt that I am going to let a far politer observer celebate the beauties of the other supreme interest of Tivoli. When Mr. Gray (as the poet loved to be called in print) visited the town with Mr. Walpole in May, 1740, the Villa d'Este by no means shared the honors of the cataracts, and Mr. Gray seems not to have thought it worth seriously describing in his letter to Mr. West, but mocks the casino with a playful mention before proceeding to speak fully, if still playfully, of the great attraction of Tivoli: "Dame Nature . . . has built here three or four little mountains and laid them out in an irregular semicircle; from certain others behind, at a greater distance, she has drawn a canal into which she has put a little river of hers called the Anio, . . . which she has no sooner done, but, like a heedless chit, it tumbles down a declivity fifty feet perpendicular, breaks itself all to shatters, and is converted into a shower of rain, where the sun forms many a bow—red, green, blue, and yellow. . . . By this time it has divided itself, being crossed and opposed by the rocks, into four several streams, each of which, in emulation of the greater one, will tumble down, too: and it does tumble down, but not from an equally elevated place; so that you have at one view all these cascades intermixed with groves of olive and little woods, the mountains rising behind them, and on the top of one (that which forms the extremity of the half-circle's horns) is seated the town itself. At the very extremity of that extremity, on the brink of the precipice, stands the Sibyls' Temple, the remains of a little rotunda, surrounded with its portico, above half of whose beautiful Corinthian pillars are still standing and entire."

For the reader who has been on the spot the poet's words will paint a vivid picture of the scene; for the reader who has not been there, so much the worse; he should lose no time in going, and drinking a cup of the local wine at a table of the restaurant now in possession of Mr. Gray's point of view. I do not know a more filling moment, exclusive of the wine, than he can enjoy there, with those cascades before him and those temples beside him; for Mr. Gray has mentioned only one of the two, I do not know why, that exist on this enchanted spot, and that define their sharp, black shadows as with an inky line just beyond the restaurant tables. One is round and the other oblong, and the round one has been called the Sibyls', though now it is getting itself called Vesta's—the goddess who long unrightfully claimed the temple of Mater Matuta in the Forum Boarium at Rome. As Vesta has lately been dispossessed there by archaeology (which seems in Rome to enjoy the plenary powers of our Boards of Health), she may have been given the Sibyls' Temple at Tivoli in compensation; but all this does not really matter. What really matters is the mighty chasm which yawns away almost from your feet, where you sit, and the cataracts, from their brinks, high or low, plunging into it, and the wavering columns of mist weakly striving upward out of it: the whole hacked by those mountains Mr. Gray mentions, with belts of olive orchard on their flanks, and wild paths furrowing and wrinkling their stern faces. To your right there is a sheeted cataract falling from the basins of the town laundry, where the toil of the washers melts into nmsic, and their chatter, like that of birds, drifts brokenly across the abyss to you. While you sit musing or murmuring in your rapture, two mandolins and a guitar smilingly intrude, and after a prelude of Italian airs swing into strains which presently, through your revery, you recognize as "In the Bowery" and "Just One Girl," and the smile of the two mandolins and the guitar spreads to a grin of sympathy, and you are no longer at the Caffe Sibylla in Tivoli, but in your own Manhattan on some fairy roof-garden, or at some sixty-cent *table d'hote,* with wine and music included.

It was a fortnight later that we paid our visit to Frascati, not proudly motoring now, but traversing the Campagna on the roof of a populous tram-car, which in its lofty narrowness was of the likeness of an old-fashionable lake propeller. The morning was, like most other mornings in Rome, of an amiability which the afternoons often failed of; but none of us passengers for Frascati doubted its promise as we gathered at the tram-station and tried for tickets at the little booth in a wall sparely containing the official who bade us get them in the car. We all did this, whatever our nation—American, English, German, or Italian—and then we mounted to the hurricane-deck of our propeller and entered into a generous rivalry for the best seats. We had a roof over our heads, and there were curtains which we might have drawn if we could have borne to lose a single glimpse of the landscape, or if we would not rather have suffered the chill which our swift progress evoked from the morning's warmth after we left the shelter of the city streets. We passed through stretches of the ancient aqueducts consorting on familiar terms with rows of shabby tenement-houses, and whisked by the ends of wide, dusty avenues of yet incomplete structure, and by beds of market-gardens, and by simple feeding-places for man and beast, with the tables set close in front of the stalls. An ambitiously frescoed casino had a gigantic peacock painted over a whole story, and the peach-trees were in bloom in the villa spaces. When we struck into the Campagna we found it of like physiognomy with the Campagna toward Tivoli.

There was very little tillage, but wide stretches of grazing-land, with those lumps of turfed or naked antiquity starting out of them, and cattle, sheep, and horses feeding over them, the colts' tails blowing picturesquely in the wind that seemed

W. D. Howells

more and more opposed to our advance. It dropped, at times, where we paused to leave a passenger near one of those suburbs which the tram-lines are building up round Rome, but on our course building so slowly that our passengers had to walk rather far from the stations before they reached home. There were other pedestrians who looked rather English, especially some ladies making for the gate of a kind, sunny walled old villa, where there was a girl singing and a gardener coming slowly down to let them in. Nearer Frascati were many neat, new stone houses, where Eoman families come out to stay the spring and fall seasons, and even the summer. But these looked too freshly like the suburban cottages on a Boston trolley-line; and we perversely found our delight in a fine breadth of brown woods for the very reason of that homelikeness which gave us pause in the houses. The trees looked American; there were American wood-roads penetrating the forest's broken and irregular extent; there was one steep-sided ravine worth any man's American money; and the dead leaves littered the sylvan paths with an allure to the foot which it was hard for the head to resist.

Elsewhere the tram-line that curved upward to Frascati was flanked, after it left the Campagna's level, with vineyards as measureless as the olive orchards of Tivoli. There was yet, at the end of March, no sign of leaf on the newly trimmed vines, which were trained on long poles of canes brought together in peaks to support them and netting the hill-slopes with the endless succession of their tops. The eye wearied itself in following them as in following the checkered wiring of the Kentish hop-fields, and was glad to leave them for the closer-set, but never too closely set, palaces of Frascati: the sort of palaces which we call cottages in our summer cities, and the Italians call casinos from the same instinctive modesty. When we began to doubt of our destination, our car passed a long, shaded promenade, and then stopped in a cheerful square amidst hotels and restaurants, with tables hospitably spread on the sidewalks before them.

We decided not to lunch at that early hour, but we could not keep our eyes from feasting, even at eleven o'clock in the morning, on the wonderful prospect that tempted them, on every hand, away from the more immediate affair of choosing one out of the many cabs that thronged about our arriving train. The cabs of Frascati are all finer than the cabs of Rome, and the horses are handsomer and younger and stronger; we could have taken the worst of the equipages that contested our favor and still fared well; but we chose the best—a glittering victoria and an animal of proud action, with a lustrous coat of bay. He wore a ring of joyous bells; he had, indeed, not a headstall of such gay colors as some others; but you cannot have everything, and his driver was of a mental vividness which compensated for all the color wanting in his horse's headstall, and of a personal attraction which made us ambitious for his company on any terms. He quickly reduced us from our vain supposition that carriages in a country-place should be cheaper than in a city; because, as he proved, there were fewer strangers to hire them and they ought logically to be dearer. So far from accepting our modest standards of time and money, he all but persuaded us to employ him for the whole day instead of a few hours at a price beyond our imagination; and he only consented to compromise on a half-day at an increased figure.

We supposed that it was the negotiation which drew and held the attention of all the leisure of Frascati, and that it was the driver and our relation to him rather than the horse and our relation to it that concentrated the public interest in us; and when we had convinced him that we had no wish but to see some of the more immediate and memorable villas, we mounted to our places in the victoria and drove out through the reluctantly parting spectators, who remained looking

W. D. Howells

after us as if unable to disperse to their business or pleasure.

Our driver decided for us to go first to the Villa Falconieri, which had lately been bought and presented by a fond subject to the German Emperor, and by him in turn bestowed on the German Academy at Rome. In the cold, clean, stony streets of Frascati, as we rattled through them, there breathed the odor of the great local industry; and the doorways of many buildings, widening almost in a circle to admit the burly tuns of wine, testified how generally, how almost universally, the vintage of that measureless acreage of grapes around the place employed the inhabitants. But there was little else to impress the observer in Frascati, and we willingly passed out of the town in the road climbing the long incline to the Villa Fal-conieri, with its glimpses, far and near, of woods and gardens. It was a road so much to our minds that nothing was further from us than the notion that our horse might not like it so well; but, at the first distinct rise, he stopped and wheeled round so abruptly, after first pawing the air, that there could be no doubt where the popular interest we had lately enjoyed in Frascati had really originated. Probably our horse's distinguishing trait was known to everybody in Frascati except his driver. He, at least, showed the greatest surprise at the horse's behavior, as unprecedented in their acquaintance, which he owned was brief, for he had bought him in Rome only the week before. With successive retreats to level ground he put him again and again at the incline, but as soon as the horse felt the ground rising under his feet he lifted them from it and whirled round for another retreat. All this we witnessed from an advantageotis point at the roadside which we had taken up at his first show of reluctance; and at last the driver suggested that we should leave it and go on to the Villa Falconieri on foot. On our part, we suggested that he should attempt some other villa which would not involve an objectionable climb. He then proposed the Villa

Mandragone, and the horse seemed to agree with us. As we drove again through the clean, cold, stony streets, with the rounded doorways for the wine-casks, we fancied something clearly ironical in the general interest renewed by our return. But we tried to look as if we had merely done the Villa Falconieri with unexampled rapidity, and pushed on to the Villa Mandragone, where, under the roof of interlacing ilex toughs, our horse ought to have been tempted on in a luxurious unconsciousness of anything like an incline. But he was apparently an animal which would have felt the difference between two rose-leaves and one in a flowery path, and just when we were thinking what a delightful time we were having, and beginning to feel a gentle question as to who the pathetic little cripple halting toward us with a color-box and a camp-stool might be, and whether she painted as well as a kind heart could wish, our horse stopped with the suddenness which we knew to be definite. The sensitive creature could not be deceived; he must have reached rising ground, and we sided with him against our driver, who would have pretended it was fancy.

It was now noon, and we drove back to the *piazza,* agreeing upon a less price in view of the imperfect service rendered, and deciding to collect our thoughts for a new venture over such luncheon as the best hotel could give us. It was not so good a hotel as the lunch it gave. It was beyond the cleansing tide of modernity which has swept the Roman hotels, and was dirty everywhere, but with a specially dirty, large, shabby dining-room, cold and draughty, yet precious for the large, round brazier near our table which kept one side of us warm in romantic mediaeval fashion, and invited us to rise from time to time and thaw our fingers over its blinking coals. The bath in which our chicken had been boiled formed a good soup; there was an admirable *pasta* and a creditable, if imperfect, conception of beefsteak; and there was a caraffe of new Frascati wine, sweet, like new cider. If we could have

W. D. Howells

asked more, it would not have been more than the young Italian officer who sat in the other corner with his pretty young wife, and who allowed me to weave a whole realtistic fiction out of their being at Frascati so out of season.

Just as I was most satisfyingly accounting for them, our late driver alarmed me by appearing at the door and beckoning me to the outside. The occasion was nothing worse than the presence of a man who, he said, was his brother, with a horse which, upon the same authority, was without moral blame or physical blemish. If anything, it preferred a mountain to a plain country, and could be warranted to balk at nothing. The man, who was almost as exemplary as the horse, would assume the unfulfilled contract of the other man and horse with a slight increase of pay; and yet I had my doubts. The day had clouded, and I meekly contended that it was going to rain; but the man explicitly and the horse tacitly scoffed at the notion, and I yielded. I shall always be glad that I did so, for in the keeping of those good creatures the rest of our day was an unalloyed delight. It appeared, upon further acquaintance, that the man paid a hundred dollars for the horse; his brother had paid a hundred and twenty-five for the balker; but it was the belief of our driver that it would be worth the difference when it had reconciled itself to the rising ground of Frascati; as yet it was truly a stranger there. His own horse was used to ups and downs everywhere; they had just come from a long trip, and he was going to drive to Siena and back the next week with two ladies for passengers, who were to pay him five dollars a day for himself and horse and their joint keep. He said the ladies, whose names he gave, were from Boston; he balked at adding Massachusetts, but I am sure the horse would not; and, if I could have hired them both to carry me about Italy indefinitely, I would have gladly paid them five dollars a day as long as I had the money. The fact is, that driver was charming, a man of sense and intelligence, who reflected credit even upon his brother and his brother's horse: one of those perfect Italian temperaments which endear their possessors to the head and heart, so that you wonder, at parting, how you are going to live without them.

We did not excite such vivid interest in Frascati at our second start as at our first; but, as we necessarily passed over the same route again, we had the applause of the children in streets now growing familiar, and a glad welcome back from the pretty girls and blithe matrons of all ages rhythmically washing in the public laundry, who recognized us in our new equipage. The public laundry is always the gayest scene in an Italian town, and probably our adventures continued the subject of joyous comment throughout the day which was now passing only too rapidly for us. We were again on the way to the Villa Falconieri, and while our brave horse is valiantly mounting the steep to its gate this is perhaps as good a place as any to own that the Villa Falconieri and the Villa Man-dragone were the only sights we saw in Frascati. We did, indeed, penetrate the chill interior of the local cathedral, but as we did not know at the time that we were sharing it with the memory of the young Stuart pretender Charles Edward, who died in Frascati, and whose brother, Cardinal York, placed a mural tablet to him in the church, we were conscious of no special claim upon our interest. We ought, of course, to have visited the Villa Aldobrandini and the Villa Ruffinella and the Villa Graziola and the Villa Taverna, but we left all these to the reader, who will want some reason for going to Frascati in person, and to whom I commend them as richly worth crossing the Atlantic for. Doubtless from a like motive we left the ruins of Tusculum unvisited, just as at Tivoli we refrained from diverging to Hadrian's Villa—the two things supremely worthy to be seen in their respective regions. But, if I had seen only half as much as I saw at Frascati—the Villa Falconieri, namely—I should feel forever over-enriched by the experience.

Slowly an ancient servitor, whose family had been in the employ of the Falconieri for a century, advanced as with the burden of their united years and opened the high gate to us and delivered us over to a mild boy. He bestowed on us, for a consideration, a bunch of wild violets, and then, as if to keep us from the too abrupt sight of the repairs and changes going on near the casino, led us first to the fish-pond, in the untouched seclusion of a wooded hill, and silently showed us the magnificent view which the top commanded, if commanded is not too proud a word for a place so pathetic in its endearing neglect. It had once been the haunt of many a gay picnicking crew in hoops and bag-wigs and all the faded fashion of the past, when hosts and guests had planned a wilder escapade than the grove before the casino invited, with its tables of moss-painted marble. There would have been an academic poet, or more than one, in the company, and they would have furnished forth the prospect with phrases far finer than any I have about me, who can only say that the Campagna, clothed in mist and cloud-shadowed, swam round the upland in the colors of a tropic sea.

Our mild boy waited a decent moment, as if to let me do better, and then led down to the casino, round through a wooded valley where there were some men with fowling-pieces, whom I objected to in tones, if not in terms. "What are they shooting?" "They are shooting larks, signore." "What a pity!" "But the larks are leaving Italy, now, and going north." It was a reason, like many another that humanity is put to it in giving, and I do not know that I missed any larks, later, from an English meadow where I saw them spiring up in song, and glad as if none of their friends had been shot at the Villa Falconieri. In fact, I did not see those fowlers actually killing any; and I can still hope they were not very good shots.

The workmen who were putting the place in repair were

lunching near the casino, in a litter of lumber and other structural material, but the casino itself seemed as yet unprofaned by their touch. At any rate, we had it quite to ourselves, let wander at will through its cool, bare, still spaces. If there was a great deal to see, there was not much to remember, or to remember so much as the satirical frescos of Pier Leone Ghezzi, who has caricatured himself as well as others in them. They are not bitter satires, but, on the contrary, very charming; and still more charming are the family portraits frescoed round the principal room. Under one curve of the vaulted ceiling the whole family of a given time is shown, half-length but life-size, looking down pleasantly on the unexpected American guests who try to pretend they were invited, or at least came by mistaking the house for another. Better even than this most amiable circle, or half-circle, of father, mother, and daughter are the figures of friends or acquaintances or kinsfolk: figures not only life-size, but full-length, in panels of the walls, in the very act of stepping on the floor and coming forward to greet their host and hostess from the other walls. They did not visibly move during our stay, but I know they only waited for us to go; and that at night, especially when there was a moon, or none, they left their backgrounds and mingled in the polite gayeties of their period. One could hardly help looking over one's shoulder to see if they were not following to that farthermost room called Primavera, which is painted around and aloft like a very bower of spring, with foliage and flowers covering the walls and dropping through the trellis feigned overhead. Of all the caprices of art, which in Italy so loved caprice, I recall no such pleasing playfulness as in the decoration of these rooms. If you pass through the last you may look from the spring within on no fairer spring without bordering the shores of the Campagna sea.

It was so pathetic to imagine the place going out of the right Italian keeping that I attributed a responsive sadness to the tall, handsome, elderly woman who had allowed us the freedom of the casino. Her faded beauty was a little sallow, as the faded beauty of a Roman matron should be, and her large, dark eyes glowed from purpling shadows.

"And the German Emperor owns it now?"

"Yes, they say he has bought it."

"And the Germans will soon be coming?"

"They say."

She would not commit herself but by a tone, an inflection, but we knew very well what she and the frescoed presences about us thought. I wish now I could have stayed behind and got the frescos to tell me just how far I ought recognize her sorrow in my tip, but one must always guess at these things, and I shall never know whether I rewarded the aged gate-keeper according to the century of service his generations had rendered those of the frescos.

We were going now to the Villa Mandragone, but we had not yet the courage for the rise of ground where we had failed before, and we entreated our driver to go round some other way, if he could, and descend rather than ascend to it. He said that was easy, and it was when we came away that we passed through that ilex avenue which we had not yet penetrated in its whole length, and where we now met many foot-passengers, lay and cleric, who added to the character of the scene, and saw again the little cripple artist, now trying to seize its features, or some of them. I did not see whether she was succeeding so well as in pity she might and as I knew she did.

In spite of our triumph with the Villa Mandragone in this

second attempt, we can never think it half as charming as the Villa Falconieri. I forget what cardinal it was who built it so spacious and splendid, with three hundred and sixty-five windows, in honor of the calendar as reformed by the reigning pope, Gregory XIII. It is a palace enclosing a quadrangle of whole acres (I will not own to less), with a stately colonnade following as far round as the reader likes. When he passes through all this magnificence he will come out on a grassy terrace, with a fountain below it, and below that again the chromatic ocean of the Campagna (I have said sea often enough). A weird sort of barbaric stateliness is given to the place by the twisted and tapering pillars that rise at the several corners, with colossal masques carven at the top and the sky showing through the eye-hollows, as the flame of torches must often have shown at night. But for all the outlandish suggestion of these pillars, the villa now belongs to the Jesuits, who have a college there, where only the sons of noble families are received for education. As we rounded a sunny wall in driving away, we saw a line of people, old and young of both sexes, but probably not of noble families, seated with their backs against the warm stone eating from comfortable bowls a soup which our driver said was the soup of charity and the daily dole of the fathers to such hungry as came for it. The day was now growing colder than it had been, and we felt that the poor needed all the soup, and hot, that they could get.

After a vain visit to Grotta Ferrata, which was signally disappointing, in spite of the traces of a recent country fair and the historical merits of a church of the Greek rite, with a black-bearded monk coming to show it through a gardened cloister, we were glad to take the tram back to Rome and to get into the snug inside of it. The roof, which had been so popular and populous in the morning, was now so little envied that a fat lady descended from it and wedged herself into a row of the interior where a sylph would have fitted

W. D. Howells

better but might not have added so much to the warmth. No one, myself of the number, thought of getting up, though there were plenty of straps to hang by if one had chosen to stand. This was quite like home, and so was it like home to have the conductor ask me to Avait for my change, with all the ensuing fears that wronged the long-delayed remembrance of his debt. In some things it appears that at Rome the Romans do as the Americans do, but I wish we were like them in having such a place as Frascati within easy tram-reach of our cities.

XV. A FEW REMAINING MOMENTS

In the days of the earlier sixties, we youth who wished to be
thought elect did not feel ourselves so unless we were deeply
read in Hawthorne's romance of *The Marble Faun*. We made
that our aesthetic handbook in Rome, and we devoutly
looked up all the places mentioned in it, which were
important for being mentioned; though such places as the
Tarpeian Rock, the Forum, the Capitoline Museum, and the
Villa Borghese might secondarily have their historical or
artistic interest. In like manner Story's statue of Cleopatra
was to be seen, because it was the "original" of the imaginary
sculptor Kenyon's Cleopatra, and a certain mediaeval tower
was sacred because it was universally identified as the tower
where the heroine Hilda lived dreaming and drawing, and
fed the doves that circled around its top. We used to show
the new arrivals where Hilda's tower was, and then stand
with them watching the pigeons which made it unmistakable.
I should then have thought I could never forget it, but I must
have passed it several times unnoting in my latest Roman
sojourn, when one afternoon in a pilgrimage to the Via del
Gambero a contemporary of that earlier day glanced around
the narrow piazza through which we were passing and,
seeing a cloud of doves wheeling aloft, joyfully shouted,
"Look! There is Hilda's tower!" and if Hilda herself had
waved to us from its battlements we could not have been
surer of it. The present vanished, and we were restored to our
citizenship in that Rome of the imagination which is greater
than any material Rome, and which it needs no archaeologist
to discover in its indestructible integrity.

No one to-day, probably, visits the Capitoline Museum for
the Faun of Praxiteles because it gave the romance its name;
but at my latest sight of it I remembered it with a thrill of the
young piety which first drew me to it, and involuntarily I

W. D. Howells

looked again for the pointed, furry ears, as I had done of old, to make sure that it was really the Marble Faun of Hawthorne. I was now, however, for no merit of mine, in official and scientific company with which it would have been idle to share my satisfaction in the verification of the Faun's ears. Instead of boasting it, I listened to very interesting talk of the deathless Dying Gladiator, who is held to have been originally looked at more from below than he has been seen in modern times, and who is presently to be lifted to something like his antique level. He, in fact, requires this from the spectator who would feel all his pathos, as we realized in sitting down and looking a little upward at him.

In his room and in the succession of the rooms filled with his immortal bronze and marble companions I was as if with ghosts of people I had known in some anterior life. They were so familiar that I felt no need to go about asking their names, even if the archaeologists had in several cases given them new names. I should have known certain of them by traits which remain in the memory long after names have dropped out of it. Julius Caesar, with his long Celtic upper-lip, still looked like the finer sort of Irish-American politician; Tiberius again surprised me with the sort of racial sanity and beauty surviving in his atrocious personality from his mother's blood; but the too Ne-ronian head of Nero, which seems to have been studied from the wild young miscreant when trying to look the part, had an unremem-bered effect of chubby idiocy. A thing that freshly struck me in the busts of those imperialities, which of course must have been done in their lifetimes, was not merely that the subjects were mostly so ugly and evil but that the artists were apparently safe in showing them so. The men might not have minded that, but how had the sculptors managed to portray the women as they did and live? Perhaps they did not live, or live long; they are a forgotten tribe, and no one can say what became of any given artist after executing the bust of an empress; his own execution may have immediately followed. But what is certain is that those ladies are no lovelier in their looks than they were in their lives; to be sure, in their rank they had not so great need of personal charm as women of the lower class. The most touching face as well as the most dignified and beautiful face among them is that of the seated figure which used to be known as that of Agrippina but which, known now as that of a Roman matron, does not relieve the imperial average of plainness. The rest could rival the average American society woman only in the prevailing modernity of their expression; imperial Rome was very modern, as we all know, and nothing in our own time could be more up to date than the lives and looks of its smart people.

The general impression of the other marbles of the Capitoline Museum remains a composite of standing, sitting, stooping, and leaning figures, of urns and vases, of sarcophaguses and bas-reliefs. If you can be definite about some such delightful presence as that old River dozing over his fountain in the little cold court you see first and last as you come and go, it is more than your reader, if he is as wise as you wish him, can ask of you. I have been wondering whether he could profitably ask of me some record of my experiences in the official and scientific company with which I was honored that day at the Campidoglio; but I should have to offer him again a sort of composite psychograph of objects printed one upon another and hardly separable in their succession. There would be the figure of Marcus Aurelius, commanding us with outstretched arm from the back of the bronze charger which would not obey Michelangelo when he bade it "Go," not because it was not lifelike, but because it was too fat to move. Against the afternoon sky, looking down into the piazza with dreamy unconcern from their vantage would be the statues on the balustrated roof of the museum. There would be the sense, rather than the vision, of the white shoulders of Castor and Pollux beside their steeds above the dark-green garden spaces on either hand; there would be the front of the Church of Ara Coeli visible beyond the insignificance of Rienzi's monument; and filling in the other end of the piazza which Michelangelo imagined, and not the Romans knew, there would be the palace of the senator, to which the mayor and the common council of modern Rome now mount by a double stairway, and presumably meet at the top in proceeding to their municipal labors. Facing the museum would be the palace of the Conservatori, where in the noblest of its splendid halls the present company would find itself in the carved and gilded arm-chairs of the conservators, seated at an afternoon tea-table and restoring itself from the fatigues of more and more antique art in the galleries about. After this there would be the gardened court of the palace, with a thin lawn, and a soft little fountain musing in the midst of it, and the sunset light lifting on the wall where the fragments of Septimius Severus's marble map of Rome order themselves in such coherence as archaeology can suggest for them.

In the palace of the Senator (who was not, as I dare say the reader ignorantly supposes, a residuum of the old Roman senate, but was the dictator whom the mediaeval republic summoned from within or withotit to be its head and its safeguard from the aristocracy) there would be, beyond the chamber where the actual city council of Rome meets under the presidency of the mayor, the great public rooms bannered and memorialled around with heroic and historic blazons; and last there would be the private room where the syndic devotes himself to civic affairs when he can turn from the sight of the Roman Forum, with a peripatetic archaeologist lecturing a group of earnest Americans, while long, velvety shadows of imperial purple stretch from the sunset on the softly rounded and hollowed ruins of the Palatine.

But, if each of these bare facts could be parted from the others and intelligently presented, what would it avail with the reader who has never seen the originals of my psychograph? It is from some such question, and not from want of a hospitable will, that I hesitate to ask him to go with me on a golden morning of March and spend it in the Villa Medici on the Pincian Hill. If I could I should like to pour its yellowness and mellowness round him, perfumed with a potpourri of associations from the time of Lucullus down through every mediaeval and modern time to that very day, when I knew Carolus Duran to be living somewhere in these beauteous bounds as the head of the French Academy which has its home in them. The academic garden-paths, with a few happy people wandering between their correctly balanced passages of box; the blond facade of the casino looking down with its statues and reliefs on these parterres; a young girl vanishing up an aisle of the grove beside the garden into whatever dream awaited her youth in the leafy dusk; an old American pair gazing after her from the terrace, with the void of the vanished years aching in their hearts for the Rome that was once young with them: does this represent to the reader an appreciable morning in the Villa Medici? He may be grateful to me if he does, and if he likes. I cannot do more for him without doing less, and yet I know it is a palette rather than a picture I am giving him.

All the while I was there, the guest of the French nation by the payment of fifty centimes gate-money, I was obscurely resenting its retention of a place which Bonaparte bestowed upon the First Eepublic with so much other loot from Italy. But now I have lately heard that the magnanimous Third Republic is going to restore it to the people rightfully its owners, and the remembrance of my morning in the Villa Medici will remain a pure joy. So few joys in this world, even in the very capital of it, are without some touch of abatement. I could not so much as visit the Catacombs of

Domatilla without suffering a frustration which, though incidental merely, left a lasting pang of unrequited interest. As we drew toward the place, I saw in a field the beginning of one of those domestic dramas which are not attributable to Italy alone. Three peasants, a man and two women, were engaged in controversy which, on his side, the man supported with both hands flapping wildly at the heads of the women, who alertly dodged and circled around him in the endeavor to close in upon him. It was instantly conjecturable, if not apparent, that they were his wife and daughter, and that he was the worse for the vintage of their home acre, and would be the better for being got into the house and into bed. The conjecture enlisted the worthier instincts of the witness on the side of the mother and daughter; but he was in no hurry to have the animated action brought to a close, and was about to tell his cabman to drive very, very slowly, when suddenly the cab descended into a valley, and when the eager spectator rose to his former level again the stone wall had risen with him, and he never knew the end of that passage of real life,

It was impossible to bid the cabman drive back for the close of the scene; the abrupt conclusion must be accepted as final; but it is proof of the charm I found in the gentle guide who presently began to marshal us among the paths of the subterranean sanctuary and cemetery that for the moment my bitter sense of loss was assuaged, and it only returns now at long intervals. Such as the woman actors in this brief scene were some early Christians might have been, and it must have been the stubborn old pagan spirit I saw surviving in the husband and father. He was probably such a vessel of wrath as, being filled with Bacchus, would have lent itself to the persecuting rage of Domitian and helped drive the emperor's gentle cousin Domatilla into the exile whence she returned to found a Christian cemetery in her villa. One understands, of course, under the villa; for the catacombs in some places reach as many as five levels below the surface. I will not follow the reader with that kind guide who will cheer his wanderings through those sunless corridors of death, where many of the sleepers still lie sealed within their tombs on either hand, and show him by the smoky taper's light the frescos which adorn the cramped chapels. I prefer to stand at the top of the entrance and ask him if he noticed how the artist sometimes seemed not to know whether he was pagan or Christian, and did not mind, for instance, putting a Mercury at the heads of the horses in an Ascent of Elijah. Perhaps the artist was really a pagan and thought a Greek god as good as a Hebrew prophet any day; art was probably one of the last things to be converted, having a presentiment of the dark and bloody themes the new religion would give it to deal with.

The earthy scent of the catacomb will cling to the reader's clothes, and he will have two minds about keeping for a souvenir the taper which he carried, and which the guide wraps in a bit of newspaper for him; he may prefer the flower which he is allowed to gather from the tiny garden at the entrance to the catacombs. Yet these Catacombs of Domatilla are among the cheerfulest of all the catacombs, and a sense of something sweet and appealing invests them from the memory of the gentle lady whose piety consecrated them as the last home of the refugees and martyrs. They are of the more recent Roman excavations, but I do not know whether later or earlier than those which have revealed the house of the two Christian gentlemen, John and Paul, of unknown surname, where they suffered death for their faith, under the Passionist church named for them. Twenty-four rooms on the two stories have been opened, and there are others yet to be opened; when all are laid bare they will perfectly show what a Roman city dwelling of the better sort was like in the mid-imperial time. The plan differs from that of the average Pompeian house as much as the plan of a cross-town New York dwelling would differ from that of the average Newport cottage. The rooms are incomparably smaller than those of the mediaeval palaces of the Roman nobles, and the decoration is sometimes crudely mixed of pagan and Christian themes and motives; the artists, like the painters of the Domatilla catacombs, were probably lingering in the old Greek tradition.

The young Passionist father who showed us through the church and the house under it made us wait half an hour while he finished his lunch, but he was worth waiting for. He was a charming enthusiast for both, radiantly yet reverently exulting in their respective treasures, and justly but not haughtily proud of the newly introduced electricity which lighted the darkness of the underground rooms and corridors. He told us he had been twenty years a missionary in Rumania, where he had possibly acquired the delightful English he spoke. When he would have us follow him he said, "All persons come this way," and he politely spoke of the wicked emperor whose bust was somehow there as Mr. Commodus. With all his gentleness, however, that good father had a certain smiling severity before which the spirit bowed. He had made us wait half an hour before he came to let us into the church, and during the hour we were with him there he kept the door locked against an unlucky lady who arrived just too late to enter with us. Not only this, but he utterly refused to go back with her singly and show her the things we had seen. Perhaps it would not have been decorous; they do not let ladies, either singly or plurally, into the garden of the convent, which is memorable among many other facts as being the retreat of Mr. Commodus when he suffered from sleeplessness, and where he once carelessly left his list of victims lying about, so that his friend Marcia found it and, reading her name in it, joined with other friends in his assassination. The sex has indeed had much restraint to bear from the Church, but in some respects it has been rendered fearless in the assertion of its rights. With poor women one of these is the indefeasible right to ask alms, and I admired the courage, almost the ferocity, of the aged crone whom I had promised charity in coming to the place and who rose up as I was being driven past her, in going away, and stayed my cabman with a clamor which he dared not ignore. Her reproaches continued through the ensuing transaction, and followed him away with stings which instinct and experience taught her how to implant in his tenderest sensibilities.

A chapter much longer than any I have written here might well be devoted to the study of the clerical or secular guides in the minor churches of Rome. They are of every manner and degree of kindliness, mixed with a fair measure of intelligence and a very fitting faith in the legends of their churches. You soon get on terms of impersonal intimacy with them, and you cannot come away without sharing their professional zeal, and distinguishing for the moment in favor of their respective churches above every other. It did not matter whether it was that newest church in the Quartiere dei Prati, or that most venerable among the oldest churches, the Church of San Gregorio: I found a reason for agreeing with the sacristan upon its singular claims. These were especially enforced by the good dame, the only woman sacristan I remember, who would not spare us a single object of interest in San Gregorio's, which is indeed for the visitor of Anglo-Saxon race supremely rich in its associations with the conversions of his ancestors from heathenism.

Being myself of Cymric blood, and of a Christianity several hundred years older than that of the ordinary Anglo-Saxon traveller, I am afraid that it was from a rather patronizing piety that I visited the church where the great St. Gregory dismissed to their mission in England St. Augustine and his fellow-apostles on one of the greatest days of the sixth

W. D. Howells

century. I might have stayed to imagine them kneeling among the people who then thronged the genially irregular piazza, but as we came up some ecclesiastical students were playing ball there, their robes tucked into their girdles for their greater convenience, and we made our way at once into the church. It forms one of a consecrated group of edifices enshrining the memory of the best of the popes, who was also the greatest; and here or in the adjacent convents a score of miracles were wrought through the heavenly beauty of his life. Of these miracles, of whose inspiration you must feel the poetry even if you cannot feel their verity, the loveliest has its substantial witness in one of the little chapels next the church. There you may see with your eyes and touch with your hands the table at which St. Gregory fed every morning twelve poor men, till one morning a thirteenth appeared in the figure of Christ the Lord, as if to own them His disciples. The chapel which enshrines the table is one of three, quaint in form and rich in art, standing in the garden called St. Silvia's, after the mother of St. Gregory. As we came out through it the westering sun poured the narrow court before the chapel full of golden light and threw the black shadow of a cypress across the way that a file of Comaldolese monks were taking to the adjoining convent. They were talking cheerily together, and swung unheeding by in their white robes so near that I could almost feel the waft of them across the centuries that parted their faith and mine.

We had come to St. Gregory's from the Baths of Caracalla, which we had set out to see on the first of our Roman holidays, and, after turning aside for the Coloseum, had now visited on next to the last of them. The stupendous ruin could scarcely have been growing in the ten or twelve weeks that had passed, but a bewildering notion of something like this obsessed me as I saw it bulking aloof in overhanging cliffs and precipices, through the cool and bright April air, against a sky of absolute blue. As if it had been cast up out of the earth in some convulsive throe of nature, it floundered over its vast area in shapeless masses which seemed to have capriciously received the effect of human design in the coping of the inaccessible steeps, in the arches flinging themselves across the spaces between the beetling crags, in the monstrous spring and sweep of the vaults, in the gloom of the cavernous apertures of its Titanic walls. For the moment its immensity dwarfed the image of all the other fragments of the Roman world and set definite bounds to their hugeness in the mind. It seemed to have been not so much a single edifice as a whole city, the dwelling instead of the resort of the multitudes that once thronged it. The traces of the ornamentation which had enriched it everywhere and which it had taken ages of ravage to strip from it, accented its savage majesty, and again the sentiment of spring in the fresh afternoon breeze and sunshine, and the innocent beauty of the blooming peach and cherry in the orchards around, imparted to it a pathos in which one's mere brute wonder was lost. But it was a purely adventitious pathos, and it must be owned here, at the end, that none of the relics of ancient Rome stir a soft emotion in the beholder, and, as for beauty, there is more of it in some ivy-netted fragment of some English abbey which Henry's Cromwell "hammered down" than in the ruin of all the palaces and temples and theatres and circuses and baths of that imperial Rome which the world is so well rid of.

VII

A WEEK AT LEGHORN

We left Rome with such a nostalgic pang in our hearts that we tried to find relief in a name for it, and we called ourselves Romesick. Afterward, when we practised the name with such friends as we could get to listen, they thought we said homesick. Being better instructed, they stared or simpered, and said, "Oh!" That was not all we could have asked, but Rome herself would understand, and, while we were seeking this outlet for our grief, she followed us as far as she could on her poor, broken aqueducts. At places they gave way under her, and she fell down, but scrambled up again on the next stretch of arches, like some fond cripple pursuing a friend on crutches; when at last our train outran them, and there was no longer an arch to halt upon, she gave up the vain chase and turned back within her walls, where we saw her domes and bell-towers fading into the heaven to which they pointed.

It was a heaven of better than absolute blue, for there were soft, white clouds in it, and the air that our Sunday breathed under it was, at the beginning of April, as bland as that of an American May-end. The orchard trees were in bloom— peach and plum, cherry and pear—whenever you chose to look at them, and all nature seemed to rejoice in the cessation of the two days' strike which had now enabled us to drive to the station instead of walking and carrying our bags and bundles. There were so many of these that we had taken two cabs, and at the station our drivers attempted to rejoice with nature in an overcharge that would have recouped them for the loss suffered in their recent leisure. But as we were then leaving Rome, and were not yet melted with the grief of absence, I had the courage to resist their demand. Long before we reached Leghorn I was so Romesick that I would have paid them anything they asked.

When we emerged from the suburbs upon the open Campagna, we passed through many fields of wheat, more than we had yet seen on the grassy waste, but there were also many flocks of sheep feeding with the cattle in pastures. Now and then we passed a wretched hut which seemed to be the dwelling of the shepherds we saw tending the flocks, and here and there we came upon a group of farm buildings, all of straw, whether for man or beast, set within a sort of squalid court, with a frowzy suggestion of old women and children about the doors of the cottages. We saw no men, though there must have been men off at work in the fields with the younger women.

As we drew near Civita Vecchia the sea widened on our view, wild with a wind that seemed to have been blowing ever since the stormy evening in 1865 when, after looking at the tossing ships in the harbor, we decided to take the diligence for Leghorn, rather than the little steamer we had meant to take. From our pleasant train we now patronized Civita Vecchia with a recognition of its picturesqueness, unvexed by the choice that then insisted on itself, though the harbor was as full of shipping as of old. There was time to run out for a cup of coffee at the station buffet, where there had been neither station nor buffet in our young time: but doubtless then as now there had been the lonely graveyard

W. D. Howells

outside the town, with its sea-beaten, seaward wall. We buried there the last of our Roman holidays under a sky that had changed from blue to gray since our journey began, and mournfully set out faces northward in the malarial Maremma.

If the Maremma is as malarial as it is famed, it does not look it. There were stretches of hopeless morass, with wide acreages under water, but mostly, I should say, it was rather a hilly country. Now and then we ran by a stony old town on a distant summit like the outcropping of granite or marble, and there were frequent breadths of woodland, oak and pine and, I dare say, walnut and chestnut. Evidently there had been efforts to reclaim the Maremma from its evil air and make it safely habitable, and the farther we penetrated it the more frequent the evidences were. There were many new buildings of a good sort, and of wood as well as stone; when we came to Grosetto, where we had spent a memorable night after being overturned in the Ombrone, in the attempt of our diligence to pass its flood, we were aware, in the evening light, of a prosperity which, if not excessive for the twoscore years that had passed, was still very noticeable. I should not quite say that the brick wall of the city had been scraped and scrubbed, but it looked very neat and new, and there was a pleasant suburb under it where the moat might have been, and people were coming and going who had almost the effect of commuters; at least, they seemed to have come out to their homes by trolley. We resisted an impulse to dismount and go up to the inn in the heart of the town where we had spent that "night of memory and of sighs."

But we searched the horizon round for the point on the highway where our diligence had failed of the track between the telegraph-poles and softly rolled with us in the muddy waters, like an elephant taking a bath, but, so far from finding it, we could not even find the highway. We began to have our doubts of what we had always believed had happened, and remained as snugly as we could in our compartment, where, to tell the truth, we were not very snug. In too fond a reliance on the almanac, the Italian government had cut off the steam which ought to have heated it, and the cold from the hills, on which we saw snow, pierced our rugs and cushions; but, if we had known what we were coming to in Leghorn, we should have thought ourselves very enviable.

I do not know exactly how far it is from the station in Leghorn to the hotel where we had providently engaged rooms with a fire in at least one of them, but I should say at a rough calculation it was a hundred miles as we covered the distance in a one-horse omnibus, through long, straight streets, after ten o'clock at night. The streets and houses were mostly dark, as houses of good habits should be at that hour, but, after passing through a wide, lonely piazza, we struck into a street longer and straighter than the others, and drew up at our hotel door opposite an hilarious cafe, where there seemed a general rejoicing of some sort. We were unable to make out just what sort, or to join in it without knowing, though it lasted well toward morning, and we were up often during the night to see that the fire did not die out of our one porcelain stove and leave us to perish of cold.

In Leghorn the good Baedeker says that all the hotels are good, and this sweeping verdict may be true if taken in the sense that one is as good as another, but they are of the old Italian type which our winter in Rome had taught us to think obsolete; now we found that it was only obsolescent. We had written to bespeak a room with fire in it, and this was well, for the hotel was otherwise heated only by the bodies of its frequenters, who, when filled with Chianti, might emit a sensible warmth; though it was very modern in being lighted with electricity, and having a lift, in which, after a tepid supper, we were carried to our apartment. We had our landlord's company at supper, and had learned from him that the most eminent of American financiers, who shall not otherwise be identified here, was in the habit, when coming to Leghorn, of letting him know that he was bringing a party of friends, and commanding of him a banquet such as he alone knew how to furnish a millionaire of that princely quality. After that we were not so much surprised as grieved to find that our elderly chambermaid had profited by our absence to gather all the coals out of our one stove into two *scaldini,* which were bristling before her where she knelt when we opened the door upon her. She apologized, but still she carried away the coals, and we were left to rekindle the zeal of our stove as best we could. It was not a large stove, and it seemed to feel its inadequacy to the office of taking the chill off that vast, dim room, where it cowered, dark and low upon the floor, with a yearning, upward stretch of its pipe lost in space before it reached the lowermost goddess in the allegory frescoed on the ceiling. If it had been a white porcelain stove, that might have helped, but it was of a gloomy earthen color that imparted no more cheer than warmth.

We rebuilt our fire, after many repeated demands for kindling, which had apparently to be sawed and split in a distant wood-yard before we could get it, and then the long, arctic night set in, unrelieved by the noisy gayeties of the cafe across the way. These burst from time to time the thin film of sleep which formed like a coating of ice over the consciousness, and then one could only get up and put more wood into the despairing stove and more clothes on the beds. Well for us that we had thought to bring all our travelling rugs with us in straps, instead of abandoning them with our other baggage in the station till next day! But, even with these heaping the hotel blankets and comforters, we shivered, and a superannuated odor that had lurked in the recesses of those rooms, to which the sun or wind had never pierced, grew with the growing cold, and haunted the night like something palpable as well as sensible—the materialization of smells dead and buried there long ago. It was wonderful how little way the electric bulb shed its beams in that naughty air; it would not even light the page which at one time was opened in the vain hope that the author would help the benumbing cold to bring torpor if not slumber to the weary brain.

It is really impossible to say where or how we breakfasted, but it was somehow managed, and then search was made by the swiftest conveyance for the hotel which we had heard of outside the city, as helping make Leghorn the watering-place it is for Italians in the summer, and in the winter as being steam-heated and appointed with every modern comfort for the passing or sojourning stranger. It was all that and more, and only for the fear that I should seem to join it in advertising its merits I should like to celebrate it by name. But perhaps it is as well not; if I did, all my readers would swarm upon that hotel, and there would be no room for me, who hope some day to go back there and spend an old age of luxurious leisure. There was not only steam-heat in the public rooms of the ground floor, but there was furnace heat in all the corridors, and there were fireplaces in certain chambers, which also looked out on the sea, to Corsica and Elba and other isles of it, and would be full of sun as soon as the cold rain closed a fortnight's activity. That which diffused a blander atmosphere than steam or radiator, register and hearth, however, was the kind will, the benevolent intelligence, which imagined us, and which would not then let us go. We had become not only agnostic as respected the possibility of warmth in Leghorn, we were open sceptics, aggressive infidels. But the landlord himself followed us from one room to another, lighting fires here and there on the hearth, making us feel the warm air rising from the furnace, calling us to witness by palpation the heat of the radiators,

W. D. Howells

soothing our fears, and coaxing our unfaith. His wife joined him in Italian and his son in English, and, if I do not say that these amiable people were worthy all the prosperity which was not then apparent in their establishment, may I never be comfortably lodged or fed again. Our daily return for what we got was a poor twelve francs each; but fancy a haughty American landlord caressing us with such sweet and reassuring civility for any sum of money! Those gentle people made themselves our friends; there was nothing they would not do, or try to do, for us, in the vast, pink palace where we were never twenty guests together, and mostly eight or ten, with the run of a reading-room where there were the latest papers and periodicals from London and Paris, and with a kitchen whence we were served the best luncheons and dinners we ate in Europe.

The place had the true out-of-season charm. There were two stately dining-rooms besides the one where we dined, and there were pleasant spaces where we had afternoon tea or after-dinner coffee, and from which a magnificent stairway ascended to the upper halls, and a quiet lift waited our orders, with the landlord or his son to take us up; and so lonely and quiet and gentle, with porters and chambermaids speaking beautiful Tuscan, and watchful attendants every-where prophesying and fulfilling our wants. It was a keeping to make the worst believe in their merit, and we were not the worst. Outside, the environment flattered or rewarded us with a garden of laurel and other evergreens, and with flower-beds where the annuals were beginning to show the gardener's designs in their sprouting seeds. Beyond these ample villa bounds a tram-car murmured to and from the well-removed city, and beyond its track lay a line of open-air theatres and variety shows and bathing establishments, as at our own Atlantic City, but here in enduring masonry instead of the provisional wood of our summer architecture.

This festive preparation intimated the watering-place supremacy which Leghorn enjoys in Italy, and which must make our quiet hotel in the season glisten and twitter and flutter with the vivid national life. The preparation includes a delightful drive by the seashore, with groves and gardens, to the city gate and indefinitely beyond it, which we one day followed as far as an old fort, where a little hotel had nestled with every promise of simple comfort. There was a neighboring village of no very exciting interest, and I do not know that the Italian Naval Academy, which we passed on the way, was very exciting, though with its villa grounds it had a pleasing rural effect. Hard by our hotel, in a piazza that seemed to have nothing to do but surround it, was the colossal bust of an Italian admiral, or the like, which had not the impressivenesa of a colossal full-length figure, but which rendered the original with the faithful realism of the Genoese Campo Santo sculpture. In compensation there was, toward the city, near the ship-yards where the great Italian battle-ships are built, the statue of their builder—a man who looked it—standing at large ease, with one hand in his pantaloons pocket, and not apparently conscious of the passer's gaze. Beyond the ship-yard, in which a battle-ship was then receiving the last touches, was a statue for which I could not claim an equal unconsciousness. In fact, it challenged the public attention and even homage as it extended the baton of command and triumphed over the four Moorish or Algerine corsairs who, in their splendid nudity, were chained to the several corners of the monument and owned themselves galley-slaves. The Medicean grand-duke who lords it over them, and who erected this monument in honor of himself for the victories his admirals had gained in sweeping the pirates from the seas, is a very proud presence, and is certainly worthy of the admiration which his bronze requires from the spectator. I instantly suspected this monument of being the chief sculpture of Leghorn, and I did not wonder that a *valet de place* was lying in wait for me there to make

W. D. Howells

me observe that from a certain point I could get all four of the galley-slaves' noses in perspective at once. Upon experiment I did not find that I could do this, but I imputed my failure to want of merit in myself and not the monument, and I willingly paid half a franc for the suggestion; if all one's failures cost so little, one could save money. I was going then to view at close quarters the port of Leghorn, which is famous for its mole and lighthouse and quarantine, the first of their kind in their time. The old port, with the fortifications, was the work of a natural son of Queen Elizabeth's Earl of Leicester, whose noble origin was so constantly recognized by the Tuscan grand-dukes that he came at last to be accepted as Lord Dudley by the English. From his day, if not from his work, the prosperity of Leghorn began, and the English have always had a great part in it. Early in the nineteenth century there were a score of great British merchants settled there, and, though afterward they declined in number, the trade with England did not decline, and the trade with America has always been such that American merchants and captains have fully shared in the commerce directly or indirectly. Both the old and the new port were a scene of pleasant activity the pleasant afternoon when I visited them, and were full of varied sail as well as many steamers, loading or unloading for or from the Mediterranean ports, east and west, and the Hanseatic cities and the far coasts of Norway.

Any seaport is charming and full of romantic interest, but an Italian port has always a prime picturesqueness. Its sailors are the most ancient mariners, and they look full of history, and capable, each of them, of discovering a continent. I cannot say that I saw any nascent Columbus in the tanned and tarry company I met, but I do not deny that there was one. Leghorn is still in her lusty youth, being not much older than our Boston in the prosperity which has not failed her since the Medici divined her importance toward the close of the sixteenth century, and fortified her harbor till she was one of the strongest places on the Mediterranean. With a hazy general consciousness of her modernity in mind, I had imagined her yet more modern, and I was somewhat surprised to read, in a rather airy and ironical but very capable local guidebook called *Su e Giu per Livorno* (or *Up and Down Leghorn),* that the place was settled twenty-six hundred and fifty-six years before Christ. The author records this with a smile, and then, by a leap over some forty centuries, he finds firm footing in the fact that the great Countess Matilde, then much bothering about in the affairs of her Tuscan neighbors everywhere, gave the Livornese coasts to Pisa in 1103. This seems to have been the signal for the Genoese, eleven years later, to ravage and destroy the Pisan settlements; but later the Pisans, confirmed in their possession by the Emperor of Germany, rebuilt and embellished the port. A century after, Charles of Anjou demolished it, and then the Pisans fortified it some more. Then, in the last years of the thirteenth century, the Florentines, Lucchese, and Genoese devastated the whole territory of Pisa, and left Leghorn only one poor little church. Well throughout the fourteenth century there were wars between these republics, and Leghorn suffered the consequences, being, as our author says, "according to custom, assailed, taken, wasted, and destroyed." But before that century was out she seems to have flourished up again, and to have received with all honor Gregory XL, returning from Avignon to Rome and bringing the papacy back from its long exile to the Eternal City.

The Genoese now sold Leghorn to Milan, and in 1407 she was sold to France for twenty-six thousand florins, which seems low for a whole city. But in less than ten years we find the Genoese back again, and strengthening and adorning her at the greatest rate. It was quite time now that she should be visited by a virulent pestilence, and that, having passed to

Florence in the meanwhile, she should have been ceded without a blow to Charles VIII. of France. But in a year she was once more in the hold of Florence and helping that republic fight her enemies the Pisans, and her other enemies under the Emperor Maximilian of Germany.

More fortifying, embellishing, and pestilence followed, and in 1429 Michelangelo came to inspect the new fortifications which the Florentine republic had built at Leghorn to repair the damages she had suffered. The next year the republic fell, and Alessandro de' Medici, who came in master at Florence, took Leghorn into the favor which his family continued to show her to the end. The first Cosimo greatly improved her harbor, dug canals, and built forts, but he let the Spaniards, for a pleasure to Charles V., place garrisons in Florence, Pisa, and Leghorn, and the Spaniards remained six years at Leghorn. In the last year of the sixteenth century Ferdinand erected to himself the superb monument with the four captive corsairs at the corners, whose noses I had failed to get in range, and in the meanwhile many great public works had been constructed and the city desolated by another plague. It was now time for the English to appear in those waters, and in 1652 they were defeated by the Dutch off Leghorn. About seventy-five years later the grippe paid Leghorn a first visit, and not long after a violent earthquake shook down many buildings and killed many women and children; but the authorities did what they could to secure the city in future by declaring the day a perpetual fast, and forbidding masking and dancing on it.

No disaster worth recording befell the city till Bonaparte came with the Rights of Man in 1796 and left a French garrison, which evacuated the place the next year, after having levied a fine of two million francs. The year after that Nelson occupied it with eight thousand English troops, and the following year the French reoccupied it and sacked the churches and imposed another fine nearly as great as the first. After the Napoleonic victories in the Italian wars, they seem to have come back again and fined the city two million francs more. They now remained five years, and in the mean time a Livornese, Giovanni Antonio Giaschi, invented a submarine-boat for attacking and destroying war-vessels, and a Spanish ship brought the yellow-fever. In 1808 Napoleon gave all Tuscany, and Leghorn with it, to his sister Elisa, but when in 1814 he was deposed, Leghorn was restored to the Tuscan grand-dukes and garrisoned for them by German troops, an earthquake having profited by the general disorder meantime to pay it another visit. The grand-duke now being driven out of Florence by Murat, he took refuge at Leghorn, which fell a prey to an epidemic of typhus. The first steam-vessel appared there in 1818, and in 1835 the Asiatic cholera; in 1847 a telegraphic line to Pisa was opened.

In 1848 the revolutions prevalent throughout Europe had their effect at Leghorn. The citizens shared in the uprising against the grand-duke, and elected among its representatives F. D. Guerrazzi, once famous as the first of Italian novelists and a man of generous mind and heart, who duly suffered arrest and imprisonment when the grand-duke was restored by the Austrians. He was sentenced to fifteen years' prison with hard labor, but later his sentence was commuted to exile. He lived to return and take part in the Italian unification in 1860, and in 1866 he led the movement against making peace with Austria unless all her Italian-speaking provinces were ceded to Italy. He died in 1873, and is remembered in Leghorn by a monument very ineffective as a whole, but singularly interesting in certain details.

I have omitted from this catalogue of events many of peaceful interest, such as visits from popes, princes, and poets, and I am not sure I have got in all the plagues and earthquakes. Perhaps I have the more willingly suppressed a

W. D. Howells

few war-like facts, in the interest of the superstition I had cherished that Leghorn was without a history, or that it had no more history than, most American cities of equal date with its commercial importance, which began with the wise hospitality of the Medici to merchants of all races and nations, religions and races, settled there, and especially to the Spanish Jews who came in great numbers to the city that it was a common saying that you had as well strike the duke as strike a Jew in Leghorn. Greeks, Turks, Armenians were protected equally with English and Dutch, and infidel and heretic were alike free in their worship. It was the great prison of the galley-slaves, who were chiefly the pirates and corsairs taken on the high seas by the duke's ships. These captives not only served as models for the Moors at the base of his monument, but they must have been very useful in the different public works which he and his successors carried out. Now they and their like are gone, and though the Greeks, the Armenians, the English, and the Scotch still have their churches, I do not suppose there is a mosque in all Leghorn.

I do not speak very confidently, because my researches in that sort were not exhaustive. I indeed visited the cathedral, not wholly because Inigo Jones had something to do in planning it, but because I had formed the habit of visiting churches in Rome, and I mechanically went into one wherever I saw it. Generally speaking, I think that they were rather bare in painting or sculpture, but they were such churches as in America one would go a long way to see and think one's self well rewarded by their objects of interest. I do not know what defence to offer for not having visited the galleries of the Museo Civico, where by actual count in the guide-book I missed one hundred and sixty-nine works of art, though just how many masterpieces I am not able to say: probably one out of every ten was a masterpiece. But, if I did not much resort to the churches and galleries in Leghorn, I roamed gladly through its pleasant streets and squares, and by the shores of the canals which once gave it the name of New Venice, and which still invite the smaller shipping up among its houses in right Venetian fashion. The streets of Leghorn are not so straight as they are long, but many are very straight, and the others are curved rather than crooked. The longest and straightest were streets of low dwelling-houses, uncommon in Italian towns, where each family lived under its own roof with a little garden behind, and a respective entrance, as people still mostly do in our towns. From the force of the mid-April sun in these streets I realized what they might be in summer, and, if I lived in Leghorn, I would rather live on the sea-front, in one of the comfortable, square, stone villas which border it. But everywhere Leghorn seemed a pleasant place to live, and convenient, with lively shops and cafes and trams and open spaces, and statues and monuments in them. The city, I understood, is of somewhat radical politics, tending from clericalism to socialism; and, like every other Italian city, it is full of patriotic monuments. There is a Victor Emmanuel on horseback, plump and squat, but heroic as always, and a Garibaldi struggling in vain for beauty in his poncho and his round, flat cap; there is a Mazzini, there is a Cavour, and, above all, there is a Guerrazzi, no great thing as to the seated figure, but most interesting, most touching in two of the bas-reliefs below. One represents him proclaiming the provisional government at Florence in 1849, after the expulsion of the grand-duke, where the fact is studied, with the wonderful realism of the Italians, in all its incidents and the costumes of the thronging spectators. The sculptor has hesitated at no top-hat or open umbrella; there are barefooted boys and bareheaded young girls, as well as bearded elders; if my memory serves, the scene is not without a dog or two. But it is the other relief which is so simply and so deeply affecting—the interior of a narrow cell, with one chair and a rude table, at which the patriot novelist wrote his greatest work, *The Siege of*

Florence, and with him standing a little way from it. In spite of the small space and the almost vacant stage, the scene is full of most moving drama, and records a whole Italian epoch, now happily past forever.

These are modern sculptures, and they scarcely contest the palm with the monument of the four galley-slaves and the Medicean grand-duke. In another piazza two princes of the Lorrainese family, if I remember rightly, face each other over its oblong—classic motives, with the figures much undraped, and one of them singularly impressive from the mutton-chop whiskers which modernized him. There are several theatres, and among them a Goldoni theatre, as there should be in a city where the sweet old playwright sojourned for a time and has placed the action of his famous comedy, "La Locandiera." But I was told that the local theatres were not so much frequented by polite people, especially for opera, as the theatre in Pisa, which, if poorer, is prouder in its society than its old-time vassal by the sea, and attracts the fashion of Leghorn during the season.

As Pisa has ceased to be the colony of literary English it once was, in the time of Byron and Hunt and Shelley, to name no others, so Leghorn has ceased to be the mercantile colony of former days. It has still a great deal of commerce with England, but this is no longer carried on by resident merchants, though here and there an English name lingers in the style of a business house; and the distinctive qualities of both colonies are united in the author of a charming book who fills the post of British consul at Leghorn. His *Tuscan Towns* must not be confused with another book called *Tuscan Cities,* though, if the traveller chooses to carry both with him about Tuscany, I will not say that he could do better. In *Tuscan Cities* there is nothing about Leghorn, I believe, but in *Tuscan Towns* there is a specially delightful chapter about the place, its people, language, and customs which I can commend to the reader as the best corrective of the errors I must have been constantly falling into here.

It was in company no less enviable than this author's that I revisited the port on a gray Sunday afternoon of my stay, and then for the first time visited the ancient fortifications which began to be in the time of the Countess Matilde and intermittently increased under the rule of the Pisan, Genoese, and Florentine republics, until the Medicean grand-dukes amplified them in almost the proportions I saw. The brutal first duke of their line, Alessandro de' Medici, who some say was no Medici, but the bastard of a negro and a washerwoman, stamped his creed in the inscription below his adoptive arms, "Under one Faith and one Law, one Lord," and it was in the palace here, the story goes, that the wicked Cosimo I. killed his son Don Garzia before the eyes of the boy's mother. Anything is imaginable of an early Medicean grand-duke, but in a manner the father's murderous fury was provoked by the fact, if it was a fact, that Don Garzia had just mortally wounded his brother Giovanni. I should like to pretend that the tragedy had wrought in my unconsciousness to the effect of the pensive gloom which the old fortress cast over me, but perhaps I had better not. There are some gray Sunday afternoons of a depressing effect on the spirit which requires no positive or palpable reason.

In any case it was a relief to go from the shadow of the past there through the pleasant city streets to the gentle quiet of the British cemetery, where so many of our race and some even of our own nation are taking their long rest. No one is now buried there, and the place, in the gradual diminution of the English colony at Leghorn, has fallen into a lovely and appealing neglect if not oblivion. Oblivion quite covers its origin, but it is almost as old as Protestantism itself, and, if the ground for it was the gift of the grand-duke who tolerated heretics as well as Jews in the impulse he gave to the city's growth, it would not be strange. The beautiful porch of the English church, for once Greek and not Gothic, fronts upon it, but the dwindling congregation has no care of it, and there is no fund to keep it so much as free from weeds and brambles and the insidious ivy rending its monuments asunder. The afternoon of our visit it was in the sole charge of a large, gray cat, which, after feasting upon the favorite herb, lay stretched in sleep on a sunny bed of catnip under the walls of a mansion near, at whose windows some young girls looked down in a Sunday listlessness, as we wandered about among the "tall cypresses, myrtles, pines, eucalyptus-trees, oleanders, cactuses, huge bushes of monthly roses, a jungle of periwinkles, sarsaparilla, wild irises, violets, and other loveliest of wild flowers." On the forgotten tombs were the touching epitaphs of those who had died in exile, and whose monuments are sometimes here while their ashes lie in Florence or Rome, or wherever else they chanced to meet their end. Among them were the inscriptions on the graves of "William Magee Seton, merchant of New York," who died at Pisa in 1803, and "Henry De Butts, a citizen of Baltimore, N. America," who died at Sarzana; with "James M. Knight, Esq., Captain of Marines, Citizen of the United States of America," who died at Leghorn in 1802; and "Thomas Gamble, Late Captain in the Navy of the United States of America," who died at Pisa in 1818; and doubtless there were other Americans whose tombs I did not see. The memorials of the English were likewise here, whether they died at Leghorn or not; but most of them seem to have ended their lives in that place, where there were once so many English residents, whether for their health or their profit. The youth of some testified to the fact that they had failed to find the air specific for their maladies, and doubtless this would account also for the disproportionate number of noble ladies who rest here, with their hatchments and their coronets and robes of state carven on the stones above them. Among others one reads the titles of "Lady Catharine Burgess born

Beauclerk; Jane Isabella, widow of the Earl of Lanesborough and daughter of the Earl of Molesworth; and Catharine Murray, only child of James Murray, . . . and the Right Honorable Lady Catharine Stewart his Spouse," with knights, admirals, generals, and other military and naval officers a many. Most important of all is the tomb of that strenuous spirit, more potent for good and ill in the English fiction of his time than any other novelist of his time, and second only to Richardson in the wide influence of his literary method, Tobias Smollett, namely, who here ended his long fight with consumption and the indifference of his country to his claims upon her official recognition. After many years of narrow circumstance in the Southern climates where he spent his later life, he tried in vain for that meek hope of literary ambition, a consulate, perhaps the very post that my companion, a hundred and fifty years later, was worthily holding. The truest monument to his stay in Italy is the book of Italian travel that he wrote, and the best effect is that sort of peripatetic novel which he may be said to have invented in *Humphrey Clinker,* and which has survived the epistolary form into our own time. It is a very simple shaft that rises over his grave, with the brief record, "Memoriae Tobiae Smollett, qui Liburni animam efflavit, 16 Sept., 1773," but it is imaginable with what wrath he would have disputed the record, if it is true, according to all the other authorities, that he exhaled his spirit two years earlier, and how he would have had it out with those "friends and fellow-countrymen" who had the error perpetuated above his helpless dust.

It was not easy to quit the sweetly solemn place or to resist the wish which I have here indulged, that some kinsman or kinswoman of those whom the blossoms and leaves are hiding would come to their rescue from nature now cleiming an undue part in them, and obliterating their very memories. One would not have a great deal done, but only enough to save their names from entire oblivion, and with the hope of this I have named some of their names. It might not be too much even for the United Kingdom and the United States, though both very poor nations, to join in contributing the sum necessary for the work. Or some millionaire English duke, or some millionaire American manufacturer, might make the outlay alone; I cannot expect any millionaire author to provide a special fund for the care of the tomb of Smollett.

VIII

OVER AT PISA

If the half-hour between Leghorn and Pisa had been spent in any less lovely transit, I should still be grieving for the loss of the thirty minutes which might so much better have been given to either place. But with the constant line of mountains enclosing the landscape on the right, in all its variety of tillage, pasture-land, vineyard, and orchard, and the unchanging level which had once been the bed of the sea, we were gainers in sort beyond the gift of those cities. We had the company, great part of the way, of more stone-pines than we had seen even between Naples and Rome, here gathering into thick woods, with the light beautiful beneath the spread of their horizontal boughs, there grouped in classic groves, and yonder straying off in twos and threes. We had the canal that of old time made Pisa a port of the Mediterranean, with Leghorn for her servant on the shore (or, if it was not this canal, it was another as straight and long), with a peasant walking beside it, under a light-green umbrella, in the showers which threatened our start but spared our arrival. We had then the city, with its domes and towers, grown full height out of the plain through which the Arno curves in the stateliest crescent of all its course.

The day had turned finer than any other day I can now think

W. D. Howells

of in my whole life, and I was once more in Pisa without the care for its history or art or even novelty which had corroded my mind in former visits. I had been there twice before— once in 1864, when I had done its wonders with all the wonder they merited, and again in 1883, when I had lived its memories on the scene of its manifold and mighty experiences. No distinct light from that learning vexed my present vision, but an agreeable mist of association, nothing certain, nothing tangible remaining, but only a gentle vague involving everything, in which I could possess my soul in peace. In this glimmer I recognized a certain cabman as having been waiting there from the dawn of time, with his dark-eyed little son, to make me his willing captive at something above the tariff rates, but destined by the same fate to serve me well, and to part with me friends at the close of the day for a franc more than the excess agreed upon. It costs so small a sum to corrupt the common carrier in Italy that I hold it wrong to fail of any chance, and this driver had not only a horse of uncommon qualities, but he spoke a beautiful Tuscan, and he had his Pisa at his fingers' ends.

We were of one mind about driving without delay to the famous group which is without rival on the earth, though there may be associated edifices in the red planet Mars that surpass the Cathedral, the Leaning Tower, the Baptistery, and the Campo Santo at Pisa. What genius it was imagined placing them in the pleasant meadow where they sit, just beyond the city streets, I do not know, but it was inspiration beyond any effect of mere taste, and it commanded my worship as much the last as the first time. The meadow still swims round them and breaks in a foam of daisies at their feet; for I take it that it is always mid-April there, and that the grass is as green and the sun as yellow on it as the afternoon we saw it. The sacred edifices are as golden as the light on them, and there is such a joyous lift in the air that it is a wonder they do not swing loose from their foundations and soar away into the celestial blue. For travellers in our willing mood there was, of course, the predestined cicerone waiting for us at the door of the cathedral, who would fix no price for the pleasure he was born to do us, yet still consented to take more than twice that he ought to have had at parting. But he was worth the money; he was worth quite two francs, and, though he was not without the fault of his calling and would have cumbered us with instruction, I will not blame him, for after a moment I perceived that his intelligence was such that I might safely put my hands in my pocket on my shut guide-book and follow him from point to point without fear of missing anything worth noting. Among the things worthiest noting, I saw, as if I had never seen them before, the unforgettable, forgotten Andrea del Sartos, especially the St. Agnes, in whose face you recognize the well-known features of the painter's wife, but with a gentler look than they usually wore in his Madonnas, perhaps because he happened to study these from that difficult lady when she was in her least celestial moods. Besides the masterpieces of other masters, there is a most noble Sodoma, which the great Napoleon carried away to Paris and which the greater French people afterward restored. At every step in the beautiful temple you may well pause, for it abounds in pictures and sculptures, the least of which would enrich St. Peter's at Rome beyond the proudest effect of its poverty-stricken grandeur. Ghirlandajo, Michelangelo, Gaddo Gaddi, John of Bologna—the names came back to me out of a past of my own almost as remote as theirs, while our guide repeated them, in their relation to the sculptures or pictures or architecture, with those of lesser lights of art, and that school of Giotto, of all whose frescos once covering its walls the fire of three hundred years ago has left a few figures clinging to one of the pillars, faint and uncertain as the memories of my own former visits to the church. I did, indeed, remember me of an old bronze lamp, by Vincenzo Possenti, hanging from the roof, which I now revered the

W. D. Howells

third time, at intervals of twenty years; from its oscillation Galileo is said to have got the notion of the pendulum; but it is now tied back with a wire, being no longer needed for such an inspiration. Mostly in this last visit I took Pisa as lightly as at the first, when, as I have noted from the printed witness, I was gayly indifferent to the claims of her objects of interest. If they came in my way, I looked at them, but I did not put myself much about for them. I rested mostly in the twilight of old associations, trusting to the guidance of our cicerone, whom, in some form or under some name, the reader will find waiting for him at the cathedral door as we did. But I have since recurred to the record of my second visit in 1883, with amazement at the exact knowledge of events shown there, which became, in 1908, all a blur of dim conjecture. It appears that I was then acquainted with much more Pisan history than any other author I have found own to. I had also surprising adventures of different kinds, such as my poorer experience of the present cannot parallel. I find, for instance, that in 1883 I gave a needy crone in the cathedral a franc instead of the piece of five centimes which I meant for her, and that the lamp of Galileo did nothing to light the gloom into which this error plunged my spirit.

It appears to have jaundiced my view of the whole cathedral, which I did not find at all comparable to that of Siena, whereas in 1908 I thought it all beautiful. This may have been because I was so newly from the ugliness of the Eoman churches; though I felt, as I had felt before, that the whole group of sacred edifices at Pisa was too suggestive of decorative pastry and confectionery. No more than at the second view of it did I now attempt the ascent of the Leaning Tower; I had discharged this duty for life when I first saw it; with my seventy-one years upon me, I was not willing to climb its winding stairs, and I doubted if I could keep it from falling, as I then did, by inclining myself the other way. I resolved that I would leave this to the new-comer; but I gladly followed our cicerone across the daisied green from the cathedral to the baptistery, where I found the famous echo waiting to welcome me back, and greet me with its angelic sweetness, when the custodian who has it in charge appealed to it; though its voice seemed to have been weakened and coarsened in its forced replies to some rude Americans there, who shouted out to it and mocked at it. One wished to ask them if they did not know that this echo was sacred, and that their challenges of it were a species of sacrilege. But doubtless that would not have availed to silence them. By-and-by they went away, and then we were aware of an interesting group of people by the font near the lovely Lombardic pulpit of Nicola Pisano. They were peasants, by their dress—a young father and mother and a little girl or two, and then a gentle, elderly woman, with a baby in her arms, at which she looked proudly down. They were in their simple best, and they had good Tuscan faces, full of kindness. I ventured some propitiatory coppers with the children, and, when the old woman made them thank me, I thought I could not be mistaken and I ventured further: "You are the grandmother?"

"Yes, signer," she answered; and then we had some talk about the age and the beauty of the baby, which I declared wonderful for both, in praises loud enough for the father and mother to hear. After that they seemed to hold a family council, from which I thought it respectful to stand apart until the grandmother spoke to me again.

I did not understand, and I appealed to our guide for help.

"She wishes you to be godfather to the child."

I had never yet been a godfather, but I had the belief that it brought grave responsibilities, which in the very casual and impermanent circumstances I did not see how I was to meet.

W. D. Howells

Yet how to refuse without wounding these kind people who had so honored me I did not know until a sudden inspiration came to my rescue.

"Tell them," I said, "and be careful to make them understand, that I am very grateful and very sorry, but that I am a Protestant, and that I suppose I cannot, for that reason, be godfather to their child."

He explained, and they received my thanks and regrets with smiling acquiescence; and just then a very stout little old priest (who has baptized nearly all the babies in Pisa for fifty years) came in, and the baptism proceeded without my intervention. But I remained, somehow, disappointed; it would have been pleasant to leave a godchild behind me there in the neighborhood of Pisa; to have sent him from time to time some little remembrance of this remote America, and, perhaps, when he grew up and came to Pisa, and learned the art of the statuary, to have had from him a Leaning Tower which he had cut in alabaster for me. I was taking it for granted he was a boy, but he may not have been; there is always that chance.

If I had been alone, I suppose I should still have gone into the Campo Santo, from mere force of habit; I always go, in Pisa, but I had now with me clearer eyes for art than mine are, and I wished to have their light on the great allegories and histories frescoed round the cloisters, and test with them the objects of my tacit and explicit reserves and misgivings. I needed such eyes, and even some such powerful glasses as would have pierced through the faded and wasted pictures and shown them at least as I had first seen them. They were then in such reasonable disrepair as one might expect after three or four centuries, but in the last thirty years a ruinous waste has set in before which not only the colors have faded, but the surfaces have crumbled under the colors; and as yet no man knows how to stop the ravage. I think I have read that it is caused by a germ; but, if not, the loss is the same, and until a parasite for the germ is found the loss must go on, and the work of Giotto, of Benozzo Gozzoli, of Memmi, must perish with that of the Orgagnas, which may indeed go, for all me. Bible stories, miracles, allegories—they are all hasting to decay, and it can be but a few years until they shall vanish like the splendors of the dawn which they typify in art.

In some things the ruin is not altogether to be regretted. It has softened certain loathsome details of the charnel facts portrayed, and in other pictures the torment and anguish of the lost souls are no longer so painful as the old painters ascertained them. Hell in the Campo Santo is not now the hell of other days, just as the hell of Christian doctrine is not the hell it used to be. Death and the world are indeed immitigable; the corpses in their coffins are as terrifying to the gay lords and ladies who come suddenly upon them as ever they were, though doubtless of no more lasting effect with such sinners than they would be nowadays. But what one must chiefly lament is the waste of the whole quaint and charming series of Scripture incidents by Benozzo Gozzoli. This is indeed most lamentable, and after realizing the loss one is only a little heartened by the gayety of certain grieving widows, sitting in marble for monuments to their husbands at several points under the arcades. What cheer they might have brought us was impaired by the sight of the sarcophaguses and the other antiques against the walls, which inflicted an inappeasable ache for the city where such things abound, and brought our refluent Romesickness back full tide upon us. More than once Pisa elsewhere did us the like involuntary unkindness; she, too, is yellow and mellow like Rome, and she had moments of the Piazza Navona and the Piazza di Spagna which were poignant. But she had moments of her own when Rome could not rival her—such, for instance, as

W. D. Howells

that when she invited us from the perishing frescos of her Campo Santo to turn our eyes on the flower-strewn field of death which the cloisters surrounded, and where in the hallowed earth which her galleys brought from Jerusalem her children, in their several turns, used to sleep so sweetly and safely.

The afternoon sunlight was prolonging the day there as well as it could, and we should have liked to linger with it as late as it would, but there were other places in Pisa calling us, and we must go. We found our driver, and his black-eyed boy beside him on the box, waiting for us at the cathedral door, and we seem to have left it pretty much to them where we should go. They decided us, if we really left it to them, mainly for the outside of things, so that we might see as much of Pisa as possible; but it appears to have been their notion that we ought to visit, at least, the inside of the Church of the Knights of St. Stephen. I do not know whether I protested or not that I had abundantly seen this already, but, at any rate, I am now glad that they took us there. As every traveller will pretend to remember, the main business of the knights was to fight the Barbary pirates, and the main business of their church is now to serve as a repository of the prows of the galleys and the flags which they took in their battles with the infidels. There are other monuments of their valor, but by all odds the flags will be the most interesting to the American visitor, because of the start that many of them will give him by their resemblance to our own banner, with their red-and-white stripes, which the eye follows in vivid expectation of finding the blue field of stars in the upper left-hand corner. It never does find this, and that is the sufficient reason for holding to the theory that our flag was copied from the armorial bearings of the Washington family, and not taken from the standard of those paynim corsairs; but there is poignant instant when one trembles.

We viewed, of course, the exterior of the edifice standing on the site of the Tower of Famine, where the cruel archbishop starved the Count Ugolino and his grandchildren to death; and we drove by the buildings of Pisa's famous university, which we afterward fancied rather pervaded the city with the young and ardent life of its students. It is no great architectural presence, but there are churches and palaces to make up for that. Everywhere you chance on them in the narrow streets and the ample piazzas, but the palaces follow mostly the stately curve of the Arno, where some of them have condescended to the office of hotels, and where, I believe, one might live in economy and comfort; or, at any rate, I should like to try. It would get rather warm there in May, and July and August are not to be thought of, but all the other year it would be divine, with such a prospect as can hardly be matched anywhere else. Pisa used once to be the resort of many seeking health or warmth, and for mere climate it ought again to come into favor. Probably there is reasonably accessible society there, and, as the Livornese believe, there is at least excellent opera. The time might grow long, but ought not to be very heavy, and there is a cafe, at the very finest point of the curve, where you can get an excellent cup of tea. Whether this attests the resort or sojourn of many English, or the growth of the tea-habit among the Pisans, I cannot say, but that cafe is very charming, with students standing about in it and admiring the ladies who come in to buy pastry, and who do not suppose there is any one there to look at them. I am sure that the handsome mother with the pretty daughter who lingered so long over their choice of little cakes could not have imagined any one was looking, or she would at once have taken macaroons and hurried away: at that cafe they have macaroons almost three inches across, and delicious.

The whole keeping was so pleasant that we hated to leave it to the lengthening shadows from the other shore, but we were to drive down the Arno into the promenade that follows it, I do not know how far; with the foolish greed of travel, we wanted to get in all of Pisa that we could, even if we tore ourselves from its most tempting morsel. But it was all joy, and I should like, at this moment, to be starting on that enchanting drive again. I leave the reader to imagine the lovely scenery for himself; almost any of my many backgrounds will serve; but I will supply him with a piece of statistics such as does not fall in everybody's way. We noted the great number of anglers who lined the opposite bank, with no appearance of catching anything, and I asked our driver if they never happened to get a bite. "Not in the daytime," he explained, compassionately, "but as soon as the evening comes they get all the fish they want."

I could pour out on the reader many other Pisan statistics, but they would be at second-hand. After long vicissitude, the city is again almost as prosperous as she was in the heyday of her national greatness, when she had commerce with every Levantine and Oriental port. We ourselves saw a silk factory pouring forth a tide of pretty girls from their work at the end of the day; there was no ruin or disrepair noticeable anywhere, and the whole city was as clean as Rome, with streets paved with broad, smooth flagstones where you never missed the rubber tires which your carriage failed of. But Pisa had a great air of resting, of taking life easily after a tumultuous existence in the long past which she had put behind her. Throughout the Middle Ages she was always fighting foreign foes without her walls or domestic factions within, now the Saracens wherever she could find them or they could find her, now the Normans in Naples, now the Corsicans and Sardinians, now Lucca, now Genoa, now Florence, and now all three. Her wars with these republics were really incessant; they were not so much wars as battles in one long war, with a peace occasionally made during the five or ten or fifteen years, which was no better than a truce.

When she fell under the Medici, together with her enemy Florence, she shared the death-quiet the tyrants brought that prepotent republic, and it was the Medicean strength probably which saved her from Lucca and Genoa, though it left them to continue republics down to the nineteenth century. She was at one time an oligarchy, and at another a democracy, and at another the liege of this prince or that priest, but she was never out of trouble as long as she possessed independence or the shadow of it. In the safe hold of united Italy she now sits by her Arno and draws long, deep breaths, which you may almost hear as you pass; and I hope the prospect of increasing prosperity will not tempt her to work too hard. It does not look as if it would.

We were getting a little anxious, but not very anxious, for that one cannot be in Pisa, about our train back to Leghorn; though we did not wish to go, we did not wish to be left; but our driver reassured us, and would not let us shirk the duty of seeing the house where Galileo was born. We found it in a long street on the thither side of the river, and in such a poor quarter that our driver could himself afford to live only a few doors from it. As if they had expected him to pass about this time, his wife and his five children were sitting at his door and playing before it. He proudly pointed them out with his whip, and one of the little ones followed on foot far enough to levy tribute. They were sufficiently comely children, but blond, whereas the boy on the box was both black-eyed and black-haired. When we required an explanation of the mystery, the father easily solved it; this boy was the child of his first wife. If there were other details, I have forgotten them, but we made our romance to the effect that the boy, to whose beautiful eyes we now imputed a lurking sadness, was not happy with his step-mother, and that he took refuge from her on the box with his father. They seemed very good comrades; the boy had shared with his father the small cakes we had given him at the cafe. At the station, in recognition of

W. D. Howells

his hapless lot, I gave him half a franc. By that time his father was radiant from the small extortion I had suffered him to practice with me, and he bade the boy thank me, which he did so charmingly that I almost, but not quite, gave him another half-franc. Now I am sorry I did not. Pisa was worth it.

IX

BACK AT GENOA

There is an old saying, probably as old as Genoa's first loot of her step-sister republic, "If you want to see Pisa, you must go to Genoa," which may have obscurely governed us in our purpose of stopping there on our way up out of Italy. We could not have too much of Pisa, as apparently the Genoese could not; but before our journey ended I decided that they would have thought twice before plundering Pisa if they had been forced to make their forays by means of the present railroad connection between the two cities. At least there would have been but one of the many wars of murder and rapine between the republics, and that would have been the first. After a single experience of the eighty tunnels on that line, with the perpetually recurring necessity of putting down and putting up the car-window, no army would have repeated the invasion; and, though we might now be without that satirical old saying, mankind would, on the whole, have been the gainer. As it was, the enemies could luxuriously go and come in their galleys and enjoy the fresh sea-breezes both ways, instead of stifling in the dark and gasping for breath as they came into the light, while their train ran in and out under the serried peaks that form the Mediterranean shore. I myself wished to take a galley from Leghorn, or even a small steamer, but I was overruled by less hardy but more obdurate spirits, and so we took the Florentine express at Pisa, where we changed cars.

The Italian government had providently arranged that the car we changed into should be standing beyond the station in the dash of an unexpected shower, and that it should be provided with steps so high and steep, with Italian ladies standing all over them and sticking their umbrellas into the faces of American citizens trying to get in after them, that it was a feat of something like mountain-climbing to reach the corridor, and then of daring-do to secure a compartment. Though a collectivist, with a firm belief in the government ownership of railroads everywhere, I might have been tempted at times in Italy to abjure my creed if I had not always reflected that the state there had just come into possession of the roads, with all their capitalistic faults of management and outwear of equipment which it would doubtless soon reform and repair. I venture to suggest now, however, that its prime duty is to have platforms level with the car-doors, as they are in England, and not to let Italian ladies stand in the doorways with their umbrellas. I do not insist that it shall impose silence and sobriety upon a party of young French people in the next compartment, but I do think it should remove those mountains back from the sea so that the trains carrying cultivated Americans can run along the open shore the whole way to Genoa. Pending this, it should provide strong and watchful employees to lower and raise the windows at the mouth of each of the eighty tunnels in every car. I do not demand that it shall change the site of the station in Genoa so that it shall not always be the city's whole length away from the hotel you have chosen, but I think this would be a desirable improvement, especially if it is after dark when you arrive and raining a peculiarly cold, disagreeable rain.

That rain was very disappointing; for, in the intervals

between tunnels, we had fancied, from the few brief glimpses we caught of the landscape, that the April so backward elsewhere in Italy was forwarder in the blossomed trees along the eastern Riviera; and we learned at our hotel that the steam-heat had just been taken off because the day had been so hot and dry, though the evening was now so cold and wet. It was fitfully put on and off during the chilly week that ensued, though in our fifth-story garden, to which we sometimes resorted, there was a mildness in the air that was absent in-doors. The hotel itself was disappointing; any hotel would be after our hotel in Leghorn; and, though there was the good-will of former days, there was not the former effect. The corridors crashed and clattered all day long and well into the night with the gayety of some cheap incursion of German tourists, who seemed, indeed, to fill the whole city with their clamor. They were given a long table to themselves, and when they were set at it and began to ply their knives and tongues the din was deafening. That would not have been so bad if they had not been so plain, or if, when they happened, in a young girl or two, to be pretty, they had not guttled and guzzled so like the plainest of their number. One such pretty girl was really beautiful, with a bloom perhaps already too rich, which, as she abandoned herself to her meat and drink, reddened downward over her lily neck and upward to her golden hair, past the brows under which her blue, blue eyes protruded painfully, all in a frightful prophecy of what she would be when the bud of her spring should be the full-blown cabbage-rose of her summer.

I dare say those people were not typical of their civilization. Probably modern enterprise makes travel easy to sorts and conditions of Germans who once would not have dreamed of leaving home, and now tempts these rude Teutonic hordes over or under the Alps and pours them out on the Peninsula, far out-deluging the once-prevalent Anglo-Saxons. The first night there was an Englishman at dinner, but he vanished after breakfast; the next day an Italian officer was at lunch, but he came no more; we were the only Americans, and now we had the sole society of those German tourists. Perhaps it was national vanity, but I could not at the moment think of an equal number of our fellow-citizens of any condition who would not have been less molestively happy. One forgot what one was eating, and left the table bruised as if physically beaten upon by those sound-waves and sight-waves. But our companions must have made themselves acceptable to the city they had come to visit; Genoa is very noisy, and they could not be heard above the trams and omnibuses, and in the streets they could not be seen at table; when I ventured to note to a sacristan, here and there, that there seemed to be a great many Germans in town, the fact apparently roused nothing of the old-time Italian antipathy for the Tedeschi. Severally they may have been cultivated and interesting people; and that blooming maiden may really have been the Blue Flower of Romance that she looked before she began to dine.

We were entering upon our third view of Genoa with the zest of our first, and I was glad to find there were so many things I had left unseen or had forgotten. First of all the Campo Santo allured me, and I went at once to verify the impressions of former years in a tram following the bed of a torrential river which was now dry except in the pools where the laundresses were at work, picturesquely as always in Italy. But here they were not alone the worthy theme of art; their husbands and fathers, and perhaps even their *fiances,* were at work with them, not, indeed, washing the linen, but spreading to dry it in snowy spaces over the clean gravel. On either bank of the stream newly finished or partly finished apartment-houses testified to the prosperity of the city, which seemed to be growing everywhere, and it would not be too bold to imagine this a favorite quarter because of its convenience to the Campo Santo. Already in the early forenoon our train was carrying people to that popular resort, who seemed to be intending to spend the day there. Some had wreaths and flowers, and were clearly sorrowing friends of the dead; others, with their guide-books, were as plainly mere sight-seers, and these were Italians as well as strangers, gratifying what seems the universal passion for cemeteries. In our own villages the graveyards are the favorite Sunday haunt of the young people and the scene of their love-making; and it has been the complaint of English visitors to our cities that the first thing their hosts took them to see was the cemetery. They did not realize that this was often the thing best worth showing them, for our feeble aesthetic instincts found their first expression in the attempt to dignify or beautify the homes of the dead. Each mourner grieved in marble as fitly as he knew how, and, if there was sometimes a rivalry in vaults and shafts, the effect was of a collective interest which all could feel. Sometimes it was touching, sometimes it was revolting; and in Italy it is not otherwise. The Campo Santo of San Miniato at Florence, the Campo Santo at Bologna, the Campo Santo wherever else you find it, you find of one quality with the Campo Santo at Genoa. It makes you the helpless confidant of family pride, of bruised and lacerated love, of fond aspiration, of religious longing, of striving faith, of foolish vanity and vulgar pretence, but, if the traveller would read the local civilization aright, he cannot do better than go to study it there.

My third experience of the Genoese Campo Santo was different only in quantity from the first and second. There seemed more of the things, better and worse, but the increasing witness was of the art which rendered the fact with unsparing realism, sometimes alloyed with allegory and sometimes not, but always outright, literal, strong, rank. The hundreds of groups, reliefs, statues, busts; the long aisles where the dead are sealed in the tableted shelves of the wall, like the dead in the catacombs, the ample space of open ground enclosed by the cloisters and set thick with white crosses, are all dominated by a colossal Christ which, in my fancy, remains of very significant effect. It is as if no presence less mighty and impressive could centre in itself the multitudinous passions, wills, and hopes expressed in those incongruous monuments and reduce them to that unity of meaning which one cannot deny them.

The Campo Santo of Genoa is a mortuary gloss of Genoese history: of the long succession of civic strifes and foreign wars common to all the Italian republics, now pacified at last by a spirit of unity, of brotherhood. At Genoa, more than anywhere else in Italy except Milan, you are aware of the North—its strenuousness, its enterprise, its restless outstretching for worlds beyond itself. Columbus came with the gift of a New World in his hand, and, in the fulness of time, Mazzini came with the gift of a Newer World in his hand: the realization of Christ in the ideal of duties without which the old ideal of rights is heathen and helpless. Against the rude force of Genoa, the aristocratic beauty of such a place as Pisa was nothing; only Florence and Venice might vie with her. But she had not the inspiration of Florence, her art, her literature; the dialect in which she uttered herself is harsh and crabbed, and no poet known beyond it has breathed his soul into it; her architecture was first the Gothic from over the Alps, and then of the Renaissance which built the palaces of her merchants in a giant bulk and of a brutal grandeur. She had not the political genius of Venice, the oligarchic instinct of self-preservation from popular misgovernment and princely aggression. Her story is the usual Italian story of a people jealous of each other, and, in their fear of a native tyrant, impatiently calling in one foreign tyrant after another and then furiously expelling him. When she would govern herself, she first made her elective chief magistrate Doge for life, and then for two years; under both forms she submitted and rebelled at will from 1359 till 1802, when, after having accepted the French notion of freedom from Bonaparte, she enjoyed a lion's share of his vicissitudes. For a hundred years before that the warring powers had fought over her in their various quarrels about successions, and she ought to have been well inured to suffering when, in 1800, the English and the Austrians besieged her French garrison, and twenty thousand of her people starved in a cause not their own. The English restored the Doges, and the Republic of Genoa fell at last nineteen years after the Republic of Venice and three hundred years after the Republic of Florence. She was given to Piedmont in 1815 by the Congress of Vienna, and she has formed part of Italy ever since the unification. I believe that now she is of rather radical opinions in politics, though the bookseller who found on his shelves a last copy of the interesting sketch of Genoese history which I have profited by so little, said that the Genoese had been disappointed in the Socialists, lately in power, and were now voting Clerical by a large majority.

The fact may have been colored by the book-seller's feelings. If the Clericals are in superior force, the clerics are not: nowhere in Italy did I see so few priests. All other orders of people throng the narrow, noisy, lofty streets, where the crash of feet and hoofs and wheels beats to the topmost stories of the palaces towering overhead in their stony grandiosity. Everywhere in the structures dating after the Gothic period there is want of sensibility; the art of the Renaissance was not moulded here in the moods of a refined and effeminate patriciate, such as in Venice tempered it to beauty; but it renders in marble the prepotence of a commercialized nobility, and makes good in that form the right of the city to be called Genoa the Proud. Perhaps she would not wish to be called proud because of these palaces alone. It is imaginable that she would like the stranger to remember the magnificence with which she rewarded the patriotism of her greatest citizen after Columbus and

Mazzini: that mighty admiral, Andrea Doria, who freed this country first from the rule of Charles V. and then from the rule of Francis I.; who swept the Barbary corsairs from the seas; who beat the Turks in battles on ship and on shore; who took Corsica from the French when he was eighty-eight years old; who suffered from civil faction; who outlived exile as he had outlived war, and who died at the age of ninety-four, after he had refused the sovereignty of the country he had served so long; who was the Washington of his day, and was equally statesman and soldier, and, above all, patriot. It is his portrait that you see in that old palace (called the Palace of the Prince because Charles V. had called him Prince) overlooking the port, where he sits an old, old man, very weary, in the sole society of his sarcastic cat, as I have noted before. The cat seems to have just passed some ironical reflection on the vanity of human things and to be studying him for the effect. Both appear indifferent to the spectator, but perhaps they are not, and you must not for all that fail of a visit to the Church of San Matteo, set round with the palaces of the Doria family—the palace which his grateful country gave the Admiral after he refused to be her master, and the palaces of his kindred neighboring it round.

I do not remember any equal space in all Europe which, through a very little knowledge, so takes the heart as the gentle little church founded by an earlier Doria, and, after four hundred years, restored by a later, and then environed with the stately homes of the race, where they could be domesticated in the honor and reverence of their countrymen because of the goodness and greatness of the loftiest of their line. It is such a place as one may revere and yet possess one's soul in self-respect, very much as one may revere Mount Vernon. The church, as well as the piazza, is full of Dorian memories, and the cloister must be visited not only for its rather damp beauty, but for the full meaning of the irony which Doria's cat in the portrait wished to convey:

against the wall here are gathered the fragments of the statue of Doria which, when the French Revolution came to Genoa, the patriots threw out of the ducal palace and broke in the street below.

We were some time in finding our way into the magnificent hall of the Great Council where this statue once stood, with the statues of many other Genoese heroes and statesmen, and I am not sure that it was worth all our trouble. Magnificent it certainly was, but coarsely magnificent, like so much elsewhere in Genoa; but, if we had been at ten times the trouble we were in seeing the Palace of the Municipality, I should not think it too much. There in the great hall are the monuments of those Genoese notables whose munificence their country wished to remember in the order of their generosity. I do not remember just what the maximum was, but the Doge or other leading citizen who gave, say, twenty-five thousand ducats to the state had a statue erected to him; one who gave fifteen, a bust; and one who gave five, an honorary tablet. The surprising thing is that nearly all the statues and busts, whether good likenesses or not, are delightful art: it is as if the noble acts of the benefactors of their country had inspired the sculptors to reproduce them not only in true character, but in due dignity. To the American who views them and remembers that we have now so much money that some of us do not know what to do with it, they will suggest that our millionaires have an unrivalled opportunity of immortality in the same sort. There is hardly a town of ten thousand inhabitants in the country where there are not men who could easily afford to give a hundred thousand dollars, or fifty, or twenty to their native or adoptive place and so enter upon a new life in bronze or marble. This would enrich us beyond the dreams of avarice in a high-grade portrait statuary; it would give work to hundreds of sculptors who now have little or nothing to do, and would revive or create the supplementary industries of casting in metal or carving in stone.

The time was in Genoa, it seems, as the time is now with us, when a great many people did not know what to do with their money. There were sumptuary laws which forbade their spending it, either they or their wives or daughters, in dress; apparently they could not even wear Genoa velvet, which had to be sold abroad for the corruption of the outside world; and this is said to be the reason why there were so many palaces built in Genoa in the days of the republic. People who did not wish to figure in that hall of fame put their surplus into the immense and often ugly edifices which we still see ministering to their pride in the wide and narrow streets of the city. Now and then a devout family built or rebuilt a church and gave it to the public; but by far the greater number put up palaces, where, after the house-warming, they dwelt in a cold and economical seclusion. Some of their palaces are now devoted to public uses; they are galleries of pictures and statues most worthy to be seen, or they are municipal offices, or museums, or schools of art or science; but part are still in the keeping of the families that contributed them to the splendor of their city. The streets in which they stand are loud with transit and traffic, but the palaces hold aloof from the turmoil and lift their lofty heads to the level of the gardens behind them. Huge, heavy they are, according to the local ideal, and always wanting the delicacy of Venetian architecture, where something in the native genius tempered to gentleness the cold severity of Palladio, and where Sansovino knew how to bridge the gulf between the Gothic and the Renascent art that would have been Greek but halted at being Roman.

The grandeur of those streets of palaces in Genoa cannot be denied, but perhaps, if the visitor quite consulted his preference or indulged his humor, he would wander rather through the arcades of the busy port, up the chasmal alleys of little shops into the tiny piazzas, no bigger than a good-sized room, opening before some ancient church and packed with busy, noisy people. The perspective there is often like the perspective in old Naples, but the uproar in Genoa does not break in music as it does in Naples, and the chill lingering in the sunless depths of those chasms is the cold of a winter that begins earlier and a spring that loiters later than the genial seasons of the South.

X

EDEN AFTER THE FALL

A few years ago an Englishman who had lived our neighbor in the same villa at San Remo, came and said that he was going away because it was so dull at San Remo. He was going with his wife to Monte Carlo, because you could find amusement every day in the week at the tables of the different games of chance, and Sundays there was a very nice little English church. He did not seem to think there was anything out of the way in his grouping of these advantages, but he did not strongly urge them upon us, and we restricted ourselves in turn to our tacit reflections on the indifference of the English to a point of morals on which the American conscience is apt to suffer more or less anguish if it offends. So far as I know they do not think it wrong to take money won at any game; but possibly their depravity in this matter rather comforted us than offended. At any rate, I am sure of the superiority of our own morals in visiting Monte Carlo after we left Genoa. If we did not look forward with our Englishman's complacency to the nice little church there, we certainly did not mean to risk our money at the tables of Roulette, nor yet at the tables of Trente et Quarante, in the Casino. What we really wished to do was to look on in the spiritual security of saints while the sinners of both sexes lost and gained to the equal hurt of their souls. We perhaps expected to hear the report of a pistol in the gardens of the Casino, if we did not actually see the ruined gambler falling among the flowers, or if not so much as this, we thought we might witness his dramatic despair as the croupier drew in the last remnant of his fortune and mechanically invited the other Messieurs and Mesdames to make their game; secretly, we might even have been willing to see something hysterical on the part of the Mesdames if fate frowned upon them, or something scandalously exuberant if it smiled. If our motives were not the worst, they were, at any rate, not the best; I suppose they were the usual human motives, and I am afraid they were mixed.

We found it rather long from Genoa to Monte Carlo, but this was not so much because of the distance as because of the delays of our train, which, having started late, grew reckless on the way, and before we reached the Italian frontier at Ventimiglia, had lost all shame and failed to connect there with the French train for the rest of our journey. So, instead of having barely time to affirm our innocence of tobacco, spirits, or perfumes to the customs officers, and to wash down a sandwich with a cup of coffee at the restaurant, we had an hour and forty minutes at Ventimiglia, which I partly spent in vain attempts to buy the poverty of the inspector so far as to prevail with him not to delay the examination of our baggage, but to proceed to it at once, in order that we might have it all off our minds, and devote our long leisure to the inquiry by what steps the ancient Ligurian tribe of the Intemelii lost their name in its actual corruption of Ventimiglia. It is a charming old town, far more charming than the stranger who never has time to walk into it from the station can imagine, and there is a palm-bordered avenue leading from the railway to the sea, with the shops and cafes of Italy on one side and the shops and cafes of France on the other. So late as six o'clock in the evening those cafes and shops preserved a reciprocal integrity which I could not praise too highly, but after dark there must be a ghostly interchange of forbidden commodities among them which no force of customs officers could wholly suppress. At any rate, I should have liked to see them try it, though I should not have liked to be kept in Ventimiglia overnight for any less reason; it seemed a lonesome place, though mighty picturesque, with old walls, and a magnificent old fort toward the sea, and a fine bridge spanning, though for the moment superfluously spanning, the perfectly dry bed of a river.

I wished to ask what the name of the river was, but out of all the files of people coming and going I chose an aged man who could not tell me; he excused himself with real regret on the ground that he was a stranger in those parts. Then there was nothing for me to do but go back to the station and renew my attempt on the inspector, who still remained proof against me. What added to the hardship of the situation was that it was Italy at one end of the station and France at the other, and in one extremity it was an hour earlier than it was at the other, by the time of Central Europe at the east and by the time of Paris at the west, so that I do not know but we were two hours and forty minutes at Ventimiglia instead of one hour and forty minutes. Of this period little could be employed at tea, and we were not otherwise hungry; we could give something of our interminable leisure to counting our baggage and suffering unfounded alarms at failing to make it come out right, but we could not give much.

The weather had turned chilly, the long station was full of draughts, and the invalid of the party, without whom no American party is perfectly national, was rapidly taking cold. We were quite incredulous when the examination actually began, but at last it really did, and it began with our pieces, with such a show of favoring us on the inspector's part, that when it was over, in about two minutes, one trunk serving as a type of the innocence of all, I furtively held up a piece of five francs in recognition of his kindness. But he slowly shook his head, whether in regret or whether in stern refusal I shall never know. He was an Italian, but in the employment of the French republic, and I have not been able since to credit with certainty his incorruptibility to his native or his adoptive country; I might easily be mistaken in deciding either way.

What I am certain of, and certainly sorry for, is the superiority of the French company's railway carriage, from Ventimiglia on, to the Italian carriage which had brought us so far, and it is still with unwillingness that I own the corporation's greater care for our comfort. If we had been in the paternal care of the administration of the gambling-house. at Monte Carlo, we could not have been more tenderly or cleanly cushioned about, or borne away on softer springs; and very possibly a measure of wickedness in the means is a condition of comfort in the end to which we are so tempted to abandon ourselves in a world which is not yet so sternly collectivist as I could wish. It was not quite dark when we arrived at Monte Carlo and began to experience, in the beautiful keeping of the place, how admirably a gambling-house can manage the affairs of a principality when it pays all the taxes. There were many two-horse landaus waiting our pleasure outside the station, and the horses were all so robust and handsome that we were not put to our usual painful endeavor in seeking the best and getting the worst. All those stately equipages were good, and the one that fell to us mounted the hill to our hotel by a grade so insinuating that the balkiest horse in Frascati could hardly have suspected it.

In our easy ascent we were aware of the gray-and-blond houses behind their walls among their groves and gardens, among flowers and blossoms; of the varying inclines and levels from which some lovely difference of prospect appeared at every step; of the admirably tended roadways, and the walks that followed them up hill and down, and crossed to little parks, or led to streets brilliant with shops and hotels, clustering about the great gambling-house, the centre of the common prosperity and animation. The air had softened with the setting sun, and the weather which had at Leghorn and Genoa delayed through two weeks of rain and cold, seemed to confess the control of the Casino administration, as everything else does at Monte Carlo, and promised an amiability to which we eargerly trusted.

It was of course warmer out-doors than in-doors, and while the fire was kindling on our hearth we gave the quarter hour before dinner to looking over our garden-wall into the comely town in the valley below, and to the palace and capital of the Prince of Monaco on the heights beyond. Nothing by day or by night could be more exquisite than the little harbor, a perfect horseshoe in shape, and now, at our first sight of it, set round with electric lights, like diamonds in the scarf-pin of some sporty Titan, or perhaps of Hercules Monoecus himself, who is said to have founded Monaco. In the morning we saw that the waters arranged themselves in the rainbow colors of such a scarf round the shores, and that there were only pleasure-craft moored in them: the yacht of the Prince of Monaco and the yacht of some American Prince, whose title I did not ascertain, but whose flag was unmistakable. There must have been other yachts, but I do not remember them, and possibly there were some workaday craft, of which I do not now recall the impression; but I am certain of the festive air of disoccupation pervading the port from the adjacent towns, both Monte Carlo and Monaco, which its wicked suburb has cleansed in corrupting, and rendered attractive by the example of its elegant leisure. There remains from both places, and from Condamine in the plain between them the sense of a perpetual round of holidays. There seemed to be no more creative business in one place than another, but I do not say there is none; there is certainly a polite distillery of perfumes and liqueurs in Condamine, but what one sees is the commerce of the shops, and the building up of more and more villas and hotels, on every shelf and ledge, to harden and whiten in the sun, and let their gardens hang over the verges of the cliffs. On the northeast, the mountains rise into magnificent steeps whose names would say nothing to the reader, except that of Turbia, which he will recall as the classic Tropaea of Augustus, who marked there the bounds between Italy and Gaul. But we were as yet in no mood to climb this height, even with the help of a funicular railway, and I made my explorations at such convenient elevations as I could reach on foot, or by the help of one of those luxurious landaus peculiar to Monte Carlo.

One such point was undoubtedly the headland of Monaco, where the Greeks of Marseilles, long enough before Augustus, built a temple to Hercules Monoecus. The Grimaldi family which gave Genoa many doges, came early into the sovereignty of Monaco, by the hook or crook those days, but whether it was they who fostered its piracy in the fourteenth century, does not distinctly appear, though it seems certain that one of the Grimaldi princes served against the English under Philip of Valois, and was wounded at Crecy. In 1524 a successor went over to the empire under Charles V. Still later the principality returned to the sovereignty of France, and in 1793 the French republicans frankly annexed it, but it was given back to the Grimaldi in 1814.

The Grimaldi on the whole were a baddish line of potentates, and only lacked largeness of scene to have left the memory of world-tragedies. They murdered one another, at least in two cases; in another, the people killed their ruler by publicly drowning him in the sea for insulting their women; the princes were the protectors of piracy, and in the very late times following their restoration by the Congress of Vienna, the reigning prince confiscated the property of the churches for his own behoof, and took into his hands the whole trade of the principality. He alone bought and ground the grain, and baked the bread, which he sold to his people at an extortionate price; he bought damaged flour in Genoa and fed it to his subjects at the same rate as good. When they murmured and threatened rebellion, he threatened in turn that he would rule them with a rod of iron, as if their actual conditions were not bad enough. Some of his oppressions were of a fantasticality bordering on comic opera: travellers had to give up their provisions at the frontier and eat the official bread of Monaco; ships entering the port were confiscated if they had brought more loaves than sufficed them for their voyage thither; no man might cut his own wood without leave of the police, or prune his trees, or till his land, or irrigate it; the birth and death of every animal must be publicly registered, with the payment of a given tax, and nobody could go out after ten at night without carrying a taxed lantern. When Nice was annexed to France in 1860 Monaco passed under French protection again, and now it is subject to conscription like the rest of France. Ten years after the beginning of this new order of things the great M. Blanc was expelled from Hombourg, and the Prince of Monaco rented to him the-gambling privilege of Monte Carlo.

Then the modern splendor of the place began. The entire population of the three towns, Monaco, Monte Carlo, and Condamine, is not above fifteen thousand, and apparently the greater part of the inhabitants depend upon the gay industry of the Casino for their livelihood. I should say that the most of the houses in Monte Carlo were hotels, or pensions, or furnished villas, or furnished apartments, and if one could be content to live in the atmosphere of the Casino, which is not meteorologically lurid, I do not know where one could live in greater comfort. It is said that everything is rather dearer than in Nice, for instance, but such things as I wanted to buy I did not find very dear. The rates at the most expensive hotels did not seem exhorbitant when reduced to dollars, and if you went a little way from the Casino the hotels were very reasonable, so that you could spend a great deal of money at the tables which in America you would spend in board and lodging. I fancy that a villa could be got there very reasonably, and as the morals of all the inhabitants are scrupulously cared for by the administration of the Casino, and no one living in the principality is allowed to frequent the gaming-tables, it is probable that domestic service is good and cheap. If I may speak from our experience at our very simple little hotel, it is admirable, one waiter sufficing for ten or twelve guests, with leisure for much friendly conversation in the office, between the breakfasts served in our rooms and the excellent dinners at the small tables in the salon. If you liked, he would speak French or Italian, though he spoke English as well as any one, and he was of that excellent Piedmontese race which has been the saving salt of the whole peninsula. As for the food, it was far beyond that of our cold-storage, and it must have been cheap, since it was provided for us at the rate we paid.

The cost of dress varies, according to the taste of and the purse, everywhere. White serge seemed the favorite wear of most of the ladies one saw in the street at Monte Carlo, especially in the region of the Casino. This may have expressed an inner condition, or it may have been a sympathetic response to the advances of the flowers in the pretty beds and parterres so fancifully designed by the gardeners of the administration, or it may have been a token of the helpless submission to which the windows of the milliners and modistes reduced all comers of the dressful sex. Many of the men with the women, or without them, were also in white serge, but they seemed more variably attired; there was a prevailing suggestion of yachting or automobiling in their dress, though doubtless most of them had not sailed or motored to the spot. Some few, say four or five, may have motored away from it, for in the centre of the charming square before the Casino there was an automobile of some newest type being raffled for in the interest of that chiefest of the Christian virtues which makes its most successful appeals in the vicinity of games of chance. Some one must have won the machine and carried a party of his friends away, and triumphantly turned turtle with it over the first of the precipices which abound at Monte Carlo. More than the tables within this opportunity of fortune tempted me, and it was only by the repeated recurrence to my principles that I was able to get away alive. In spite of myself, I did not get away without, however guiltlessly, having yielded to the spirit of the place. It was at the Administrational Art Exhibition, where there were really some good pictures, and where, on my entering, I was given a small brass disk. On going out I attempted to restore this to the door-keeper, but he went back with me to a certain piece of mechanism, where he instructed me to put the disk into a slot. Then the disk ran its course, and a small brass ball came out at the bottom. The door-keeper opened this, and showed me that it was empty; but he gave me to understand that it might have been full of diamonds, or rubies, or seed-pearls, which might have implanted in me a lust of gambling I should never have overcome. Monte Carlo was in every way tempting. A vast oblong, brilliant with flowers in artistic patterns, stretched upward from the Casino, and there was an agreeable park where one might sit. On every other side there were costly hotels and costly restaurants, including that of the unexampled, the insurpassable Giro, where one saw people eating and drinking at the windows whenever one passed, by day or night. Beyond the Casino seaward were the beautiful terraces, planted with palms and other tropic growths, where people might come out and kill themselves when they had nothing left to lose but their lives; and against the dark green of their fronds the temple of fortune lifted a frosted-cake-like front of long extent. I do not know just what type of architecture it is of, but it distinctly suggests the art of the pastry cook when he has triumphed in some edifice crowning the centre of the table at a great public dinner. What mars the pleasing effect most is a detail which enforces this suggestion, for the region of the Casino is thickly frequented by a species of black doves, and when these gather in close lines of black dots along the eaves, they have exactly the effect of flies clustering on the sugary surfaces of the cake. At intervals are bronze statues of what seem a sort of adolescent cherubs, but which have, I do not know why, a peculiarly devilish appearance. No doubt they are harmless enough; but certainly they do nothing to keep the flies off the cake.

In fine, as an edifice the Casino disappoints, and if one is not pressingly curious about the interior, one rather lingers on the terrace overlooking the sea, and the lines of the railroad following the shore, and the panorama of the several towns. It is charming to sit there, and if it is in the afternoon, you may see an artist there painting water-colors of the scenery. Even if he were not painting, you could not help knowing him for an artist, because he wears a black velvet jacket and knickerbockers, and a soft slouch hat, and has a curled black mustache and pointed beard; there is no mistaking him; and at a given moment, after he has been working long enough, he puts above his sketch the sign, "For Sale," as artists always do, and then, if you want a masterpiece, you go down a few steps from where you are sitting and buy it. But I never did that any more than I took tickets for the charity automobile, though there is no telling what I might not have done if I had broken the bank when at last I went into the Casino.

It seems to open about eleven o'clock in the morning, for gamblers are hard-working, impatient people, and do not want to lose time. A broad stretch of red carpet is laid down the steps from the portal and they begin to go in at once, and people keep going in until I know not what hour at night. But I think mid-afternoon is the best hour to see them, and it is then that I will invite the reader to accompany me, instructing him to turn to the left on entering, and get his gratis billet of admission to the rooms from the polite officials there in charge, who will ask for his card, and inquire his country and city, but will not insist upon his street and his number in it. This form is apparently to make sure that you are not a resident of the principality, and that if you suffer in your morals from your visit to the Casino you shall not be a source of local corruption thereafter. They bow you away, first audibly pronouncing your name with polyglottic accuracy, and then you are free to wander where you like. But probably you will want to go at once from the large, nobly colonnaded reception-hall or atrium, into that series of salons where wickeder visitors than yourself are already closely seated at the oblong tables, and standing one or two deep round them. The salons of the series are four, and the tables in each are from two to five, according to the demands of the season; some are Trente et Quarante-tables, and some, by far the greater number, are Roulette-tables. Roulette seems the simpler game, and the more popular; I formed the notion that there was a sort of aristocratic quality in Trente et Quarante, and that the players of that game were of higher rank and longer purse, but I can allege no reason justifying my notion. All that I can say is that the tables devoted to it commanded the seaward views, and the tops of the gardens where the players withdrew when they wished to commit suicide. The rooms are decorated by several French painters of note, and the whole interior is designed by the famous architect Gamier, to as little effect of beauty as could well be. It is as if these French artists had worked in the German taste, rather than their own, and in any case they have achieved in their several allegories and impersonations something uniformly heavy and dull. One might fancy that the mood of the players at the tables had imparted itself to the figures in the panels, but very likely this is not so, for the players had apparently parted with none of their unpleasing dulness. They were in about equal number men and women, and they partook equally of a look of hard repression. The repression may not have been wholly from within; a little away from each table hovered, with an air of detachment, certain plain and quiet men, who, for all their apparent inattention, may have been agents of the Administration vigilant to subdue the slightest show of drama in the players. I myself saw no drama, unless I may call so the attitude of a certain tall, handsome young man, who stood at the corner of one of the tables, and, with nervously working jaws, staked his money at each invitation of the croupiers. I did not know whether he won or lost, and I could not decide from their faces which of the other men or women were winning or losing. I had supposed that I might see distinguished faces, distinguished figures, but I saw none. The players were of the average of the spectators in dress and carriage, but in the heavy atmosphere of the rooms, which was very hot and very bad, they all alike looked dull. At a psychological moment it suddenly came to me in their presence, that if there was such a place as hell, it must be very dull, like that, and that the finest misery of perdition must be the stupid dulness of it. For some unascertained reason, but probably from a mistaken purpose of ornament, there hung over the centre of each table, almost down to the level of the players' heads, lengths of large-linked chains, and it was imaginable, though not very probable, that if any of the lost souls rose violently up, or made an unseemly outcry, or other rebellious demonstration, those plain, quiet men, the agents of the Administration, would fling themselves upon him or her, and bind them with those chains, and cast them into such outer

W. D. Howells

darkness as could be symbolized by the shade of the terrace trees. The thing was improbable, as I say, but not impossible, if there is truth in Swedenborg's relation that the hells are vigilantly policed, and from time to time put in order by angels detailed for that office. To be sure the plain, quiet men did not look like angels, and the Administration of which they were agents, could not, except in its love of order, be likened to any celestial authority.

Commonly in the afternoon there is music in the great atrium from which the gambling-rooms open, and then there is a pleasant movement of people up and down. They are kept in motion perhaps by their preference, somewhat, but also largely by the want of seats. If you can secure one of these you may amuse yourself very well by looking on at the fashion and beauty of those who have not secured any. Here you will see much more distinction than in the gambling-rooms; the air is better, and if you choose to fancy this the limbo of that inferno, it will not be by a violent strain. In the crowd will be many pretty young girls, in proper chaperonage, and dressed in the latest effects of Paris; if they happen to be wearing the mob-cap hats of the moment it is your greater gain; they could not be so charming in anything else, or look more innocent, or more consciously innocent. You could only hope, however, such were the malign associations of the place, that their chaperons would not neglect them for the gaming-tables beyond, but you could not be sure, if the chaperons were all like that old English lady one evening at the opera in the Casino, who came in charge of her niece, or possibly some friend's daughter. She remained dutifully enough beside the girl through the first act of the stupid musical comedy, and even through the ensuing ballet, and when a flaunting female, in a hat of cart-wheel circumference, came in and shut out the whole stage from the hapless stranger behind, this good old lady authorized her charge to ask him to take the seat next them where he could see something of the action if he wished. But at the end of the ballet, she rose, and bidding the girl wait her return, she vanished in the direction of the gaming-rooms. She may merely have gone to look on at a spectacle which, dulness for dulness, was no worse than that of the musical comedy, and I have no proof that she risked her money there. The girl sat through the next act, and then in a sudden fine alarm, like that of a bird which, from no visible cause, starts from its perch, she took flight, and I hope she found her aunt, or her mother's friend, quietly sleeping on one of those seats in the atrium. It was one of those tacit, eventless dramas which in travel are always offering themselves to your witness. They begin in silence, and go quietly on to their unfinish, and leave you steeped in an interest which is life-long, whereas a story whose end you know soon perishes from your mind. Art has not yet learned the supreme lesson of life, which is never a tale that is told within the knowledge of the living.

Nowhere, I think, is the "sweet security of streets" felt more than in Monte Carlo. Whether the control of that good Administration of the Casino reaches to the policing of the place in other respects or not, I cannot say, but one walks home at night from the theatre of the Casino with the same sense of safety that one enjoys under that paternal roof. At eleven o'clock all Monte Carlo sleeps the sleep of the innocent and the just in the dwellings of the citizens and permanent residents; though it cannot be denied that there appear to be late suppers in the hotels and restaurants surrounding the Casino, which the iniquitous may be giving to the guilty. Away from the flare of their bold lights the town reposes in a demi-dark, and presents to the more strenuous fancy the effect of a mezzotint study of itself; by day it is a group of wash-drawings near to, and farther off, of water-colors, very richly and broadly treated. I could not insist too much upon this notion with the reader who has never been there, or has not received picture postal-cards from sojourning correspondents. These would afford him a portrait of the chief features and characteristics of the place not too highly flattered, for in fact it would be impossible for even a picture postal-card to exaggerate its beauty. They will besides convey one of the few convincing proofs that in spite of the Blanc Casino and the French Republic the Prince of Monaco is still a reigning sovereign, for the postage-stamps bear the tastefully printed head of that potentate. If the visitor requires other proofs he may take a landau at the station in Monaco, and drive up over the heights of the capital into the piazza before the prince's palace. When the prince is not at home he can readily get leave to visit the palace for twenty minutes, but on my unlucky day the prince was doubly at home, for he was sick as well as in residence. I satisfied myself as well as I could, and I am very easy to satisfy, with my drive through the pleasant town, which is entirely Italian in effect, with its people standing about or looking out of their windows in their Sunday leisure, and quite Roman in the cleanliness of its streets. I took due pleasure in the unfinished exterior of the Oceanographic Museum and the newly finished interior of the Monaco Cathedral. The cathedral, which is so new as to make one rejoice that most other cathedrals are old, is of a glaring freshness, but is very handsome; somehow in spite of its newness it contains the tombs of the reigning family, and perhaps it has only been newly done over. The museum which is ultimately to be the greatest of its kind in the world, already contains somewhere in its raw inaccessible recesses the collections made by Prince Albert in his many cruises, and is of a palatiality worthy of a sovereign with a tenant so generous and prompt in its rent as the Administration of the Casino of Monte Carlo.

This fact, namely, that the princely grandeur and splendor of Monaco all came out of the gaming-tables, was something that the driver of my landau made me observe, when our intimacy had mounted with our road, and we paused for the magnificent view of the sea from the headland near the museum. He was otherwise a shrewd and conversible Piedmontese who did not make me pay much above the tariff, and who had pity on my poor French after awhile, and consented to speak Italian with me. In the sort of French glare over the whole local civilization of the principality, everybody will wish to seem Erench, but after you break through the surface, the natives will be as comfortably and endearingly Italian as anybody in the peninsula. Among themselves they speak a Ligurian patois, but with the stranger they will use an Italian easily much better than his, and also much better than their own French. I think they prefer you in their racial parlance after you have shown some knowledge of it, and two kind women of whom I asked my way in Monte Carlo, one day when I was trying for the station of the funicular to Turbia, grew more volubly kind when I asked it in such Tuscan as I could command. That station is really not hard to find when once you know where it is, and at three o'clock in the afternoon I was mounting the precipitous incline of the alp on whose summit Augustus divided Italy from Gaul, and left the stupendous trophy which one sees there in ruins to-day.

I should like to render the sense of my upward progress dramatic by pretending that we mounted from a zone of flowers at Monte Carlo into regions where only the hardiest blossoms greeted us, but what I really noticed was that by-and-by the little patches of vineyard seemed to grow less and the olive-trees scraggier. Perhaps even this was partly fancy; as for the flowers, I cannot bring myself to partake of their deceit; for they are the most shameless fakers, as regards climate, in nature. It is, for instance, perfectly true that they are in bloom along the Riviera all winter long, but this does not prove that the winter of the Riviera is always warm. It merely proves that flowers can stand a degree of cold that nips the nose bent to hale their perfume, and brings tears into the eyes dwelling in rapture on their loveliness. They are like women; they look so fragile and delicate that you think they cannot stand anything, but they can stand pretty much everything, or at least everything they wish to. Throughout that week at Monte Carlo, while we cowered round our fires or went out into a frigid sunshine, the flowers smiled from every garden-ground in a gayety emulous of that of their sisters passing in white serge. So probably I gave less attention to the details of the scenery through which my funicular was passing than to the stupendous prospects of sea and shore which it varyingly commanded. If words could paint these I should not spare the words, but when I recall them, my richest treasure of adjectives seems a beggarly array of color tubes, flattened and twisted past all collapsibility. Nothing less than an old-fashioned panoramic show would impart any notion of it, and even that must fail where it should most abound, namely, in the delicacy of that ineffable majesty.

We climbed and climbed, with many a muted hope and many a muted fear of the mechanism which carried us so safely, and then we ran across a stretch of comparative level and reached the last station, under the cliff on which the local hotel stood, with the mighty ruin behind it. Our passengers flocked up to the terrace of the hotel, much shoved and shouldered by automobiles bearing the company which seems proper to those vehicles, and dispersed themselves at the many little tables set about for tea, and the glory of the matchless outlook. While one could yet have the ruin mostly to one's self, it seemed the most favorable moment to visit the crumbling walls and broken tower, whose fragments strewed the slopes around. The tower was of Augustus, and the fortress into which it was turned in the Middle Ages was of unknown authority, but the ruin was the work of Marshal

Villars, who blew up both trophy and stronghold sometime in the French king's wars with the imperialists in the first half of the eighteenth century. The destruction was incomplete, though probably sufficient for the purpose, but as a ruin, nothing could be more admirable. There seems to be at present something like a restoration going on; it has not gone very far, however; it has developed some fragments of majestic pillars, and some breadths of Roman brick-work; a few spaces about the base of the tower are cleared; but the rehabilitation will probably never proceed to such an extreme that you may not sit down on some carven remnant of the past, and closing your eyes to the surrounding glory of alp and sea find yourself again on the Palatine or amid the memorials of the Forum.

W. D. Howells

ABOUT THE AUTHOR

 **William Dean Howells** (March 1, 1837 May 11, 1920) was an American realist author and literary critic.

Born in Martins Ferry, Ohio, originally Martinsville, to William Cooper and Mary Dean Howells, Howells was the second of eight children. His father was a newspaper editor and printer, and the father moved frequently around Ohio. Howells began to help his father with typesetting and printing work at an early age. In 1852, his father arranged to have one of Howells' poems published in the Ohio State Journal without telling him.

He wrote his first novel, The Wedding Journey, in 1872, but his literary reputation took off with the realist novel, A Modern Instance, published in 1882, which described the decay of a marriage. His 1885 novel The Rise of Silas Lapham is perhaps his best known, describing the rise and fall of an American entrepreneur in the paint business. His social views were also strongly reflected in the novels Annie Kilburn (1888) and A Hazard of New Fortunes (1890). He was particularly outraged by the trials resulting from the Haymarket Riot.

In 1904, he was one of the first seven chosen for membership in the American Academy of Arts and Letters, of which he became president.

Choose from Thousands of 1stWorldLibrary Classics By

A. M. Barnard
Ada Leverson
Adolphus William Ward
Aesop
Agatha Christie
Alexander Aaronsohn
Alexander Kielland
Alexandre Dumas
Alfred Gatty
Alfred Ollivant
Alice Duer Miller
Alice Turner Curtis
Alice Dunbar
Allen Chapman
Alleyne Ireland
Ambrose Bierce
Amelia E. Barr
Amory H. Bradford
Andrew Lang
Andrew McFarland Davis
Andy Adams
Angela Brazil
Anna Alice Chapin
Anna Sewell
Annie Besant
Annie Hamilton Donnell
Annie Payson Call
Annie Roe Carr
Annonaymous
Anton Chekhov
Archibald Lee Fletcher
Arnold Bennett
Arthur C. Benson
Arthur Conan Doyle
Arthur M. Winfield
Arthur Ransome
Arthur Schnitzler
Arthur Train
Atticus
B.H. Baden-Powell
B. M. Bower
B. C. Chatterjee
Baroness Emmuska Orczy
Baroness Orczy
Basil King
Bayard Taylor
Ben Macomber
Bertha Muzzy Bower
Bjornstjerne Bjornson

Booth Tarkington
Boyd Cable
Bram Stoker
C. Collodi
C. E. Orr
C. M. Ingleby
Carolyn Wells
Catherine Parr Traill
Charles A. Eastman
Charles Amory Beach
Charles Dickens
Charles Dudley Warner
Charles Farrar Browne
Charles Ives
Charles Kingsley
Charles Klein
Charles Hanson Towne
Charles Lathrop Pack
Charles Romyn Dake
Charles Whibley
Charles Willing Beale
Charlotte M. Braeme
Charlotte M. Yonge
Charlotte Perkins Stetson
Clair W. Hayes
Clarence Day Jr.
Clarence E. Mulford
Clemence Housman
Confucius
Coningsby Dawson
Cornelis DeWitt Wilcox
Cyril Burleigh
D. H. Lawrence
Daniel Defoe
David Garnett
Dinah Craik
Don Carlos Janes
Donald Keyhoe
Dorothy Kilner
Dougan Clark
Douglas Fairbanks
E. Nesbit
E. P. Roe
E. Phillips Oppenheim
E. S. Brooks
Earl Barnes
Edgar Rice Burroughs
Edith Van Dyne
Edith Wharton

Edward Everett Hale
Edward J. O'Biren
Edward S. Ellis
Edwin L. Arnold
Eleanor Atkins
Eleanor Hallowell Abbott
Eliot Gregory
Elizabeth Gaskell
Elizabeth McCracken
Elizabeth Von Arnim
Ellem Key
Emerson Hough
Emilie F. Carlen
Emily Bronte
Emily Dickinson
Enid Bagnold
Enilor Macartney Lane
Erasmus W. Jones
Ernie Howard Pie
Ethel May Dell
Ethel Turner
Ethel Watts Mumford
Eugene Sue
Eugenie Foa
Eugene Wood
Eustace Hale Ball
Evelyn Everett-green
Everard Cotes
F. H. Cheley
F. J. Cross
F. Marion Crawford
Fannie E. Newberry
Federick Austin Ogg
Ferdinand Ossendowski
Fergus Hume
Florence A. Kilpatrick
Fremont B. Deering
Francis Bacon
Francis Darwin
Frances Hodgson Burnett
Frances Parkinson Keyes
Frank Gee Patchin
Frank Harris
Frank Jewett Mather
Frank L. Packard
Frank V. Webster
Frederic Stewart Isham
Frederick Trevor Hill
Frederick Winslow Taylor

Friedrich Kerst
Friedrich Nietzsche
Fyodor Dostoyevsky
G.A. Henty
G.K. Chesterton
Gabrielle E. Jackson
Garrett P. Serviss
Gaston Leroux
George A. Warren
George Ade
Geroge Bernard Shaw
George Cary Eggleston
George Durston
George Ebers
George Eliot
George Gissing
George MacDonald
George Meredith
George Orwell
George Sylvester Viereck
George Tucker
George W. Cable
George Wharton James
Gertrude Atherton
Gordon Casserly
Grace E. King
Grace Gallatin
Grace Greenwood
Grant Allen
Guillermo A. Sherwell
Gulielma Zollinger
Gustav Flaubert
H. A. Cody
H. B. Irving
H.C. Bailey
H. G. Wells
H. H. Munro
H. Irving Hancock
H. R. Naylor
H. Rider Haggard
II. W. C. Davis
Haldeman Julius
Hall Caine
Hamilton Wright Mabie
Hans Christian Andersen
Harold Avery
Harold McGrath
Harriet Beecher Stowe
Harry Castlemon
Harry Coghill
Harry Houidini

Hayden Carruth
Helent Hunt Jackson
Helen Nicolay
Hendrik Conscience
Hendy David Thoreau
Henri Barbusse
Henrik Ibsen
Henry Adams
Henry Ford
Henry Frost
Henry James
Henry Jones Ford
Henry Seton Merriman
Henry W Longfellow
Herbert A. Giles
Herbert Carter
Herbert N. Casson
Herman Hesse
Hildegard G. Frey
Homer
Honore De Balzac
Horace B. Day
Horace Walpole
Horatio Alger Jr.
Howard Pyle
Howard R. Garis
Hugh Lofting
Hugh Walpole
Humphry Ward
Ian Maclaren
Inez Haynes Gillmore
Irving Bacheller
Isabel Cecilia Williams
Isabel Hornibrook
Israel Abrahams
Ivan Turgenev
J.G.Austin
J. Henri Fabre
J. M. Barrie
J. M. Walsh
J. Macdonald Oxley
J. R. Miller
J. S. Fletcher
J. S. Knowles
J. Storer Clouston
J. W. Duffield
Jack London
Jacob Abbott
James Allen
James Andrews
James Baldwin

James Branch Cabell
James DeMille
James Joyce
James Lane Allen
James Lane Allen
James Oliver Curwood
James Oppenheim
James Otis
James R. Driscoll
Jane Abbott
Jane Austen
Jane L. Stewart
Janet Aldridge
Jens Peter Jacobsen
Jerome K. Jerome
Jessie Graham Flower
John Buchan
John Burroughs
John Cournos
John F. Kennedy
John Gay
John Glasworthy
John Habberton
John Joy Bell
John Kendrick Bangs
John Milton
John Philip Sousa
John Taintor Foote
Jonas Lauritz Idemil Lie
Jonathan Swift
Joseph A. Altsheler
Joseph Carey
Joseph Conrad
Joseph E. Badger Jr
Joseph Hergesheimer
Joseph Jacobs
Jules Vernes
Julian Hawthrone
Julie A Lippmann
Justin Huntly McCarthy
Kakuzo Okakura
Karle Wilson Baker
Kate Chopin
Kenneth Grahame
Kenneth McGaffey
Kate Langley Bosher
Kate Langley Bosher
Katherine Cecil Thurston
Katherine Stokes
L. A. Abbot
L. T. Meade

L. Frank Baum
Latta Griswold
Laura Dent Crane
Laura Lee Hope
Laurence Housman
Lawrence Beasley
Leo Tolstoy
Leonid Andreyev
Lewis Carroll
Lewis Sperry Chafer
Lilian Bell
Lloyd Osbourne
Louis Hughes
Louis Joseph Vance
Louis Tracy
Louisa May Alcott
Lucy Fitch Perkins
Lucy Maud Montgomery
Luther Benson
Lydia Miller Middleton
Lyndon Orr
M. Corvus
M. H. Adams
Margaret E. Sangster
Margret Howth
Margaret Vandercook
Margaret W. Hungerford
Margret Penrose
Maria Edgeworth
Maria Thompson Daviess
Mariano Azuela
Marion Polk Angellotti
Mark Overton
Mark Twain
Mary Austin
Mary Catherine Crowley
Mary Cole
Mary Hastings Bradley
Mary Roberts Rinehart
Mary Rowlandson
M. Wollstonecraft Shelley
Maud Lindsay
Max Beerbohm
Myra Kelly
Nathaniel Hawthrone
Nicolo Machiavelli
O. F. Walton
Oscar Wilde

Owen Johnson
P.G. Wodehouse
Paul and Mabel Thorne
Paul G. Tomlinson
Paul Severing
Percy Brebner
Percy Keese Fitzhugh
Peter B. Kyne
Plato
Quincy Allen
R. Derby Holmes
R. L. Stevenson
R. S. Ball
Rabindranath Tagore
Rahul Alvares
Ralph Bonehill
Ralph Henry Barbour
Ralph Victor
Ralph Waldo Emmerson
Rene Descartes
Ray Cummings
Rex Beach
Rex E. Beach
Richard Harding Davis
Richard Jefferies
Richard Le Gallienne
Robert Barr
Robert Frost
Robert Gordon Anderson
Robert L. Drake
Robert Lansing
Robert Lynd
Robert Michael Ballantyne
Robert W. Chambers
Rosa Nouchette Carey
Rudyard Kipling
Saint Augustine
Samuel B. Allison
Samuel Hopkins Adams
Sarah Bernhardt
Sarah C. Hallowell
Selma Lagerlof
Sherwood Anderson
Sigmund Freud
Standish O'Grady
Stanley Weyman
Stella Benson
Stella M. Francis

Stephen Crane
Stewart Edward White
Stijn Streuvels
Swami Abhedananda
Swami Parmananda
T. S. Ackland
T. S. Arthur
The Princess Der Ling
Thomas A. Janvier
Thomas A Kempis
Thomas Anderton
Thomas Bailey Aldrich
Thomas Bulfinch
Thomas De Quincey
Thomas Dixon
Thomas H. Huxley
Thomas Hardy
Thomas More
Thornton W. Burgess
U. S. Grant
Upton Sinclair
Valentine Williams
Various Authors
Vaughan Kester
Victor Appleton
Victor G. Durham
Victoria Cross
Virginia Woolf
Wadsworth Camp
Walter Camp
Walter Scott
Washington Irving
Wilbur Lawton
Wilkie Collins
Willa Cather
Willard F. Baker
William Dean Howells
William le Queux
W. Makepeace Thackeray
William W. Walter
William Shakespeare
Winston Churchill
Yei Theodora Ozaki
Yogi Ramacharaka
Young E. Allison
Zane Grey